MW00333279

To - ∿

From. Grandma and Grandpa

Don't ever give up - God is
still in control !!

We Didn't Fight for SOCIALISM:

America's Veterans Speak Up

By
Oliver L. North and David L. Goetsch

FIDELIS
PUBLISHING

FIDELIS PUBLISHING
ISBN: 9781735856346
ISBN (eBook): 9781735856353

We Didn't Fight for Socialism:
America's Veterans Speak Up

Cover Design by Diana Lawrence
Interior Design by Xcel Graphic - www.xcelgraphic.com

Manufactured in the United States of America
10 9 8 7 6 5 4 3 2

For information about special discounts for bulk purchases, please contact BulkBooks.com, call 1-888-959-5153, or email cs@bulkbooks.com

Unless otherwise noted, all biblical quotations are from The Holy Bible, English Standard Version. ESV® Text Edition: 2016. Copyright © 2001 by Crossway Bibles, a publishing ministry of Good News Publishers.

Fidelis Publishing, LLC
Sterling, VA • Nashville, TN
fidelispublishing.com

CONTENTS

WE DIDN'T FIGHT FOR SOCIALISM

People who call themselves progressives are at the forefront of movements to shut down debates on college campuses and restrict freedom of speech. They are eager to cut corners, bend the Constitution, make up laws through question- able court rulings, and generally ignore the rules to get their way. In Marine Corps boot camp, our drill instructors often told us that making it to graduation was about mind over matter. They would tell us, "We don't mind and you don't matter." Today's progressives are of the same mindset. They don't mind, and conservative principles of God and country don't matter.

—P. Henly Shelton, United States Marine Corps, 1968–1969

Shelton served as 106mm recoilless rifle/mortar man in First Battalion, Third Marines at Quang Tri, Vietnam, where he was wounded in combat. For his service he received the Purple Heart, and was awarded the Navy Achievement Medal with Combat V. Following his service in the Marine Corps, Shelton enjoyed a successful career in executive management, sales, marketing, and consulting, rising to president for North American opera- tions of his company. He earned a bachelor of science degree from the University of West Florida and an MBA from Georgia State University, and he completed the AMP Program at Harvard Business School.

November 3, 2020, will go down in American history as a watershed date, equal in importance to July 4, 1776, when intrepid Americans declared their independence from tyrannical government. Opting for freedom from the British Crown, these early Americans risked their lives, fortunes, and sacred honor for the cause of liberty. Thousands died in the ensuing War for Independence to make that dream come true. Since then, hundreds of thousands more have died in wars at home and abroad to preserve the dream.

Sadly, on November 3, 2020, more than seventy million Americans turned their backs on the sacrifices made by their predecessors and voluntarily surrendered their hard-won independence by opting for socialism in the presidential election. They voted to become, once again, subservient subjects of an all-controlling government, this one led by extreme Leftists who ran on a platform of socialism. What no enemy from outside our borders has been able to accomplish by force, socialist ideologues accomplished without firing a shot (well, mostly).

The conversation took place in a national military cemetery. Several veterans were paying their respects to fallen comrades and the conversation turned to the results of the presidential election of November 3, 2020. The veterans gathered there were dismayed that so many Americans had cast their votes for a candidate whose political platform was undeniably socialist. They were also concerned the election was corrupt, fraudulent, and tainted. To these veterans, Joe Biden had cheated his way into the White House, making him an illegitimate president.

One of the veterans made a comment worth remembering. "Looking out over the great expanse of this hallowed place, you see acres and acres of crosses and Stars of David. Every one of them represents a hero who served our country and fought to protect it. What were they fighting to protect? They fought for freedom, individual rights, rule of law, the opportunity to build a better life, and all the other things making America historically great. What they fought for might vary somewhat from person to person, but there is one thing I know for certain: not one of these heroes fought for socialism."

A few weeks later, another conversation involving veterans took place, this one in a barbershop. It was a Saturday morning, and the barbershop was full to overflowing. Both barber chairs were occupied, and there was standing room only in the waiting area. This particular barbershop is not just a place to get a haircut; it is also an establishment catering to veterans who come to talk about politics, sports, and world affairs while waiting their turn in the chair. The shop's walls are covered with military memorabilia, and the magazine rack overflows with periodicals covering America's armed conflicts from all eras.

Because they share a common bond forged by their service in uniform, the veterans who patronize this shop are comfortable sharing their thoughts, opinions, and concerns with one another. Consequently, they don't hold back. You don't have to wonder what these veterans think about current events or political issues. Listen for few minutes and you will know. Not only that, you will be expected to offer your own opinions. To these veterans, participation is a requirement, not an option.

As is often the case, the topic of conversation this particular morning was politics. More specifically, it was about the sharp Left turn America has taken toward socialism. The majority opinion among the veterans was that too many Americans have been lured into embracing an inherently flawed concept they know little about, a concept some of the veterans had witnessed firsthand during their military service. One of the veterans commented that if Americans who'd voted the Biden/Harris ticket had ever lived in a socialist country, they would have voted differently.

Others commented on the failure of socialism in the former Soviet Union, Cuba, and Venezuela. One veteran had been stationed in Germany when the Berlin Wall came down and that long-divided nation was finally reunited. Reunification was a joyful event for the German people, but once the celebrations ran their course, a problem emerged. Germans in the capitalist west were soon confronted by a harsh reality: the lackluster work ethic of Germans from the socialist east. This veteran echoed the frustration of many West Germans in stating that decades under socialism had robbed the East Germans of their initiative and work ethic.

Another veteran attempted to recite a quote he had recently read about socialists sharing nothing but misery. He couldn't recite the quote word for word or remember its author, but he got the gist of it. The author, as it turned out, was Winston Churchill, and the full quote reads as follows: "The inherent vice of capitalism is the unequal sharing of blessings. The inherent virtue of Socialism is the equal sharing of miseries." Churchill issued this warning in the House of Commons on October 22, 1945, when Britain's Labour Party was transitioning the country to a socialist economy.[1]

After about thirty minutes of discussion, one of the veterans summed up the prevailing opinion in the room by firmly stating he hadn't joined the military to fight for socialism. His statement received a round of applause, and everyone crammed into the barbershop that morning joined in with enthusiasm. This veteran's comment painted a clear picture of the battle of ideas being waged in America—a battle splitting the American electorate right down the middle.

America arrived at a crossroads on November 3, 2020. One path led to a revival of the Founders' vision for our country, one characterized by freedom, liberty, self-determination, and opportunity. The other path led to socialism, a philosophy leading to tyranny, corruption, and despotism everywhere it has been tried. Yet in spite of socialism's inherent flaws and well-documented failures, ideologues on the extreme Left have successfully seduced Americans with their false promises of a socialist utopia. After decades of Leftist indoctrination in our schools and colleges, socialist advocates have finally hoodwinked half of the American electorate into believing their false promises.

Beginning with the War for Independence, more than a million Americans have given their lives to protect the principles upon which our country was built. In developing this book, we surveyed and interviewed hundreds of military veterans to determine their views on America's turn toward socialism. These veterans and thousands of others we have talked to over the years made it clear they hadn't served in the military to fight for socialism. Rather, they had fought to protect the principles our Founders espoused when they risked everything to establish our nation. Those principles included freedom, individual liberty, self-determination, God-given rights, equal opportunity, the rule of law, and private property. They did not include collectivism, groupthink, or government control of every aspect of the individual's life—the defining characteristics of socialism.

A battle is raging in America, a clash over ideas and philosophies. On one side in this battle are Americans who love our country and what it has always represented. On the other side are socialist ideologues who want to tear down the America established by our Founders and replace it with a hopelessly flawed philosophy that has failed everywhere it has been tried. That philosophy is socialism. For decades advocates of this flawed philosophy have used indoctrination, misdirection, deception, division, and distortion to convert gullible Americans to their cause. Socialists now control the Democratic Party and the White House. This means socialists are on the verge of controlling you.

Americans must know the truth about this irreparably flawed and repeatedly failed philosophy that so many have bought into. In the following pages, we present hard facts, uncomfortable truths, and objective analysis of socialism. We also present feedback from veterans who are concerned that the America they see emerging in the wake of the November 3, 2020 elections is not the one they fought for. Finally, we provide a plan for winning the battle of ideas pitting the philosophy of America's founders against the philosophy of socialists.

This battle of ideas may be the most important battle Americans have ever fought. Our prayer is that in this battle of ideas, freedom-loving Americans will emulate the courage and commitment of their predecessors who fought in hot wars to protect the vision of our Founders.

Freedom, liberty, individual rights, self-determination, opportunity, and the rule of law have long characterized the American ideal. These principles are why for more than four hundred years immigrants from all over the world have left their homelands, seeking better lives here. These uniquely American principles, taken together, are the foundation upon which our country was built starting with the 1620 landing of the Pilgrims. They are also the antithesis of socialism, a philosophy based on collectivism, group-think, and government control of every aspect of your life—a philosophy inevitably leading to corruption, despotism, and tyranny.

THE FOUR Ds OF SOCIALISM

Over the past one hundred years, when socialist ideologues have gained power anywhere in the world, they have done so by *deceiving, distorting, dividing,* and *destroying*. We call these "the four Ds of socialism." Because of this propensity, the following questions become more important every day:

Do you want to be governed by Leftist ideologues . . .

- who want to tear down everything good and right about America?
- who are so hungry for power that they'll stoop to using deception and distortion to gain it?
- whose method of operation is to divide and conquer by fomenting discord based on race, gender, age, national origin, income level, and other factors used to divide people in a pluralistic nation?
- who not only refuse to condemn violence, but side with rioters, looters, and arsonists while at the same time demonizing police officers, who are trying to maintain law and order?
- who try to destroy the lives of anyone who disagrees with them by encouraging, promoting, and participating in the cancel culture?
- who confuse making noise with making progress and who think tearing down historic statues, burning down police stations, looting businesses, and attacking law-abiding citizens amounts to progress?
- who tell the have-nots in America they are victims and encourage them to make excuses instead of helping them make progress?
- whose overarching goal is to control the government and use it to control you?

- who attained office under a cloud of suspicion of systematic voter fraud?

These are not just hypothetical questions, and they are even more pertinent now in the aftermath of the national elections in November 2020. Through the unrelenting application of deception, distortion, division, and destruction, socialist ideologues have gained control of the White House. With their foot in the door, their plan is to use the government to control you. This is not just political rhetoric. It's a fact proven over and over throughout history when socialists gain government control.

This is why it is so important for Americans to know the truth about socialism. Leftist ideologues are deceptive in their efforts to replace America's traditional values with their failed philosophy, and they have made substantial progress in doing so. They are steadily supplanting traditional American values with their inherently flawed political theory—one that advocates a societal system that suppresses the rights of the individual in favor of government control. If you remember nothing else written in this book, remember this: socialists want to control the government for one reason and one reason only: so they can use the government to control you. This is the story of socialism everywhere it has been tried.

Throughout this book, we present concerns expressed by military veterans about the acceptance of socialism in the United States by people who have never lived it. As one of these veterans commented, it is discouraging to realize that many Americans who enjoy all the benefits of capitalism and individual liberty are using their positions of influence to advocate for socialism. Prominent among these socialist ideologues are radical Democrats, Leftist politicians, entertainers, mainstream media commentators, print journalists, and Marxist college professors.

The most effective way to gain complete control of your life is to make you dependent on government for your essential needs. Even worse than the hubris of Marxist college professors and Leftist politicians is the hypocrisy of entertainers, actors, and athletes who become wealthy and famous because of capitalism, and then use their wealth and stardom to influence young people in favor of socialism. Ironically, it is often those who have benefited most from capitalism who claim to prefer socialism.

Socialist ideologues have convinced a lot of Americans to cast off the philosophy and values that made our country great and replace them with a fatally flawed ideology. Why would any thinking person do this? The answer is simple: a thinking person wouldn't. We wrote this book to encourage Americans to think critically about the messages coming from Leftist ideologues, to question those messages, and to speak up about inconsistencies in the facts, diversions from the historical record, and lapses in reason.

Remaining silent in the face of a movement meant to tear down everything good and great about our country amounts to aiding and abetting the advance of that movement. Therefore, we encourage you to make your voice heard and push back against the rising tide of socialism in our country. We pray readers will take to heart what we write and what our veterans say in this book. Don't let your silence make you complicit in tearing down the America envisioned by the Founders more than 240 years ago.

AMERICA'S DANGEROUS TURN TOWARD SOCIALISM

Looking back on the years and months leading up to the presidential election of 2020, one of the veterans surveyed for this book said he never thought the day would come when an avowed socialist would be a serious contender in a presidential primary. But, of course, this is exactly what happened in the Democrats' presidential primary in 2020. Senator Bernie Sanders, an ardent, unapologetic socialist who ran on a far-Left platform, not only bested a field of more than twenty other Democratic candidates; he came in second place and almost won the nomination.

Sanders was so popular with the Democratic base that he forced all the other candidates to shift their platforms far to the Left. Even though he fell short of winning the nomination, Sanders retained his influence in the Democratic primary. In fact, he was so influential that the eventual primary winner—former vice president Joe Biden—not only adopted much of the Sanders platform but also selected the most Left-leaning member of the U.S. Senate, Kamala

Harris, as his running mate. Harris leans even farther to the Left in her views than Bernie Sanders. Now that Biden and Harris are in the White House, Sanders has finally won his long-sought victory for socialism even though he lost the primary race.

HOW DID SOCIALISTS WIN IN 2020?

Was the COVID-19 pandemic the reason socialists won the presidency and control of the senate in 2020, as some have suggested? There is little question that politicizing the coronavirus and resorting to the politics of fear helped Democrats gain votes. Would they have won the presidency had there been no pandemic? Probably not.

Before the pandemic, President Trump helped give Americans the best economy many had ever known. Consumer confidence was at an all-time high, and the stock market was breaking records every day. Although we readily acknowledge the COVID-19 pandemic and election manipulation as factors in the presidential election of 2020, it took more than a virus from China to convince more than eighty million Americans to cede control of the White House to an extreme Leftist candidate, even if some of them were dead when they voted.

The seeds of what happened in November 2020 were planted decades before the coronavirus was imported from China. Those seeds have been persistently watered by the extreme Left of the Democratic Party for years. In November 2020, the seeds of socialism finally blossomed into a full-fledged thornbush. Socialists got a welcome boost from the coronavirus, and they used every nefarious scheme imaginable—including voter fraud, media dominance, and electronic warfare—to take full advantage of that boost. However, the main reason they were able to prevail in the national elections of 2020 was the deception, distortion, division, and destruction they have perpetrated on the American public for decades.

How completely have the tentacles of socialism enfolded American society? A poll taken by the Victims of Communism Memorial Fund before the national elections of 2020 revealed that 44 percent of millennials—Americans between the ages of twenty-one and thirty-six—favor socialism over capitalism.[2] A Pew poll, also taken before the 2020 elections, found that almost 70 percent of voters under age thirty would be willing to vote for a socialist candidate for president.[3] The accuracy of these polls was borne out by the November 2020 election results.

Enticed by the unrealistic promises of unscrupulous politicians, indoctrinated by Leftist educators, and deceived by the mainstream media, many Americans have adopted socialism as their governmental philosophy of choice. This should come as no surprise. After all, advocates of socialism promise Americans free health care, free college tuition, student-debt forgiveness, and lifelong welfare with no work requirement. That so many Americans are willing to accept these false promises is a serious blot on the academic integrity of public schools, colleges, and universities. At a time when critical thinking is needed more than ever by American citizens, years of indoctrination have turned many into easily deluded sheep who accept without question the false narrative and deceptive promises of the Left.

It should come as no surprise that promises of student-debt forgiveness resound with college graduates who face the burden of paying off student loans, particularly those who are now toiling away in jobs they could have gotten with just a high school diploma. In fact, these disgruntled, disillusioned degree holders often find themselves supervised by someone with only a high school diploma but more years of experience. Their "less educated" supervisors gained valuable experience on the job while the college students were wasting their time pursuing watered-down but expensive degrees with no value in the job market.

Young people about to begin college are also targeted by unscrupulous Leftist politicians who make false promises of "free tuition" to win their support. To young people looking to matriculate at pricey universities, "free tuition" must sound especially enticing. What these naive young people fail to grasp is a simple but profound truth: nothing is free. When something is said to be "free," it means someone else is paying for it. Unfortunately, this is acceptable to an increasing number of people in America—specifically, those who have adopted an entitlement mentality.

Perhaps the most enticing of the false promises made by socialist ideologues is the promise of free health care. Such a promise is bound to appeal to Americans who lack common sense and are unschooled in the basics of economics, and it certainly did during the 2020 elections. One of the veterans surveyed for this book commented that any American who falls for the false promise of free health care should be required to spend time in line at a Veterans Administration hospital, waiting for treatment. This veteran, who had endured the experience on several occasions, was certain it would cure them of their blind faith in "free" health care.

Another veteran found it especially disturbing that college students are willing to take out huge loans to pursue unmarketable degrees and then expect others to pay their debts. Again, what socialist advocates conveniently forget to tell economically illiterate young people is that nothing in the world is free; somebody has to pay. "Forgiving" their student loans doesn't mean making them go away. Rather, it means making someone else pay them. That someone else is you.

This veteran pointed out that by rewarding irresponsible behavior in college students, the government is just encouraging more irresponsible behavior. He wondered how Leftist politicians and government bureaucrats could expect college graduates to pay their car loans, credit card bills, and home mortgages if they aren't held accountable for paying their student loans. What they learn in school they will expect to apply in the real world.

WHAT HAPPENS WHEN SOCIALISTS RULE?

As Marine Corps veterans, we often talk with fellow veterans from all of the service branches and from all over the country. Over the years we have talked with thousands of veterans, many of whom are concerned about the rise of socialism in our country. Their concerns mirror those of the veterans we interviewed and surveyed for this book. One retired veteran expressed a concern shared by many of his fellow veterans: "If a socialist is elected president, are veterans and elderly people going to lose the retirement pensions they spent a lifetime earning?"

It's not that this veteran thought a socialist president and congress would intentionally take away his military pension, although he didn't rule out the possibility. Rather, he feared America's economy would become so overburdened by "free" health care, "free" college tuition, and lifelong welfare that the federal treasury would be depleted and the economy would crash. One need only look to Venezuela to validate this veteran's concerns. Venezuelans duped by the false promises of free everything elected the very politicians who transformed their previously wealthy nation into an economic cesspool in which a starving population was forced to scrounge for meals in the trash.

SOCIALISTS UNDERMINE TRADITIONAL AMERICAN VALUES

If our conversations with veterans are any indication, many of the men and women who have served our country in uniform are concerned about the attack on traditional American values by socialist ideologues. According to the veterans with whom we interact, these traditional values make America a nation worth fighting for. As one veteran claimed, if we lose our traditional values, we lose America.

Here are some of the values veterans believe made America great but are now being undermined by Leftist politicians using false promises to buy the votes of naive citizens: freedom, personal responsibility, accountability, initiative, competition, self-reliance, achievement, individual rights, self-discipline, private-property rights, entrepreneurship, meritorious advancement, and Christian morality. These traditional American values are the polar opposite of those subscribed to by socialists.

Veterans and other Americans who worry about our country's movement toward socialism are justified in their concerns. There is a growing divide in our country between citizens who believe in the values and economic philosophy that made America the envy of the entire world and those who reject these values, preferring socialism over capitalism. As of the 2020 elections, the latter group is in the ascendency. It was America's traditional values that made the veterans we talked to proud to serve our country and even go in harm's way to preserve those values, but a declining number of Americans share that pride and commitment.

For example, a Gallup poll taken before the 2020 elections revealed that 76 percent of Republicans are "extremely proud" to be Americans, but only 22 percent of Democrats make this claim.[4] The latter percentage represents a major decline from earlier polls, in which more than 50 percent of Democrats indicated they were proud to be Americans.[5] Will young people who have been indoctrinated to view America with disgust rather than pride be willing to defend our country in uniform? Will they willingly go in harm's way to defend America from its enemies when necessary? Many of the veterans we talked to believe the answer to both questions is no. They doubt the willingness of entitled young people to serve. No wonder these veterans are concerned. All Americans should be.

Increasingly, it appears Americans who accept the socialist narrative reject the traditional values our veterans fought for. Listen to extreme Leftists in the Democratic Party and there is no doubt they prefer socialist despots to the heroes and visionaries who founded our country. To socialist ideologues, George Washington, Thomas Jefferson, James Madison, and their fellow founders were just a bunch of old, racist, chauvinistic white men who built a nation to benefit themselves, to the exclusion of women and people of other races. In the socialist's view, the Founders were men whose statues should be torn down and tossed on the dust heap of history.

Admittedly, America's founders had their flaws, as do all people, but it is irresponsible, not to mention ungrateful, to forget that without them there would be no United States. Further, it is hypocritical to judge our founders out of historical context based on today's cultural values or to hold them to a standard their critics don't live up to themselves. It is also disingenuous to judge people solely on their flaws while ignoring their contributions.

IS A SOCIALIST AMERICA WORTH FIGHTING FOR?

Veterans we questioned for this book, as well as veterans we have talked to over the years, made it clear that they did not join the military to fight for socialism. Many of the veterans interviewed and surveyed for this book said they'd served in the military because they loved the freedom and opportunity afforded them by our country as well as the values long characterizing America. To them, America has always been the good guy in the community of nations. A socialist America, in the eyes of these veterans, will no longer be a good guy.

For nearly 250 years, Americans have responded to our nation's call in the same way the prophet Isaiah responded to the Lord's call when he said, "Here I am! Send me" (Isaiah 6:8). American citizens have donned the uniform many times to defend our nation and its allies from the forces of tyranny and evil. Some of those enemies have been socialist tyrants. For example, Adolf Hitler and his Nazi cronies led the National Socialist Party in Germany up to and during World War II. They called their party *national socialists* to distinguish it from the international socialists of the Soviet Communist Party, but they were socialists nonetheless.

Much of the danger in today's turbulent world comes from Communist/socialist nations, including China and North Korea. One of the veterans we surveyed posed two pertinent questions: (1) Can you imagine fighting to defend Nazi Germany, Cuba, China, or North Korea? and (2) Why would anybody go in harm's way to defend a government that cares nothing about its own people? These questions have important ramifications for Americans in the present and the future.

It is critical not just to our national defense but to our very survival as a nation that American citizens remain willing to join the military and go in harm's way to protect the God-given freedoms set forth in our Constitution. We are concerned that if America continues on its current path of increasing socialism, the day will come when young Americans will no longer be willing to serve in the military, much less put themselves in harm's way to defend our country. It is worth noting that during World War II, Soviet Army officers had to station themselves behind their own troops and threaten to shoot them in the back if they didn't fight. Obviously, socialism does not inspire loyalty to country.

A NOTE ABOUT OUR VETERANS

The title of this book is the statement "We Didn't Fight for Social-ism." We wish to make an important point before proceeding. Not all military personnel fight in combat. Consequently, not all veter-ans are combat veterans. All branches of the military consist of two components: combat arms and support troops. Yet we that believe that all who served in the military, in any capacity—combat or sup-port—fought for our country. This is because every job in the military, whether in the combat arms or a support billet, plays an important role in the defense of our great nation. The military doesn't just make up jobs. Every job in every branch of the military contributes in some way to our national defense.

For every warrior who carries a rifle, drives a tank, fires artillery, or flies a jet in combat, there must be support troops to train, equip, assist, crew, and care for that individual. Without these support troops, those who go in harm's way would go into battle untrained, without effective planning, improperly equipped, poorly armed, and left on their own when wounded. Some of the veterans we surveyed and interviewed for this book served in combat; others served in support roles. But *all* served; therefore, all fought for our country.

A NOTE ABOUT OUR INTERVIEWS AND SURVEY

We interviewed a lot of veterans in preparation for writing this book. We also surveyed more than five hundred others. Further, we have both spent the last several decades in constant communica-tion with veterans from all branches of the military and from all over the country. A number of the veterans we interviewed are quoted herein, and comments they made on survey forms are paraphrased throughout the book. We do not claim this to be a statistically rep-resentative sample of all veterans. Military veterans tend to be more conservative as a whole than the general population, but there are plenty of veterans at both ends of the political spectrum and all points in between.

What we can claim is this: many veterans are concerned about America's growing acceptance of socialism. We know this to be true not just because of the interviews and survey we conducted but even more because we are constantly in touch with veterans from across the nation, and have been for a long time. Both of us interact regularly with veterans—old and young, north and south, east and west, urban and rural—from all branches of the military. These veterans have no qualms about expressing their views on the state of the nation they fought for.

Our more recent conversations with veterans have, more often than not, focused on the rising tide of socialism in our country. The concerns expressed in these conversations mirror the results of our interviews and survey for this book. If the veterans we have talked to over the years and more recently for this book have these concerns, it stands to reason other veterans have them too. If veterans have these concerns, it stands to reason other Americans have them too. Further, because they sacrificed to serve our country, we believe veterans and the views they express should be given due consideration by Americans of all stripes.

A CALL TO ACTION FOR ALL AMERICANS

We wrote this book as a call to action for all Americans. Securing America's future is not a liberal versus conservative or Democrat versus Republican issue. Rather, it is a challenge for all Americans. At its root, this is a spiritual battle ignited in the garden of creation. From the beginning, we've been allowed the choice between good and evil, the Creator and the destroyer. Our purpose in writing this book was to encourage citizens of all worldviews and political persuasions to look beyond the politics of the moment and be good stewards of America's future.

To be a good steward in the current context means to pass along our country to the next generation in better condition than when we inherited it. Americans of all stripes are responsible for determining what our nation's future will be. We are all called to be good stewards of what made America a nation worth fighting for, and that most assuredly is not socialism. As citizens of a free and self-governed nation, we have it in our power to craft a bright future for America or to pen its obituary.

Unless we want to spend our golden years apologizing to our grandchildren for squandering their national inheritance, Americans on the left, right, and in the middle need to work together to reestablish the core values at the foundation of America's greatness that will guarantee a brighter future for all Americans for generations to come. It's time for Americans who believe in what our country has historically stood for to speak up for those things. Our prayer is that this book will encourage everyone who reads it to join the battle of ideas currently raging in our country; to fight the good fight on behalf of what has long made our country what President Reagan called that bright, "shining city upon a hill."[6]

CHAPTER 1

SOCIALISM: WHAT IT ISN'T, WHAT IT IS, AND WHY IT APPEALS TO SOME

Gaining a clear understanding of the foolishness and evil nature of socialism is worth more to Americans at this point in history than our nation's gross national product. Such an understanding will enable us to grasp the errors of social- ist thinking, deceitfulness of socialist ideologues, and moral and economic destructiveness of this flawed concept when compared with the practical superiority of private property, limited government, and economic freedom.

—Archie Jones, PhD, United States Marine Corps, 1960–1964

Dr. Jones is a longtime Christian educator and professor. He is the author of *The Gateway to Liberty* (American Vision Press, 2010) and coauthor of *Liberal Tyranny in Higher Education,* (American Vision Press, 2009).

It is both ironic and disturbing that so many Americans claim to be favorably disposed toward socialism when they don't really know what it is. Worse, it's not just indoctrinated college students and naive citizens who lean toward socialism without knowing anything

about it. Many of socialism's most prominent proponents and prac-
titioners cannot define the concept. There are politicians on the
extreme Left who advocate for blatantly socialist programs who still
claim they aren't socialists. Then there are socialist ideologues who
speak with enthusiasm and authority about the concept but have no
understanding of the harsh realities associated with it.

It is no exaggeration to say that ignorance of the inherent failings
of this flawed concept is one of the main reasons many people claim
to prefer socialism to capitalism. Even those proponents who do
understand what socialism means appreciate it only in theory. As
one of the veterans we surveyed for this book commented, if ever
they were forced to live under the conditions that accompany socialism, those favorable to this faulty philosophy would quickly change
their opinions.

To favor socialism and government control over capitalism and
individual liberty, people must be willing to uncouple themselves
from reality and operate solely in the realm of theory or even fantasy. One of the veterans we surveyed said that people who think
they prefer socialism to capitalism probably also think Disney World
is real life. Socialism is like Disney World: what you see behind the
scenes is much different from what you see publicly.

To be an advocate for socialism, you must be willing to ignore
evidence that abounds concerning the documented failings and
inherent flaws of the concept. In fact, evidence of its failings is so
convincing that socialist ideologues must ignore it, cover it up,
distort it, or stoop to lying about it. This is precisely what is happening in America today. The extreme Left of the Democratic Party
proposes a long list of socialist programs but refuses to use the term
socialism in association with these programs. They are like the man
who is constantly stumbling drunk but claims he isn't an alcoholic.

The only Leftist Democrat honest enough to admit he is a
socialist is Senator Bernie Sanders, and he admits the fact openly.
Because of socialism's tarnished history, his fellow Leftists in the
Democratic Party avoid the term like the plague, all the while adopting the same political platform as Sanders—some going even farther
to the left. For example, in the presidential election of 2020, Joe
Biden adopted much of the Sanders platform and went even further

to the left on the rest of his platform. As a senator, Kamala Harris had a voting record further to the left than Bernie Sanders. Yet Biden and his vice president claim they aren't socialists. Apparently, Democrats have never heard the old maxim "If it walks like a duck . . ." For this reason, we begin with an explanation of what socialism isn't, what it is, and why it appeals to certain people.

WHAT SOCIALISM ISN'T

Here is the bottom line when it comes to defining socialism: it is not the utopian paradise promised by Leftist ideologues wherein a benevolent nanny government supplies all of your wants and needs. A government taking care of you from cradle to grave is the promise socialist ideologues make to win the support of the naive and ignorant, but this is a false promise. Even if socialist governments were the benevolent nannies its advocates claim them to be, instead of the tyrannical monoliths they invariably become, no government can make good on the promises of socialism. A little common sense would tell gullible supporters of socialism that anything that sounds too good to be true probably is.

During the course of his thirty-year military career, one of the veterans surveyed for this book spent time in several socialist countries where he witnessed the harsh realities of life in "Utopia." Having observed socialism up close, this veteran had nothing good to say about it. Consequently, he finds it especially disturbing to hear people who have never even visited a socialist country claim they favor socialism over capitalism. He said it's like the owner of a Rolls-Royce claiming to prefer a Russian Lada although he has never seen or driven one. If you aren't familiar with the Russian Lada, think of a bulldozer without the creature comforts. This automobile, produced by socialist workers, has the aesthetic appeal of an outhouse and the dependability of the weather. He went on to say that shopping for groceries in a socialist country is like shopping in America the day before a hurricane hits or the day after the coronavirus lockdown was announced. The shelves are bare. In socialist countries, the shelves are often bare, and not just during times of crisis. Immigrants from Venezuela who had to ward off starvation by searching for food scraps in dumpsters can tell you about bare shelves in socialist countries.

One of the reasons many people find socialism appealing, particularly millennials and Americans at the bottom of the socioeconomic ladder, is they are being exploited by deceitful politicians and other corrupt players who promise them the proverbial pot of gold at the end of the rainbow. Socialism attracts millennials because it promises them something for nothing, an enticing concept to young people accustomed to parents paying for everything. It appeals to people at the bottom of the socioeconomic ladder in the same way playing the lottery does. They actually believe they are going to win. In defense of the lottery, at least people who play it have a one-in-a-gazillion chance of winning.

With socialism everybody loses except top-level bureaucrats controlling the government, economy, treasury, and you. In an attempt to advance their wicked agenda, Leftist ideologues claim that with socialism everything is free. The false promise of free everything can be seducing to people who are unschooled in the basics of economics. Again, anyone who believes anything is free is living in fantasy land. Everything comes with a cost, and somebody has to pay it.

To the poor, socialism advocates promise free health care and lifelong welfare with no work requirement. To college students they promise free tuition. To college graduates they promise student-debt forgiveness. Unfortunately, because they have been indoctrinated rather than educated, many Americans are taken in by the false promises of socialism. The ability to see through the fog of misinformed self-interest that serves socialism advocates so well is why schools and colleges used to teach students to think critically. Unfortunately, critical thinking has no place in the Leftist curricula prevalent today—curricula designed to indoctrinate.

Were they not economically illiterate because of an academically anemic education system, hoodwinked Americans would know what the veterans we surveyed and interviewed pointed out over and over: nothing is free, everything costs, and someone has to pay. Unfortunately, just convincing people to think critically about socialism is not enough. Knowing everything costs and somebody has to pay is not necessarily a deterrent to socialism. There are a lot of people in America who don't care if somebody has to pay as long as that somebody is not them. People in this category are the easiest prey for socialist ideologues.

To college graduates drowning in student debt while toiling away in jobs they could have gotten with just a high school diploma or GED, the promise of student-loan forgiveness must seem like a life jacket thrown to a drowning man. Like fish, college graduates drowning in debt soon learn it is difficult to get away once hooked, and they are quick to take the bait socialist ideologues offer. Even those who eventually come to understand the downside of government entitlements find it difficult to wean themselves from them. People who grow accustomed to handouts are seldom willing to give them up. We all know what happens to the hooked fish hauled into the boat's live well.

One of the things advocates of socialism fail to tell debt-ridden college students is if their loans are paid by American taxpayers today, they are going to find themselves paying off the loans of future students tomorrow. Once a government entitlement is granted to one generation, it is demanded by the next generation and the next and the next. This is why government entitlements seldom go away; they just keep getting bigger and bigger. People become as addicted to government handouts as they do to drugs: even those who sincerely want to break the habit find it difficult and sometimes impossible.

Another consideration is that a student loan, no matter how large and burdensome, at least has a defined payoff date. Unless the debtors default, at some point their student loans will be paid off. This is not the case with taxes. The taxes required to pay off "forgiven" student loans and to finance other socialist give-away programs are a lifelong burden for all Americans, and it only increases over time.

Taxes represent only the monetary cost of socialist give-away programs. The hidden cost is even higher. Forgiving student loans reinforces irresponsible behavior and an entitlement mentality. If we want college students to become responsible, contributing citizens, the worst thing we can do is reward their irresponsibility. College students whose loans are forgiven by the government will expect other debts to be forgiven—but they will find that banks and credit card companies are not as forgiving as pandering politicians trying to buy their votes.

As one of the veterans we surveyed pointed out, with people you get more of what you reward. If their student loans are forgiven, won't college students come to expect *all* of their debts—home mortgages, credit card balances, automobile loans, and lines of credit—to be forgiven too? When this kind of expectation sets in, we all suffer the consequences, even the irresponsible folks who demanded their student loans be forgiven. When an economy collapses, it's like the roof of a house falling in. It falls on everyone, including those who caused it to collapse. This is why there is so much suffering in socialist countries. With socialism, the economy almost always collapses.

The key point to grasp here is socialism does NOT mean everything is free. As appealing as this false promise sounds to the ill-informed, it's not just a myth; it's a lie propagated by bad actors trying to advance a dangerous agenda. Their agenda is to control every aspect of your life by making you wholly dependent on government, meaning wholly dependent on them. Once you have to depend on government for your health care and other basic human needs, the government controls you. As one of our veterans pointed out, this is what gave rise to the claim that "a government big enough to give you everything you want is a government big enough to take from you everything you have."[1] This adage is sometimes credited to Thomas Jefferson and at other times to Gerald Ford, but regardless who originated it, the message is prescient.

In addition to claiming socialism means everything is free, some advocates make the even more ludicrous claim that the concept is biblical. As proof, they quote Acts 2:45, "And they were selling their possessions and belongings and distributing the proceeds to all, as any had need" or Acts 4:32, "No one said that any of the things that belonged to him was his own, but they had everything in common." As one of the veterans we surveyed made clear, to take these verses out of context and suggest they mean socialism is biblical demonstrates ignorance of both the Bible and socialism.

Acts 2 contains the apostle Peter's sermon on Pentecost, in which he exhorts the men of Judea to devote themselves to the apostles' teaching and to the fellowship of Christ. Those who cite Acts 2:45 to claim socialism is biblical point out how the people who heard Peter's sermon responded by giving away their "possessions and belongings" to those in need. The point these socialist advocates miss is the people in question voluntarily gave up their private property; it was not taken from them by the government and redistributed. Hence, those who claim socialism is biblical are way off base.

Voluntarily giving private possessions to the poor is hardly a socialist concept; it is a biblical expectation of all Christians. With socialism, you don't voluntarily give away your private possessions or property; the government takes them. With socialism you don't distribute your belongings to others; the government does the distributing. With socialism, you don't decide what is given to others or how much; the government decides. Voluntarily giving to the poor is a Christian practice in keeping with the second greatest commandment, not a socialist principle. In case you aren't familiar with that commandment, it reads like this: "Love your neighbor as yourself" (Mark 12:31).

Further, for socialists to seek validation of their philosophy in the Bible is the height of hypocrisy since they don't worship the God of Holy Scripture in the first place. To a socialist, government is god. Therefore, the rights of citizens as well as their sustenance come from government. Of all the flaws of socialism, this one is the worst. In spite of the claims of socialist ideologues to the contrary, government cannot possibly do what God can. Of all the reasons socialism fails, putting government in the place of God tops the list.

WHAT SOCIALISM IS

Now that we have explained what socialism does not mean, let's look at what it does mean. Socialism is a philosophy in which the government controls every aspect of the individual's life, whether by coercion or by the imposition of laws, regulations, and taxes.

With socialism, the larger group takes precedence over the individual, and that group, ultimately, is the government. Therefore, anything done in the name of the government is deemed appropriate and even praiseworthy no matter how much it hurts individuals.

Government control is the essence of socialism, no matter how the concept is otherwise defined. There are two reasons for this. First, the approach socialists use to gain control over the individual is evolving. Socialists in Western nations, including the United States, have adopted the label of "social Democrats" to distinguish themselves from socialist tyrants such as Hitler, Stalin, Mao, Pol Pot, Castro, Chávez, and Maduro. Social Democrats still want to control every aspect of the individual's life but by making them dependent on government rather than through physical coercion, as was the case with the socialist despots just named.

Second, traditional definitions have focused on how socialist governments manage to control individuals as opposed to focusing on the fact that control is the overriding goal of socialism. For example, traditionally socialism has been defined as an economic system in which the government owns and operates the means of production and distribution. The goods and services needed by a nation's citizens are produced and provided by the government. In theory, this definition sounds benign enough. However, as is often the case with theories, it breaks down in its application.

A VETERAN SPEAKS UP

Socialism has brought misery everywhere it has been tried. Here is what one veteran had to say about this aspect of socialism:

The underlying premise of socialism is belief in the inherent goodness and perfectability of man. You would think thousands of years of human history would have put this delusion to rest. Over the past one hundred–plus years, socialism has been responsible for more misery, suffering, and death than any other philosophy or dogma . . . Socialism presupposes there is a small group of people who know how we all should live, and history repeatedly reveals they are more than willing to use all of the coercive force and power of government to ensure we all comply.

—Samuel Nelson, United States Air Force, 1980–1985

Nelson is a distinguished graduate of the United States Air Force Academy (1980) with a master's degree from Air University. His civilian career, spanning nearly four decades, has been spent in the research and development of air-launched weapons for the Air Force.

The thing that should leap off the page at you from this definition is when you are dependent on the government as the sole-source provider of your basic human needs, you have become a slave to the government. This is why so-called social democracy is a lie. Social democrats may not use armed force to coerce you into complying with government mandates, but forced compliance based on total dependence is still coercion. In a democracy, the people control the government. With socialism, including social democracies, the government controls the people.

Whether the government owns and operates the means of production or uses total dependence as its method of control, the outcome is the same for the individual. If you have ever stood in a long line at a social security office, waited months to be treated at a Veterans Administration (VA) clinic, or taken a number at the local office of the Department of Motor Vehicles, you have experienced the inherent problems with the government being the sole-source provider of services you need. But we digress. Before getting into the systemic weaknesses of big government, we need to continue with our definition of socialism.

Socialism is known to economists as a *command* economic system. Capitalism, on the other hand, is a *demand* system. The differences between these two systems are stark, and you need to understand the differences. In a command system, the government dictates what is made and in what quantities as well as what services are provided and how extensively. These decisions are made by government bureaucrats known as *central planners*.

Once a plan has been developed, government-owned and operated organizations are given their quotas and commanded to fill them; thus, the name "command system." Not surprisingly, central planners typically decide how much of a product to produce based on the previous year's plan rather than the demands of consumers. Consequently, fluctuations in consumer demand are not accounted for in the planning. Worse yet, there is no incentive for central planners to get their estimates right. In a socialistic system, the central planners are paid the same whether their quotas meet consumer needs or not. Further, because the government is the sole provider of human essentials, it doesn't matter whether or not consumers are happy. In a socialist command system, unhappy consumers are out of luck; they have only one provider for the things they need: the government.

Contrast government-as-the-sole-source-provider with what happens in a capitalist economy. If you are tired of standing in line at the local post office, you can ship your items through Federal Express, United Parcel Service, DHL, or several other private providers. If you don't like the prices or service at one store, you have the option of taking your business to another one. If you doubt the capabilities of one health-care provider, you can choose another. Freedom of choice for consumers exists throughout a free-market economy and is a basic principle of capitalism.

For now, VA health-care facilities come as close as anything we have in the United States to socialized medicine. The reputation of VA hospitals for quality of patient care and other services has suffered for years. In 2019, Congress decided to solve some of the problems associated with VA facilities, such as long lines, waiting lists, and poor service, by allowing veterans to use their benefits at private hospitals. The strategy worked. Waiting lists were reduced and veterans got the care they needed.

It is instructive to note that improving VA health-care services required a capitalistic solution. Not surprisingly, falling back on capitalism in times of economic distress is a common practice in socialist countries. For example, China's current economic prosperity is based on the establishment of enterprise zones in which capitalism is allowed. In fact, China no longer qualifies as a fully socialized nation. Rather, it has joined the ranks of what are known as "emerging nations." These are historically socialist nations moving toward capitalism.

Imagine for a moment how your life would change if bureaucrats in Washington, DC were responsible for deciding how many of the products you use in your daily life were going to be produced each year and how much they would cost. While mulling this over, consider that the least respected institution in America is the U.S. Congress (although the mainstream media is giving Congress some serious competition). Now consider further that the government bureaucrats in this situation would be under intense pressure not to overproduce because the production budget was set and could not be altered without severe repercussions.

The smart approach for bureaucratic central planners, therefore, is to under-produce because it is better to deal with shortages than to face the music for overproducing. Central planners have nothing to fear from disgruntled consumers who complain about scarcity caused by underproduction, but they have much to fear from their bureaucratic superiors. Add to this that there are no penalties for under-producing and you begin to understand why shortages of essential goods and services are a normal part of life in socialist countries.

Think about the shortages of certain items and the "one per customer" signs in grocery stores because of the COVID-19 pandemic. The bare shelves in grocery stores and pharmacies at the beginning of the pandemic were exceptions in capitalist countries, but they are an everyday reality in socialist countries. In other words, what people in capitalist countries view as exceptions occurring only in emergency situations, people in socialist countries view as normal.

Contrast the *demand* system of capitalism with the *command* system of socialism. In a demand system you, the consumer, decide what will be produced and in what quantities by how much you consume and how much you are willing to pay for the items you consume. In a free-market economy, private-sector businesses survive and thrive by providing what their customers demand at prices they are willing to pay and, ironically, by anticipating what innovations consumers will want, often before consumers know themselves.

The necessity of developing new and improved products and getting them to the market first is why innovation is indigenous to capitalism but missing with socialism. Central planners in socialist countries are always looking backward at last year while free-market planners are always looking forward to the future. The incentive of profits drives innovation in a capitalist economy. There are no such incentives in a socialist economy. Bureaucratic planners in socialist countries work to meet government-mandated quotas, not consumer demand.

Incentives: Why capitalism always outperforms socialism

The key to the efficiency, innovation, and entrepreneurship associated with capitalism is the concept of incentives. People and businesses respond to incentives because the concept grows out of the human instinct for survival, coupled with the human desire to prosper. Socialism, on the other hand, is based on the expectation that people will work cooperatively and collaboratively for the good of the larger group—meaning the government—even when doing so is detrimental to the individual. This expectation may sound appealing in theory, but it completely disregards the basics of human nature, a serious flaw of socialism. Socialism typically ignores human nature. The only time socialism takes human nature into account is when it appeals to its worst aspects (e.g., laziness, entitlement, irresponsibility, idleness, etc.).

For example, trying to convince their employees to work together for the greater good of the business is why organizations in the United States spend millions every year on teamwork training, an investment that brings mixed results at best. Ironically the businesses achieving the best teamwork are organizations providing incentives to the individual team members. In other words, they incentivize teamwork by making it financially attractive to individual team members to cooperate and collaborate. When the team performs better, the individuals on the team are rewarded. But for socialists, individual rewards are anathema. Everyone must be equal; everyone must be paid the same.

Appealing to the best interests of the individual is why capitalism always outperforms socialism. Capitalism is based on the concept of individualism while socialism is based on the concept of collectivism. With no evidence to support their belief and a lot to refute it, socialists believe human nature can be perfected so group collaboration trumps individual interests. Capitalists know better. They understand human perfection comes only in the hereafter, not the here and now. Capitalists also understand that people respond to individual incentives, and they use this knowledge for good. Responding to personal incentives is not selfishness on the part of individuals; it is the outworking of human nature.

What applies to individuals also applies to organizations. With capitalism the most successful private-sector businesses are those accurately anticipating your needs and meeting them in the right amounts, at the right price, at the right time, and with greater than expected quality. This is how they survive. Those failing in this regard are left on the dust heap of history. Unlike government-owned- and -operated organizations, capitalist businesses cannot rely on ever-increasing taxes to compensate for poor planning, inefficient operations, and the lack of innovation. Thus, private-sector businesses are incentivized by a desire to survive and prosper, as are the individuals employed by them.

Consider just one example of how a command economy is not just unresponsive but almost guarantees shortages. In 2020, when the world was stricken by COVID-19, panic buying set in. People flocked to stores to purchase personal hygiene items to help protect themselves from the virus. As a result, retailers quickly ran out of certain supplies, creating nationwide shortages. In a socialist country where producers of personal hygiene products had already met their quotas, consumers would be out of luck.

Central planners had already dictated how many personal hygiene items would be produced that year, based, no doubt, on last year's numbers. Hence, government-operated organizations would be unprepared to respond to the changing need and probably unwilling to do so since there would be no incentive for them to respond. Central planners and command-oriented producers require predictability. They are not geared for rapid or sudden changes in demand or other circumstances. A demand system, on the other hand, approaches unexpected emergencies as new opportunities, rather than unwelcome exceptions.

In a demand economy there would be shortages of the needed products for a brief period, but private-sector producers would immediately go into production overdrive to meet consumer demand. Additionally, innovative producers of different products would rapidly switch gears and start manufacturing those in highest demand. This is exactly what happened in the United States when the coronavirus created shortages in personal-hygiene products.

There were temporary shortages, but only temporary. Because they are driven by consumer demand rather than quotas enforced by central planners, private-sector producers are flexible, innovative, and responsive when sudden, unexpected changes in consumer demand occur. For example, within just days of learning about a nationwide shortage of hand sanitizer, several whiskey distillers began using some of their raw material—alcohol—to produce this high-demand product. Other companies switched their production focus to manufacturing disposable face masks, disposable gloves, ventilators, and other badly needed products. Not only did this help satisfy consumer demand; for some businesses it resulted in an increase in the company's bottom line.

Sneaking socialism in the back door

Socialist ideologues are the personification of hypocrisy. For example, well-known socialist Senator Bernie Sanders used to criticize millionaires unmercifully as greedy, uncaring money-grubbers. But then a sharp-eyed pundit pointed out that he, Sanders himself, is a millionaire. Not to be deterred in his anti-capitalist rants, Sanders simply switched the target of his diatribes from millionaires to billionaires. He got away with this sleight-of-hand trick, but even the most ardent advocates of socialism cannot get away with trying to cover up the abject failure of central planning, the proven inefficiency of government-owned organizations, or the stifling effects of government control.

In the United States, socialist ideologues know better than to suggest the government take over private-sector businesses, at least by coercion and at least for now. Consequently, they have been quietly taking a new approach in their ongoing attack on capitalism. They have dropped their longtime goal of creating a "workers' paradise" in which workers own the businesses employing them and have substituted the more palatable-sounding goal of "income equality."

Their new goal certainly sounds more appealing until you consider what socialists mean by "income equality." As is often the case when dealing with the Left, caution is in order. They are masters at finding palatable terms for unpalatable practices. We call this tactic *semantic subterfuge*. With semantic subterfuge, words are carefully chosen to obfuscate rather than communicate, to blur rather than clarify, and to deceive rather than inform. Perhaps the best example of this practice is calling abortion "choice." The term *abortion* conjures up images of innocent children being ripped apart in their mothers' wombs, but calling it "choice" makes this heinous practice sound not just acceptable but appealing. After all, who doesn't want choice?

The biggest problem with the Left's definition of income equality is to them it means equal results, not equal opportunity. Not surprisingly, equal results are to be achieved by government coercion. The problem with mandating equal results is it ignores the fact that people are not equal when it comes to intelligence, talent, motivation, ambition, creativity, or any of the other factors that make people excel. People do not contribute equally to the success of their employers. They never have and never will. Therefore, expecting equal results is not just wishful thinking; it's absurd.

Some people are motivated to work hard and some are not. Some people are smart and some are not. Some people are highly talented and some are not. Some people think creatively and some don't. Some people will persevere when the work gets hard and some won't. These facts make equal results impossible, and trying to force them through government coercion just takes away the incentives for more intelligent, motivated, and creative people to put their God-given talents to good use.

Socialism advocates claim income equality means the poor get richer and the rich get poorer. Their claim is actually half-true. With socialism, the rich do indeed become poorer—excluding, of course, those who control the government. Unfortunately, the poor become poorer too. This is not just contention. Our claim has been proven over and over by experience and history. For example, while the people of Venezuela were starving, Hugo Chávez—their socialist president—became an obese, bloated billionaire. In a socialist nation only the few government decision makers at the top get richer. Everyone else gets poorer.

Socialists like to criticize capitalism by claiming the rich can use their money to gain influence and power. This is another oft-used socialist ruse: accuse your opponents of what you are guilty of. For example, in the 2020 senatorial elections, Democrats pumped millions of dollars into campaigns in an attempt to unseat incumbent Republican senators and gain control of the Senate. An unprecedented amount of money—from out-of-state sources—was spent trying to buy Senate seats, a clear attempt to use money to gain power.

Let's look at just one representative example. In an attempt to unseat Republican senator Lindsey Graham in South Carolina, Democrat Jaime Harrison spent an unprecedented $109 million, most of which came from sources outside South Carolina. Fortunately, even his record spending wasn't enough to buy the election. Unprecedented spending by Democrats also occurred in the 2020 Senate elections in Arizona, Kentucky, and Maine. The Senate races in 2020 were proof positive of the hypocrisy of the Left. They accuse Republicans of doing what they themselves are guilty of doing.

While criticizing capitalists for using money to gain power—something we have just shown that socialists do—Leftist ideologues also use their power to gain money. This fact has been borne out time and again by experience and history. We have already mentioned the example of Hugo Chávez in Venezuela. While his people were starving, Chávez used his power to bleed Venezuela's coffers dry, becoming a multibillionaire in the process. Another example of a socialist kleptocrat is Fidel Castro. Although he played the part of the penniless leader dressed in military fatigues and living at the same level as the poor people of Cuba, Castro was in fact a billionaire who used his power to amass a well-hidden fortune.

Closer to home, Joe Biden mysteriously went from being the self-acknowledged poorest man in the U.S. Senate to becoming wealthy as vice president. How did this happen? You don't become wealthy on the salary of the vice president. So, where did the money come from? To date Biden has provided no answer to this question. His silence on the subject has cast a cloud of suspicion around him that will make it difficult for many Americans to trust him as their president. The suspicion surrounding the president grows out of the sordid affair in which his son, Hunter, received huge amounts of money from a foreign government and a job for which he wasn't qualified. This affair raised questions concerning then vice president Biden's use of his office to secure money from a foreign government or, at the very least, to do so for his son. This is precisely what socialists do. They use the power of position to feather their own nests.

To achieve their goal of controlling a government that, in turn, controls the people, socialist ideologues are using the old boil-the-frog strategy. They are sneaking socialism in through the back door. Rather than have the government own the means of production and distribution, their new approach is to transform America into a welfare state in which citizens are completely dependent on the government. The first step toward complete government control is the provision of *single-payer health care*, a euphemism for socialized medicine and another example of semantic subterfuge. With this backdoor plan, other essential services will eventually fall under government control, but slowly enough, the American people—the frog—don't realize they are being boiled.

Single-payer health care is just one strategy ideologues are using to sneak socialism in the back door. A complementary strategy is the progressive income tax. Nobel laureate Friedrich Hayek, author of *The Road to Serfdom*, originally became famous for warning of the tyranny, loss of individual freedom, and oppression that inevitably accompany central planning and government control of the economy, the two mainstays of socialism. Later, in the foreword to a new edition of his book written in 1976, Hayek added a new warning about using the progressive income tax to sneak socialism in the back door. Hayek acknowledged that socialist ideologues were no longer openly advocating government control of the means of production and distribution. Rather, they have begun to use the progressive income tax and income redistribution to convert capitalist economies into welfare states by default.

Leftists in the Democratic Party claim the progressive income tax, properly applied, to the wealthiest Americans—often referred to as the top 1 percent—will pick up the tab for socialized medicine and all the other big-government programs they want to implement. What they refuse to reveal or even admit is taxing the wealthiest Americans at even a one-hundred percent rate would not raise enough money to pay for just one of their socialist programs: single-payer healthcare. That still leaves free college tuition, lifelong welfare, student-debt forgiveness, and the Green New Deal on the socialist's wish list to name just a few.

To socialist ideologues the progressive income tax is a backdoor way to control the means of production without having to actually take over and operate businesses. By imposing exorbitant taxes on businesses and business owners, the government can "own" them without actually acquiring the deed. This is the ultimate plan of those who call themselves "social democrats": control the government and then use the power of government to control individuals and organizations.

Achieving fairness and income equality by manipulating the progressive income tax is just one more myth perpetuated by socialist ideologues who prey on economically illiterate citizens. History has shown citizens of socialist countries are indeed equal, but only in their suffering and lack of life's essentials. This is why so many people in socialist countries resort to bribery and cronyism to become more equal among supposed equals. When inefficiency and poor planning lead to chronic shortages of life's essentials, socialist citizens are forced to bribe government officials to obtain the few items available. This is one more reason why those who prosper in a socialist economy are always the few at the top who control the government.

SOCIALISM AND PRIVATE PROPERTY

William Howard Taft was the twenty-seventh president of the United States and later a Supreme Court justice. His views on private property were prescient. Taft claimed, "Next to the right of liberty, the right of private property is the most important individual right guaranteed by the Constitution and the one which, united with that of personal liberty, has contributed more to the growth of civilization than any other institution established by the human race."[2] President Taft's statement is a powerful endorsement of capitalism over socialism.

To college students who don't yet own anything purchased with money they had to earn, government ownership of property may sound like a reasonable idea. After all, they are probably living in government-owned dormitories on their college campuses. But they do own automobiles, smartphones, and personal computers, even if their parents paid for them, which is likely. This fact can be used to teach college students an important lesson about socialism.

One veteran we interviewed, who is a college professor, recommended trying an experiment she sometimes uses. She encouraged those who are not fooled by the false promises of socialism to ask college students how they would like it if they had to turn their smartphones and computers over to the government. Then, if they wanted to have one of these devices, they had to put their names on a government-controlled waiting list to get one. If they were fortunate enough to be among the few to actually receive a smart phone or computer from the government, the only apps or software they could have would be those approved by the government. According to this veteran, the typical response from college students to this experiment is, "You're kidding, right?"

This same veteran/college professor has a ready answer for students who complain about the drabness, overcrowding, and stifling rules of their college dormitories. She tells the complaining students, "This is what you get with government housing. If you lived in a private home you owned instead of a government-owned dormitory, you would have the freedom to make your own decisions and choose your own roommates." Her response often leads to some interesting and, for the students, edifying discussions about private property versus government-owned property.

Government confiscation of private property was one of the most fundamental aspects of the philosophy advocated by Karl Marx and Friedrich Engels in *The Communist Manifesto*. It is still central to the thinking of ardent socialists in spite of the blatant failures of countries that have tried this deceived approach. The historical record concerning government confiscation of private property is instructive. The best example of this failed concept comes from China.

Once he gained control in China, Mao Tse-tung confiscated private farms and replaced them with agricultural collectives. Predictably, China suffered a major famine. Tens of thousands of Chinese citizens died as a result. Pol Pot did the same thing in Cambodia, resulting in widespread starvation in that country.

Few people know collective farming has already been tried in America. Shortly after landing at Plymouth Rock, the Pilgrims experimented with collective farming, a mistake that almost wiped out their original colony. It is no exaggeration to say socialism almost undermined the establishment of what became the United States of America.

After landing in the new world, Pilgrim governor William Bradford established a collectivist economy in which the community rather than individuals owned the land. The Pilgrims were supposed to work the land cooperatively. They were expected to share not just the harvest but the work necessary to raise the crops needed to survive. Because there were no individual incentives to work hard, what the Pilgrims shared, predictably, were misery, scarcity, and starvation.

Only by dividing the land up and converting it to private property so each family owned its own plot was Governor Bradford able to save the Pilgrim colony from famine and ruin. This is why we now celebrate Thanksgiving every November. The original Thanksgiving was a celebration of the Pilgrims' survival, something occurring in part because the governor had the good sense to privatize land and apply the farming techniques learned from friendly Native Americans.

According to Governor Bradford, converting the land to private property "had very good success; for it made all hands very industrious."[3] This is what private property does. The right of private property may be the most powerful incentive there is for motivating hard work, innovation, and productivity. Take away incentive and you get what Bradford's Pilgrims, Mao's peasants, Pol Pot's farmers, and Maduro's Venezuelans got: chronic shortages leading to privation and starvation.

The collectivization of agriculture is not the only aspect of socialism's habitual failure. Another is government housing. One of the veterans surveyed for this book shared an interesting story about living in government-owned housing. It occurred while he served in the Air Force many years ago. This veteran painted an instructive picture of the inherent failings of government-owned property. He served before the all-volunteer military brought about better conditions. Stationed in Okinawa, he and his family had to live in base housing. He described the houses provided by the government as plain, drab, and cookie-cutter.

If "equality" was the goal, it was certainly achieved. All the military families living in base housing were equal in their discomfort, inconvenience, and misery. All of the houses they lived in were equal in their drab sameness. They were also equal in having constant plumbing and electrical problems, as well as roof leaks. Finally, the military personnel were equal in their powerlessness to have needed household repairs made. The military families had to put their names on a waiting list and then wait for weeks and sometimes months for government employees or contractors to finally show up to make the needed repairs.

This veteran claimed he and his wife felt like cattle living in a leaky, poorly insulated barn. When he talked with neighbors who lived in the same conditions about making improvements to their houses, the idea was shot down immediately. His neighbors asked him why he would want to waste the little money he had making improvements to property he didn't own. The government would not reimburse him for improving its property. In fact, the government wouldn't even thank him. Rather, he would probably be disciplined for violating some arcane government regulation. In other words, since he didn't own the property, there was no incentive to improve it or to even take care of it. The veteran who shared this experience said he never appreciated the value of private property until he was forced to live in government housing.

REFUTING THE RACE CAR–AND–DRIVER RATIONALE FOR SOCIALISM

As thousands flee socialist countries such as Venezuela, seeking food and freedom, proponents of socialism are finding it increasingly difficult to justify their support of this flawed philosophy. This is why Leftists in the Democratic Party refuse to accept the socialist label even as they adopt socialist policies. It is also why the most ardent among them have begun to use the race car–and–driver analogy as their new apologetic.

This analogy posits socialism as a fundamentally sound race car but with a poor track record because of bad drivers. According to socialist advocates, their race car (socialism) would win if it had a competent driver. In other words, they claim socialism is a legitimate philosophy that will work if implemented by competent leaders. They, of course, view themselves as competent leaders.

Modern-day socialists admit socialism failed miserably in the former Soviet Union, but they blame the failure on the incompetent Soviet leaders. Never mind that these same supposedly incompetent Soviet leaders were able to put the first satellite in space and develop some of the most advanced military technologies in the world. And while it is true socialist leaders such as Castro, Pol Pot, Mao, and Hugo Chávez were despots, they weren't incompetent. They could not have gained control of their respective countries if they were incompetent. They lost the race not because they were incompetent but because they were driving a faulty car: socialism.

When socialism was tried in the Nordic countries, the leaders there certainly weren't incompetent. In fact, they were smart and well-intentioned, albeit duped. If anyone could make socialism work, it would have been these Nordic leaders. However, as the record shows, they couldn't. This was not because they were incompetent, but because socialism is a fundamentally flawed concept even the most competent leaders cannot make work. To stay with our analogy, even the best driver cannot win the race in a poorly designed race car.

The fatal flaws of socialism have given rise to the concept of *emerging economies*. Economists use this term to describe countries with traditionally high levels of government control but out of economic necessity, are moving toward free markets and private property. In other words, they are *emerging* from the darkness of socialism. To various degrees, these countries currently include Indonesia, China, Thailand, Vietnam, South Africa, India, Chile, Mexico, and Brazil. How ironic, then, as other countries around the world that have actually tried socialism are giving it up in favor of capitalism, the United States, historically the world's bastion of capitalism, is moving toward the pit of socialism.

WHAT DO SOCIALIST IDEOLOGUES REALLY WANT?

One of the veterans we surveyed asked a pertinent question: What do socialist advocates really want? This question is so important that before proceeding with the remainder of this book, we must answer it. When you know the answer to this question, you will know what drives the difficult-to-understand machinations of socialist ideologues.

In all human nature there is no temptation stronger than the allure of power. In fact, the allure of other common temptations, such as money, sex, and longevity, pale in comparison. It is in the nature of human beings to covet power. When our natural human tendencies are allowed to proceed unchecked by morality and common decency, we covet the ability to get what we want, do what we want, and say what we want whenever we want. These tendencies go unchecked in socialists because they reject the God who is the basis of morality and human decency.

An even worse human tendency shows up in some people in the desire to be able to force others to do what they want them to do. Because people who harbor this desire live in a world where others have the same desire, they need power. Power allows some people to exert control over others and bend them to their will, something necessary if they are to get what they want, say what they want, do what they want, and require others to do what they want them to do. Although they refuse to admit it, all these things are goals of socialist ideologues.

The desire for power—what we call the "god syndrome"—is why socialist ideologues are willing to ignore the inherent flaws of their failed philosophy. The desire for power can blind people to reality. This is precisely what it does to advocates of socialism. Socialist ideologues want to be able to control the world so they can get what they want, say what they want, do what they want, and more important, believe what they want without opposition. This last desire—without opposition—is important to understand. Socialists want to be able to believe their distorted view of the world, but they don't stop there. They also want to be able to force you to believe it or, barring that, coerce you into meekly accepting it without opposition. To understand why socialist advocates want power and how they will use it, memorize the following three-part formula:

1. The government controls the people.
2. Socialists control the government.
3. Socialists control the people.

To achieve the third element in this formula, socialist ideologues must first replace personal liberty and individual freedom with government control. With this achieved, they must gain control of the government. Once they have achieved these two parts of the formula, the third element—control of the people—will fall into place. Socialists in the Democratic Party made significant progress toward achieving step 1 in this formula when the Biden/Harris ticket, aided by questionable vote counts, eked out a slim majority in the presidential election of 2020.

During the 2020 national elections, Democrats made it clear that if they take control of the government, they will use that control to put measures in place to ensure conservatives never again control the White House, Senate, House of Representatives, or Supreme Court. When they gain total control of the government, socialist ideologues will never surrender it, at least not willingly. History has proven that once socialist ideologues gain control of the government and, in turn, the people, they use the power of government to retain power.

WHY SOCIALISTS REJECT AMERICAN EXCEPTIONALISM

If you want to stir up a hornet's nest, tell a group of socialist ideologues America is not just good and great, but uniquely so among the other nations. Tell them America is exceptional. Few things raise the hackles of Leftist ideologues more than the concept of American exceptionalism. The reason for this is simple: If America is exceptional, why adopt socialism? Socialist ideologues have no answer for this simple but profound question. Consequently, their only option is to deny that America is good, great, or exceptional. As one of the veterans we surveyed commented, to a socialist ideologue America is exceptional only in that it is exceptionally bad.

It is important to understand what is meant by *American exceptionalism* and why we believe America is an exceptional nation. American exceptionalism means the United States is unique among the community of nations because our founders adopted a governing philosophy providing unprecedented, unsurpassed levels of freedom, stability, and prosperity for nearly two and a half centuries.[4] That governing philosophy comes straight from Holy Scripture. This is why no other nation in the world has enjoyed the level of governmental stability, freedom, or prosperity as the United States.

The United States is the longest-standing constitutional republic in the world. To appreciate what an accomplishment this is, consider that during the time America has been governed according to the Constitution, France has gone through seventeen different constitutions and governments. Since 1848, France's neighbor, Germany, has had five different constitutions and forms of government.[5] Then there are the third-world nations that change governments with mind-numbing regularity. The Constitution is like the roots of a mighty oak, anchoring our country to the ground laid by the Founders. Unfortunately, Leftist justices on the Supreme Court and socialist politicians have been hacking away at those roots for decades.

In addition to the stability, freedom, and prosperity America has enjoyed under it, the U.S. Constitution has been and continues to be one of the most influential documents in world history. Elements of the Constitution have been adopted by numerous other countries, including Australia, Canada, West Germany, Switzerland, Yugoslavia, Nigeria, Argentina, Brazil, and Mexico.[6] The ideas codified in our constitution have improved lives throughout the world. This level of positive influence alone makes America exceptional.

To understand why American citizens have enjoyed an unmatched level of stability, freedom, and prosperity as well as governmental continuity, one must begin with the Declaration of Independence. This document provides the philosophical foundation for the U.S. Constitution. American exceptionalism can be traced back to four specific elements in the Declaration of Independence that make America not just different but exceptional. The Declaration established the following:[7]

- There is an authority higher than government. That authority is God
- The rights of American citizens come from God, not government
- The primary purpose of government is to protect the God-given rights of citizens from all sources, including the government
- There is a fixed moral law that is higher than man-made laws. This fixed moral law establishes universal absolutes of right and wrong. It comes directly from Scripture.

The U.S. Constitution was written by individuals who knew well these elements of the Declaration of Independence and believed them. As a result, the Constitution was written as a *user's manual* for putting the philosophy espoused in the Declaration into practice. Later in this book we refute the claim of socialist ideologues that the U.S. Constitution is a "Godless document." At this point we focus on a foundational fact that readers must understand. To wit, socialists must reject these four elements of the Declaration of Independence because they are antithetical to everything socialists believe and want the American public to believe. This is because if America is exceptional, we don't need socialism.

WHY YOUNG AMERICANS ARE SUSCEPTIBLE TO THE FALSE PROMISES OF SOCIALISM

Leftist college professors, the media, historical revisionists, and the entertainment industry all play a role in hoodwinking the public about socialism, but the susceptibility of young people begins at home with their parents. Parents are often unwittingly complicit in the growing acceptance of socialism by their children. This happens when helicopter parents shield their children from responsibility and accountability during their formative years, accept mediocrity from them instead of encouraging excellence, and do for them what their children should do for themselves.

Not surprisingly, when these pampered children become adults, they expect the government to do for them what their parents have always done. Knowing this, socialist advocates promise the government will do just that: take care of them from cradle to grave. This is precisely the message entitled young adults want to hear. Consequently, they are easily deluded into thinking the government is going to play the nanny role their parents have always played in their lives.

A lot of parents in America give their children too much while requiring too little. Ironically, many of these parents were poor or middle-income when they were young and had to work long and hard for the material advantages they now enjoy. Not wanting their children to have to suffer the hardships they endured, these parents sometimes fall into the trap of "protecting" them from the consequences of idleness, bad attitudes, poor decisions, and unacceptable behavior. They also give their children what the children should earn. This is unfortunate because, ironically, we appreciate more what we earn through our own efforts than what we are freely given. These same parents often make the same well-intentioned but misguided mistake of shielding their children from any sort of obligation and refusing to hold them accountable for poor performance and misbehavior.

Shielding children in this way doesn't help them; it harms them. Letting children confront the hard lessons of life while they are young and able to learn from the experience is the best way to prepare them for life outside the protective cocoon of the parental home.

But that's not what today's parents are doing. Is it any wonder, then, so many young Americans develop an aversion to responsibility, a dislike of accountability, and an entitlement mentality? This aversion is behind the phenomenon of the thirty-year-old son moving back in with his parents because he is unable to cope with the everyday realities of life on his own. Such unprepared, immature adults are easily hoodwinked by the false promises of socialism.

As a rule, young people today have been raised in unprecedented affluence, a condition many of them take for granted. What their parents had to work hard to achieve, they have been given, so they don't appreciate it as they would if they'd worked for it. Think of automobiles. When we were in high school, only a privileged few of our classmates had automobiles. Drive by a high school today and look around. It is the rare student of driving age who doesn't have a car or truck. Even people who qualify as poor by today's standards have air conditioning, automobiles, cell phones, and microwave ovens. What is considered poverty in America today would be considered affluence in many countries around the globe.

Young people shop in stores or at online sites overflowing with abundance from all over the world. They can purchase things earlier generations didn't even know existed. Unfortunately, too many young people today don't realize it wasn't always this way. They also fail to grasp that the affluence they enjoy is the result of capitalism. Consumer demand is a powerful force for creating abundance, and capitalism, unlike socialism, puts the consumer in the driver's seat.

We grew up without air conditioning or central heating, as did many of the veterans interviewed and surveyed for this book. One of these veterans pointed out that not only do youngsters today take air conditioning and central heating for granted; they think having to share a room with a brother or sister—something most Americans from earlier generations had to do—amounts to child abuse. Our lives of abundance in the United States exist because of capitalism coupled with the Christian work ethic. No matter where it has been tried, socialism has failed to come close to providing the material advantages of capitalism. Further, its collective approach to enterprise undermines the work ethic.

Even with its acknowledged imperfections, capitalism is better by far than any other economic philosophy ever imagined. Coupled with the Christian work ethic, capitalism has allowed the United States to create a standard of living that is the envy of the world. One veteran commented that it is no accident so many people from all over the world want to resettle in America. What immigrants seek in America exists because of capitalism and freedom, not socialism and government control. Socialism's failure is what drives thousands of immigrants to America's shores every year.

Historians claim no great civilization has ever survived its own affluence. Affluent living can make people soft physically, mentally, and morally. One of the veterans we surveyed stated that had America been settled by the entitled youth of today and led by socialist ideologues, we would still be just thirteen British colonies on the Atlantic Seaboard, if that many. Several of the veterans we interviewed wondered what was going to happen to America when we have to rely on entitled "snowflakes" to protect us from the hardened tyrants and terrorists of the world.

WHY A FAILED PHILOSOPHY CONTINUES TO APPEAL TO SOME AMERICANS

Young people are not the only constituent groups taken in by the false promises of socialist ideologues. There are several other groups that advocates of socialism target because of their inherent susceptibility or economic naivety. One of the veterans we surveyed wanted to know which groups in America, other than young people and college students, support socialism and why. This is a good question.

The groups most susceptible to the machinations of socialist ideo-logues include the following:

- *Displaced workers whose jobs have been eliminated by technology or sent overseas where labor is cheaper.* The hostility of displaced workers toward capitalism is understandable, but through retraining they can still secure better positions in the labor force than they will under socialism. While starting a new career in midlife can be a challenge, the need to retrain is a small price to pay when the alternative is a daily grind in which every aspect of the individual's life is monitored, controlled, and dictated by the government; individual freedom is lost; and chronic shortages of daily essentials are common. Further, the demands of socialist ideologues to continually raise the minimum wage just ensures more workers will be displaced when employers either send their work overseas or replace people with technology

- *Working poor who find it difficult to make ends meet and who can-not afford health insurance.* The susceptibility of people in this group is also understandable, yet they still have more and bet-ter options available under capitalism than they would under socialism, a fact proven over and over wherever socialism has been tried

- *Americans for whom welfare has become a way of life rather than a temporary safety net.* People in this group don't realize that in a socialist setting they would have to work, but they would have no choice concerning the kind of work required of them. Additionally, their income level and access to essential goods and services would decrease under socialism

- *College professors whose lives, careers, and views are shielded from reality because they operate in an insular environment funded by taxes, donations, and government grants rather than a free market that demands results.* College professors are so insulated from reality they assume a socialist government would allow them to continue professing their naive beliefs and promoting their loathsome agendas when history suggests just the opposite.

Never forget: Mao sent more than forty-six thousand college professors to their deaths. College professors also assume a socialist economy would be able to financially support the huge number of colleges and universities currently feeding at the public trough in America. History has shown this to be a foolish assumption

- *Government bureaucrats who are intent on protecting their careers by ensuring the government continually increases in size.* The careers of federal government bureaucrats are currently protected by civil-service policies making it difficult to weed out even the most unmotivated and incompetent personnel. Bureaucrats assume that under socialism this kind of protection would continue to be enforced. However, history has shown that in a socialist setting, civil-service policies quickly fall victim to cronyism. Bureaucrats who find themselves on the wrong side of the governing elite or who occupy a position desired by a crony of a government leader soon find themselves out of their government jobs.

CHAPTER 2

SOCIALISM ENCOURAGES CORRUPTION AND TYRANNY

As a veteran with more than thirty-five years of service to our nation as an Air Force officer, I still adhere to the pledge I took at the outset of defending our nation and complying with the U.S. Constitution. I fought for freedom during my time in the service seeing both cold-war tactics and hot-war devastation. That short thirty-five years saw tyrants, despots, and dictators try to take over nations through the influence of socialism, in spite of the fact that socialism has proven to be unsuccessful in the human equation. It takes away from the desire to reach the pinnacle of success, a desire that leads to a nation's growth and prosperity.

—Gordon "Gordy" Fornell, United States Air Force, 1958–1993

Lieutenant General (retired) Gordon "Gordy" Fornell had a distinguished thirty-five-year career in the Air Force, during which he flew more than fifty different kinds of aircraft, logged more than 7,000 hours of flight time, earned parachute wings, and was certified as a Level III program manager.

The list of socialist leaders past and present alluded to in General Fornell's opening quote for this chapter reads like a Who's Who of rogues, despots, and tyrants. As one of the veterans we surveyed noted, socialism seems to attract the worst kind of leaders, a claim borne out by history. There was Stalin in the Soviet Union, who oversaw the murder of more than twenty million of his own citizens. Then there was Stalin's contemporary, Chairman Mao, who was in a league of his own. He murdered or starved at least sixty million Chinese citizens. Cambodian despot Pol Pot murdered or starved more than two million of his citizens, creating what has come to be known as the "killing fields."

In more recent times, Hugo Chávez transformed the once-prosperous democracy of Venezuela into a socialist hellhole. He became obese and wealthy while his citizens starved and lost everything. His successor, Nicolas Maduro, picked up where Chávez left off and continued the subjugation of Venezuelan citizens. Under his rule, Venezuela has experienced inflation exceeding 700 percent, critical shortages of food and medicine, and a mass exodus of citizens to other countries, mostly to the United States.

In Maduro's socialist "paradise," the people of Venezuela are fighting over scraps from garbage cans to stay alive. The nation's doctors—who now earn only about $1.20 per day—have to purchase the critical medical supplies they need on the black market. Not surprisingly, Venezuelans are fleeing their country in droves. They now comprise the largest number of people from anywhere in the world petitioning the United States for asylum. The socialist paradise promised by Hugo Chávez and Nicolas Maduro has become hell on earth for Venezuelans.

The historical record is clear when it comes to the types of folks who typically rise to the top in socialist nations: people with no respect for individual freedom, personal liberty, common decency, or Christian morality. They are willing to imprison, starve, torture, and murder their own citizens to gain control and enforce conformity. Even the less violent of them are willing to deceive, distort, and divide to secure their positions in government. The despots rising to the top in socialist regimes have been willing to do anything to advance their perverse agendas, all the while justifying their depraved deeds in the name of creating a socialist utopia.

Anything seen as serving the government is considered acceptable to socialist ideologues, even if it impinges on the freedom of individuals, which it often does. This is why to a socialist the desire for individual liberty or personal freedom is considered "selfishness." Theoretically, the larger group to be served is composed of all citizens in a socialist nation. In reality, the only group served is the government elites. Nobody prospers or benefits in a socialist economy except the corrupt cronies at the top, who control the government controlling the people.

CORRUPTION AND TYRANNY IN SOCIALIST COUNTRIES

Corruption and tyranny are as indigenous to socialism as fleas to a dog. They manifest in the forms of mass murder, oppression, famine, terror, false imprisonment, purges, censorship, suppression of religion, banning of dissent, confiscation of private property, disarming of citizens, pilfering of the public treasury, and voter fraud, to name just a few examples. The veteran who claimed socialism seems to attract the worst kinds of leaders was right. In fact, the reality of socialist leaders is probably even worse than he thought.

If you find yourself thinking the kinds of things that happened in the Soviet Union, China, Cambodia, Cuba, and Venezuela could never happen in the United States, think back to the presidential election of November 2020. Accusations of voter fraud were widespread, triggering numerous legal challenges to the eventual voter count. These accusations involved: (1) mass ballot mailouts allowing people to vote more than once, dead people to vote, and unregistered citizens to cast ballots; (2) waiting to count mail-in ballots until the in-person count was complete so unscrupulous election personnel would know how many votes their preferred candidate needed to win; (3) declaring vote totals complete before absentee ballots were received from military personnel; (4) providing some military bases an insufficient number of absentee ballots to allow all the troops to vote; (5) defying the elections laws of the states where the corruption was taking place; (6) defying court orders pertaining to the counting of votes; (7) tainted surveys of voter preferences; (8) media outlets blatantly promoting one candidate over the other; and (9) censoring supporters of one candidate on social media and the Internet.

Voter fraud, media bias, and censorship don't rank as high on the list of corrupt activities as murdering and imprisoning political opponents, but they are a first step down a slippery slope that should not be ignored or downplayed. Corruption is corruption regardless of the fraudulent methods employed. Whether the corrupt methods involve violence or voter fraud, they are intended to coerce, manipulate, and control people whose rights are supposed to be protected by the government, not trampled on by it.

In these lesser acts of corruption are found the seeds of more frightening forms of corruption. Never forget that during the 2020 presidential election, supporters of the Democratic Party's candidate were assembled in numerous major cities across the country, preparing to riot, loot and burn should their candidate lose. These cities were spared from mob violence only because their candidate was declared the winner.

In this chapter we summarize some of the more widely known facts about the corruption and tyranny associated with prominent socialist leaders, facts directly from the historical record. Some of the more blatant examples of corruption and tyranny in socialist countries were committed by Joseph Stalin, Mao Tse-tung, Pol Pot, and Hugo Chávez. These despots' regimes should be studied by all who think they prefer socialism to capitalism. The actions of these tyrants explain why its advocates find it necessary to conceal, distort, and rewrite the historical record of socialism. By studying the past, we can avoid making the same mistakes in the future. With a view to learning from the past, we present herein a brief history of socialist regimes.

Joseph Stalin: Corruption and tyranny in the Soviet Union

Joseph Stalin became the leader of the Soviet Union through acts of corruption. He remained in power using these same tactics.

Stalin maintained his chokehold on the Soviet people through mass murder, repression, terror, false imprisonment, and censorship. During Stalin's reign of terror, no one was safe. He came to power by murdering opponents of Bolshevism on a broad scale. In America this would be like a newly elected president initiating the mass murder of those who voted against him in the presidential election or who might try to unseat him in a future election.

Killing off those who opposed socialism and communism wasn't enough for Stalin. Once he seized the reins of power, Stalin turned on fellow socialists and Communists, including members of his own Bolshevik party. He ruthlessly attacked Bolshevik leaders who'd played key roles in the early years of the Soviet Union. Viewed by Stalin as potential opponents, these fellow Bolsheviks had to go. Hence, Stalin had them eliminated. Try to imagine George Washington having John Adams or Alexander Hamilton killed to prevent him from opposing him for a second term as president. This is precisely what Stalin did to other Soviet leaders.

Stalin tried to legitimize his purges of political opponents by conducting "show trials" during what came to be known as the period of the Great Terror (1936–1938). During this infamous period, Leon Trotsky, Grigory Zinovyev, Sergei Kirov, and Lev Kamenev—all key Bolshevik leaders—were expelled from the Communist Party and later executed on false charges or simply assassinated to ensure they couldn't challenge Stalin's leadership.

In addition to ruthlessly eliminating fellow members of his own party, Stalin sent millions of Soviet citizens to prison or labor camps to solidify his hold on power. In America this would be like a Democratic president rounding up millions of Republican citizens or a Republican president rounding up millions of Democratic citizens and sending them to death camps. Many of these citizens were worked to death or simply killed, which is why Stalin's labor camps (the Gulag) became known as death camps. The most common "crime" committed by those sent to the Gulag was questioning Stalin's plans for his version of a socialist *paradise* in the Soviet Union.

Stalin's most feared and oft-used weapon for ensuring Soviet citizens toed the party line was his secret police. The first version of the Soviet secret police—the Cheka—was established during the reign of Vladimir Lenin, before Stalin murdered his way to power. The Cheka's original responsibilities amounted to investigating those who spoke out against Communist/socialist orthodoxy. But the role of the Cheka evolved quickly, transforming the organization into a ruthless instrument of terror used to coerce citizens into compliance, punish dissenters, and eliminate opposition. As a result, the most dreaded experience Soviet citizens could face during Stalin's reign of terror was a late-night knock on their door. It meant only one thing: Stalin's secret police had come calling.

Over time the Soviet secret police became known as the People's Commissariat for Internal Affairs (NKVD). Stalin used the NKVD with brutal efficiency to eliminate anyone and everyone who might be perceived as a threat—not just to communism and socialism—but even more so to him. He was especially hard on intellectuals and religious believers; particularly Protestants, Catholics, and Jews. Stalin's goal when it came to religion was simple: eliminate it.

To this end, the government confiscated church property, atheism became the official "religion" of the Soviet Union, and church leaders were imprisoned. The only god Stalin wanted his people to worship was the god of government, which he controlled. Again, if you think these kinds of attacks on the church could not happen in the United States, remember how government officials in Leftist-controlled states shut down churches during the COVID-19 pandemic but allowed bars and liquor stores to operate.

Try to imagine an American president transforming the Federal Bureau of Investigation (FBI) into his own personal police force to spy on and terrorize American citizens who speak out against his views. Or sitting in church one Sunday when armed FBI agents in riot gear burst in, arrest your pastor, and confiscate all church property. If all of this sounds far-fetched to you, it shouldn't. It can happen in the United States if the philosophical descendants of Stalin and other socialist despots continue to gain ground.

This is why so many Americans were disturbed by the FBI's activities during Donald Trump's first run for the presidency and leading up to the partisan impeachment hearings in which Democrats tried to remove Trump as president after he defeated Hillary Clinton. Some felt the FBI was behaving too much like the

NKVD—minus, of course, the torture and death camps. But don't discount this incident. Using the federal police as a weapon of coercion against citizens is tyranny whether they employ torture and death camps or limit their methods to spying, trumped-up charges, and false accusations. Coercion is coercion regardless of the methods used, and tyranny is tyranny whether it is of the hard or the soft variety.

Russian intellectuals were particular targets of Stalin and his henchmen. Even before Stalin murdered his way to power, anyone who could present a cogent argument against communism/socialism, along with anyone who questioned Stalin's brutal tactics, became a target of the government. Artists, writers, and academics were singled out and dealt with harshly. Newspapers and magazines were taken over by the government and became little more than mouthpieces for Stalin. Periodicals taking a stand against Stalin's murderous methods were eliminated altogether. The government also took over book publishers, libraries, and bookstores to control the reading material that got into the hands of Soviet citizens.

In America, this would be like all media outlets, newspapers, social media, the Internet, and magazines being confiscated by the government and then being heavily censored by bureaucrats beholden to the party in power. Americans got a taste of this kind of tyranny when President Donald Trump ran for reelection against former vice president Joe Biden in 2020. Social media giants blatantly and unapologetically censored input from conservative sources, and media outlets refused to air speeches, political rallies, and press briefings by President Trump. These social media giants used their control of the Internet to promote the narrative of the Far Left while refusing to circulate opposing views. This reached its peak when the major social media platforms permanently banned former president Trump and shut down platforms such as Parler.

Imagine Barnes & Noble, Books-a-Million, Amazon, ABC, CBS, NBS, CNN, MSNBC, Facebook, and Twitter being confiscated and controlled by the government. This is precisely what happened in the socialist "paradise" of the Soviet Union under Stalin. Again, if you think these things could never happen in the United States, we challenge you to watch mainstream news programs. As several of the veterans interviewed for this book pointed out, the majority of them have become little more than propaganda organs for the Left wing of the Democratic Party. No longer objective in their coverage or outlook, they are simply advocates for Leftist politicians and their socialist principles. In other words, excluding government confiscation, what happened in the Soviet Union is already happening in the United States.

There is one final act of repression Stalin undertook to solidify his hold on power that should be considered by those who claim to prefer socialism to capitalism. He *cleansed* the Soviet Union's universities of professors whose views were at odds with his. Thousands of professors, along with artists, journalists, and other members of what Soviets called the "intelligentsia" were summarily packed off to the Gulag to be starved and worked to death. Professionals intelligent enough to understand what Stalin was doing and how he was going about it were considered enemies of the state. Socialists need an intellectually malleable citizenry. Less-than-compliant professors in the Soviet Union who spoke out against Stalin paid dearly for doing so.

In America this would be like a Republican president arresting all liberal college professors nationwide and sending them off to the worst prisons in this country, or a Democratic president taking the same action against conservative professors. The former would shut down American universities, because the overwhelming majority of college professors in this country are liberal. Of course, there would be little gained for socialists by removing conservative professors from colleges and universities since there are so few of them. Liberals have so solidified their stranglehold on professorial appointments that colleges and universities might as well erect signs reading, "No conservatives allowed." But we digress. The stranglehold Marxist professors have on higher education is dealt with later in this book. For now, let's return to Stalin.

Ideologues tend to discount Stalin when it comes to the historical record of socialism, ignoring him when possible. But when forced to acknowledge his reign of terror, they claim he was an anomaly, that he doesn't represent the views or methods of most socialist leaders. However, as you will see in the summaries of other socialist leaders, this defense is full of holes. When it comes to the most prominent socialist leaders in history, Stalin represents the rule, not the exception. In fact, even though he killed more than twenty million of his own citizens during his reign of terror, Stalin isn't even the worst example of a corrupt socialist tyrant. That dubious distinction goes to his contemporary, Chairman Mao of China.

Mao Tse-tung: Corruption and tyranny in China

No person is more venerated in China than Mao Tse-tung, patriarch of that nation's Communist Party and its chairman from 1949 to 1976. The reverence for Chairman Mao among modern-day Chinese is difficult to understand. After all, he murdered more than sixty million of their predecessors in transforming China into what was supposed to be a Communist/socialist utopia. In fact, Mao still holds the dubious distinction of being the worst mass murderer of the twentieth century.

When one veteran observed how socialism seems to attract the worst kinds of leaders, he could have been talking specifically about Mao Tse-tung. As evil as they were, Hitler, Stalin, and Pol Pot were amateurs compared to Mao. He sent more of his own citizens to death camps than the other three combined. During Mao's reign, nobody was allowed to so much as question his vision of complete government control in China or his control of the Communist Party, which controlled the government.

Like most socialist ideologues, Mao viewed anyone who opposed him as an enemy. All tyrants view opponents as enemies who must be eliminated, but Mao's contempt for the Chinese people was legendary. To put his tyranny into perspective, try to imagine George Washington murdering, working to death, or starving every colonist who did not share his vision for our country or who questioned his conduct of the war for independence from Great Britain. Historians will tell you Washington's opponents amounted to a surprisingly large portion of the colonial population, including a few of his own officers in the Continental Army. Mao's opponents amounted to a lot of people in China too.

Mao didn't discriminate when it came to terrorizing Chinese citizens who questioned his vision or tactics, but like Stalin, he was especially hard on intellectuals. Mao feared the influence they could have on the Chinese people. Consequently, he tortured and terrorized them unmercifully. If these tactics didn't work, he had them murdered. In fact, Mao was fond of boasting that he killed forty-six thousand intellectuals in China. Try to imagine an American president rounding up dissenting scholars, professors, scientists, artists, and writers; having them executed; and then bragging about it.

Mao called the most ill-fated of his socialist reforms the "Great Leap Forward." Despite this positive-sounding title—a blatant example of semantic subterfuge—his Great Leap Forward was a human tragedy of epic proportions. The misnamed Great Leap Forward was Mao's plan for transforming China's weak economy into a socialist powerhouse. His plan worked about as well as Ford's Edsel.

The biggest and most tragic failure of Mao's Great Leap Forward was the collectivization of Chinese agriculture, in which private farms were confiscated and controlled by the government. Farmers forced to work on the collective farms were told by central planners what to plant and when. Many farmers who had successfully raised certain kinds of crops for decades were now required to raise different kinds of crops unfamiliar to them. In a devastating blunder, the Chinese government implemented collectivization on a massive scale with centralized planning and state control of farming methods. Mao's confiscation and collectivization of private farms would have failed under even the best of circumstances, but inept planning, poor farming methods, and an inefficient distribution system turned failure into tragedy.

Not surprisingly, individuals who had farmed their own land for generations were reluctant to go along with Mao's plan for confiscation and collectivization. Many resisted. But Mao was brutal in his determination to force collectivization to work. Like most socialists, he thought the government could simply coerce people into making a bad idea work. But a bad idea is a bad idea no matter whose idea it is, and the Great Leap Forward was a bad idea, a situation not to be rectified by government coercion.

Mao's Great Leap Forward led to one of the worse famines in recorded history. Add to the list of Chinese citizens who starved to death during the famine to those who were worked to death or murdered for resisting, and Chairman Mao oversaw the deaths of more than forty-five million Chinese citizens during just four years in this period of *socialist reform*. Before his death, Mao would add another fifteen million Chinese citizens to the list of those murdered, worked to death, or starved during his reign of terror.

During the famine resulting from Mao's forced collectivization of agriculture, Chinese citizens sometimes resorted to stealing food to stay alive, an understandable response to starvation. Mao was especially harsh on those caught pilfering food, including children. These *criminals* were punished in the most brutal of ways. Some had their noses or ears cut off; others were branded like cattle. Some were burned alive, while others were tied up and thrown into rivers or lakes to drown. The worst form of punishment employed by Mao's goons was forcing parents to bury their own children alive.[1]

Mao is the worst tyrant on the list of socialist despots. He was willing to starve, torture, and murder in a failed effort to force a flawed concept to work. His disdain for human life is unmatched in modern history. On the other hand, his commitment to a flawed concept—socialism—was so strong nothing and no one could turn him from his course of implementing it in China. Mao was a blindly committed ideologue. The same can be said of the Leftist politicians and professors who use their platforms to advocate for socialism in America in spite of what the historical record shows.

Pol Pot: Corruption and tyranny in Cambodia

Mao Tse-tung was the greatest mass murderer of the twentieth century, but that might be because Pol Pot of Cambodia had a much smaller population to terrorize. While it is true Mao murdered, starved, and worked to death at least sixty million of his own people during his reign of terror in China, that number represented approximately 12 percent of China's population at the time. Pol Pot murdered two million people, but that number represented 22 percent of Cambodia's population, and he ruled that country for just four years (1975–1979). In comparison, Mao had twenty-seven years (1949–1976) to do his horrific work.

Like Mao, Pol Pot was a Marxist ideologue and tyrannical despot who forced socialism on his country. Also like Mao, he brutally tortured, terrorized, or murdered anyone who stood in his way. Pol Pot's barbaric regime was known as the Khmer Rouge. Its goal was to transform Cambodia into a socialist agrarian nation. Unfortunately for the Cambodian people, Pol Pot's confiscation of private farms, collectivization of agriculture, and forced relocation of people from the cities to government farms had the same predictable effect as Mao's misnamed Great Leap Forward. It resulted in famine.

Cambodian citizens who resisted or spoke out against Pol Pot's socialist plans were arrested and bused to what became known as Cambodia's "killing fields." Pol Pot became famous for claiming it is better to kill innocent people than to let dissidents escape. But killing innocent people and dissidents wasn't enough for Pol Pot. Like Hitler, he planned to "purify" his country and create a master race. Under his rule, Pol Pot classified anyone who wore glasses or spoke a foreign language as an "undesirable" to be bused to the killing fields for extermination.

Located in Choeung Ek, the killing fields were just that: fields where Pol Pot's henchmen brutally murdered dissenters and anyone else Pol Pot deemed unfit for the Cambodian master race he envisioned. Of course, many starved to death during the famine caused by his forced collectivization of agriculture, but others were beaten to death in the killing fields. One tree in particular in the killing fields was used to bash in the heads of babies who were swung into its trunk by their feet. Adults were either beaten to death with blunt instruments or thrown into ditches and covered with lethal poisons.[2]

Like Mao and Stalin, Pol Pot was blindly committed to socialism. He, too, thought this fatally flawed philosophy could be forced on the population by torture, murder, starvation, and genocide.

Two things he and other socialist tyrants did not understand—and today's socialists still don't—is (1) you cannot force an unworkable system to work no matter how many people you kill, and (2) people can be brutally coerced into going along with government plans, but even in the worst conditions, they will find ways to resist a philosophy that violates their beliefs and personal interests. In other words, socialist tyrants like Pol Pot can strong-arm a nation into compliance, but they cannot change hearts. This is one of many reasons socialist regimes fail.

Hugo Chávez: Corruption and tyranny in Venezuela

One of the veterans we surveyed wondered how one man could transform the most prosperous, oil-rich country in South America into a hellhole of poverty and starvation. He was speaking, of course, of Venezuela's Hugo Chávez. For Chávez, transforming Venezuela from prosperity to poverty was a four-step process: (1) He got himself elected by convincing voters through false promises that socialism would improve their lives. (2) He replaced Venezuela's capitalist economy with socialism. (3) He used the power of government to stay in office even after his socialist programs had so damaged the economy that Venezuelans were starving. (4) He discouraged dissent and rebellion by disarming all Venezuelan citizens.

The Chávez government, claiming it was acting to reduce crime, outlawed firearms in Venezuela in 2012 for all but his police force and military. Citizens eventually realized they'd been hoodwinked by their own government, as the murder rate actually *increased*. This fact is important because socialist ideologues use the same arguments used by Chávez in their attempts to disarm American citizens. Predictably, when the Venezuelan government disarmed its citizens, only government-controlled police and military personnel—and criminals—had guns. This is precisely what will happen in the United States if anti-gun Leftists have their way. In fact, it may be worse in the United States, where the Far Left wants to eliminate police altogether.

A VETERAN SPEAKS UP

Socialist tyrants typically disarm their citizens by force, but you can disarm citizens without actually taking their guns from them. Could this be happening in America already? Here is what one veteran had to say:

In Venezuela a socialist dictator and his henchmen removed all firearms from citizens when he feared rebellion against the government after destroying his nation's economy. Could this happen in America? Perhaps it is happening already without the government actually taking our firearms away from us. In my state citizens are not allowed to use deadly force to protect their homes, personal property, churches, or synagogues against rioting mobs, even though the mobs may be toppling crosses, burning vehicles, or looting. Is this another step toward America becoming like Venezuela?

—Kenneth Geis, United States Army, 1979 – 1982

Geis is a firearms and firearms safety instructor certified by the National Rifle Association.

Ironically, when Hugo Chávez was elected president of Venezuela, socialist ideologues thought they finally had the right person in the right place at the right time. He was lauded by Leftists everywhere as the leader who would demonstrate once and for all the viability of socialism as the path to equality, fairness, and prosperity. Hugo Chávez was going to transform Venezuela into a socialist utopian model for the rest of the world, one that would render capitalism and democracy obsolete.

Predictably, the socialist programs implemented by Chávez failed miserably, and he responded in the same way socialist leaders have always responded: by becoming a dictatorial tyrant and using coercion in a vain attempt to force a square peg through a round hole. Chávez, like Stalin, Mao, Pol Pot, and other socialist despots, was forced to opt for coercion when, predictably, central planning and government control transformed Venezuela into a humanitarian disaster instead of a model of economic reform.

Rather than become an example for future socialist utopias, Venezuela became a model of corruption, bullying, cronyism, authoritarianism, and kleptocracy. A kleptocracy is a nation in which government bureaucrats exploit the citizens and resources of their country for their own personal gain. The worst kleptocrat of them all was Hugo Chávez. Eventually Chávez became an embarrassment to socialist ideologues who proclaimed Venezuela would be a model of social democracy leading the way to a transformed world.

Under Chávez, Venezuela did become a model—of futility, hopelessness, inefficiency, corruption, hyper-inflation, starvation, and mass out-migration. Writing for the *New York Times*, Bret Stephens chronicled what actually happened in Venezuela during the reign of Hugo Chávez:

> *Government overspending created catastrophic deficits when oil prices plummeted. Worker co-ops wound up in the hands of incompetent and corrupt political cronies. The government responded to its budgetary problems by printing money, leading to inflation. Inflation led to price controls, leading to shortages. Shortages led to protests, leading to repression and the destruction of democracy. Thence to widespread starvation, critical medical shortages, an explosion in crime, and a refugee crisis to rival Syria's.*[3]

The same things can happen in the United States if the Left is able to gain and keep complete control of the government and implement their destructive socialist programs.

While starving Venezuelan citizens were rummaging through dumpsters for food and coping with inflation ranging between 700 and 1,000,000 percent, billionaire Hugo Chávez got fat. To disguise his expanding girth from starving citizens, he had his suits specially tailored to make him appear slimmer. After all, how could he be seen on television looking fat and jowly when his citizens were starving? Finally, when even the best tailors in the world could no longer hide the obvious, Chávez stopped making public appearances. But he didn't stop lining his pockets with money extorted from Venezuela's oil companies or stolen from the public treasury. When Chávez died, he was worth more than $2 billion. His daughter and heir is thought to be the wealthiest person in Venezuela.

Starvation inevitably results in crime, violence, and riots, and it did in Venezuela. In an effort to quell social unrest in his country, Chávez blamed Venezuela's problems on greedy business owners and the United States. When this charade didn't work, he disarmed his citizens. One U.S. veteran warned that Americans who support the Second Amendment should learn from what happened in Venezuela.

One of the main goals of Leftist politicians and socialist ideologues in America is abolishing the Second Amendment and disarming the American public. Joe Biden wasted no time pushing for strict gun controls after moving into the White House in January 2021. Not only did the nationwide disarming of Venezuelan citizens leave them helpless and at the mercy of a tyrannical government; it rendered them unable to defend themselves, their homes, and their families against the criminal element in that country. Our veteran friend claimed that what happened in Venezuela is precisely why the Founders included the Second Amendment in the Bill of Rights.

Writing for *National Review*, Roberto González and Liza Gellerman summed up Hugo Chávez's legacy of socialist reform in Venezuela. "Today 90 percent of Venezuelans are living below the poverty line and inflation rates exceed 1 million percent. Record numbers of children are dying from malnutrition, and nearly all of the country's hospitals are either inoperative or in critical need of basic medical supplies. Frequent nationwide power outages have left, at times, 70 percent of Venezuela in darkness."[4] Make no mistake about this situation. It occurred not because Hugo Chávez was incompetent but because socialism doesn't work. Yet, in the United States, Leftist politicians are still advocating for the kinds of policies that will bankrupt our nation and turn it into another Venezuela.

Starvation, lawlessness, and government repression initiated a mass exodus of Venezuelan citizens from that beleaguered country. The destination for most of them is the United States, a nation, ironically, moving ever closer to the philosophy that transformed Venezuela into an economic and humanitarian disaster. One of the veterans we surveyed has relatives in Venezuela. "Why do socialists in America refuse to learn from what happened in Venezuela?" he asked.

Why indeed?

A VETERAN SPEAKS UP

Survived the war without a gun, now back home I carry one
It's sad I have to live this way, my homeland
in the U.S.A.
Today the threat is from within, this type of war
is hard to win
We don't know friend from foe, I'd rather be a GI Joe
Panama looks good to me, like many countries overseas
Well, with the exception of Seoul, a long way from home
is my only goal

—David Rose, United States Army, 1969–1971

David Rose, a conscientious objector, served in Vietnam as a combat trauma medic in the emergency room of the Seventy-First Evacuation Hospital in Pleiku and as a "dust-off medic." Following his military service, Rose had a long and successful career as a surgery assistant. After retiring, he returned to college to qualify as a park ranger and served in Yosemite National Park. At age sixty-five, Rose's PTSD began to overtake him. Writing poetry about his experiences, such as the one above, is part of his therapy. Rose is secretary of the board of directors of the Florida Veterans' Hall of Fame and is actively engaged in supporting veterans nationwide.

CHAPTER 3

SOCIALISM BREEDS LAZINESS AND ENTITLEMENT

Exceptionalism through structure and competition is what our military provides, which might make it the last bastion of true exceptionalism, the backbone of capitalism.

—Brian Haugen, U.S. Army Special Forces, 1986–2008

Lieutenant Colonel Brian Haugen served our country for twenty-three years as an Army Ranger and member of the Army's elite Special Forces. He was commissioned in 1986 through the Reserve Officers Training Corps (ROTC) at Marion Military Institute in Alabama. His commissioning was followed by duties including service as an airborne platoon leader, a battalion support company commander, a group support company commander (Twentieth Special Forces Group [Airborne]), and the chief of the joint operations center (Combined Joint Special Operations Task Force) in Bagram, Afghanistan. Haugen's military commendations and decorations include the Combat Infantry Badge, the Master Parachutist Badge, Honduran Jumpmaster Wings, the German Parachute Badge, a Meritorious Service Medal, the Joint Services Commendation Medal, an Army Commendation Medal with one oak leaf cluster, an Army Achievement Medal, a Southwest Asia Service Medal with one star device, an Army Meritorious Unit Citation (Desert Shield), the Global War on Terrorism Expeditionary Medal, the Afghanistan Campaign Medal, and two Liberation of Kuwait Medals (Saudi Arabia and Kuwait). As a civilian, Haugen has built a successful career in business as a certified financial advisor.

In the opening quote for this chapter, Lt. Col. Brian Haugen made an excellent point about the importance of competition and an attitude of exceptionalism. It is a point that advocates of socialism would do well to consider. One of the veterans interviewed for this book spent time in several socialist countries during his career in the military. He saw firsthand how socialism affects the attitudes of individuals toward work. Based on his observations of the work ethic in those countries, he was adamant that socialism breeds laziness and entitlement. Observably, the lack of personal responsibility, incentives, and competition associated with socialism robs people of their motivation to work and their ambition to succeed.

The lack of motivation inherent in socialism manifests itself in a variety of ways in the workplace. For example, in socialist countries it is not uncommon for employees to sleep through their work shifts. What is worse, there is little or no peer pressure to discourage this type of counterproductive behavior. In capitalist countries, although there are certainly lazy employees, they do not represent the majority or the norm. Workers in capitalist countries, including lazy ones, feel a sense of pressure to do the work they are paid to do. This pressure comes not only from their peers but also from feelings of personal responsibility, ambition, and competition for incentives (e.g., raises, promotions, bonuses, recognition). The difference between employees in socialist settings and those in capitalist settings is not so much the individuals but the system they work in. It is the lack of personal responsibility, competition, and incentives in socialist settings that dampens the individual's drive.

In his book *The Case against Socialism*, Rand Paul tells the story of a group of farmers in Communist China who risked their lives to ensure their families got enough food.[1] Just one simple but powerful incentive—food—drove a group of Chinese peasants to take their lives in their hands by engaging in something strictly forbidden during Mao Tse-tung's reign of terror.

These farmers worked on a government-owned agricultural collective. Each year, at harvesttime, the crops grown on their collective farm were turned over to the government. The government, under the direction of the Chinese Communist Party, doled out a portion of the crops to each of the farmers who had raised them. Every farming family received the same share regardless of how much or how little they had contributed to sowing, nurturing, and reaping the harvest. So, the farmer who'd worked from sunup to sundown got the exact same share as the farmer who had contributed little or nothing to the harvest. Worse yet, the identical share each family received was just an equal-sized piece of an undersized pie, a share too small to adequately feed a family.

Out of desperation, several of the farmers came together and formed a secret pact. Each farmer would continue to work on the Chinese Communist Party–owned collective farm, but in addition, he would carve out a portion of the land to farm for himself and his family. Not surprisingly, the farmers who had their own parcels of land to cultivate worked many extra hours on it to ensure a good crop and a plentiful harvest. At harvesttime, each farmer kept enough of the crops he had raised on his secret plot to sufficiently augment the meager share of the harvest received from the Communist Party. The rest of what they raised was added to the crops the government took.

In spite of the farmers' precautions, the Communist officials noticed the increase in the overall harvest and figured out what was happening. The incentive of more food for their families coupled with an unexpected motivating factor had driven the farmers to produce more food than could be hidden. That unexpected factor was *competition*. One of the farmers later explained that all of his coconspirators competed against one another to raise the largest crop on their private plots. None wanted to be accused of devoting insufficient time or effort to a project that could cost them their lives.

Fortunately for these agricultural entrepreneurs, their experiment in capitalism occurred as the leadership of the Chinese Communist Party was passing from Mao to Deng Xiaoping. Because Deng inherited an economic disaster from Mao, he and his cronies at the top of the Communist Party decided to look the other way as these microenterprises sprang up throughout China. Allowing entrepreneurship, competition, and incentives has since been the single most important factor in the transformation of China's economy from global disaster to global powerhouse.

As a result, Chinese officials now struggle with maintaining Communist rule over what is becoming a quasi-capitalist economy; a difficult balancing act at best. To see how they are maintaining this difficult balance, one need only look to the measures the Chinese Communist Party has taken to suppress demands for freedom and capitalism in Hong Kong. Citizens of this longtime bastion of freedom and enterprise are regularly beaten, tortured, and jailed—often for life—for demanding the freedoms they have enjoyed for decades. One can't help but wonder if what is happening in Hong Kong is but a precursor to what the future holds for the Chinese mainland. History has shown in battles between freedom and suppression that freedom eventually wins, but the cost in blood is often as high as it was in the American Civil War.

The reason a group of Chinese peasants turned entrepreneurs could produce a harvest too big to conceal from their Communist overseers can be summarized as follows: (1) Each farmer was personally responsible for his own parcel of *private* land; therefore, he felt ownership and was held accountable by his coconspirators to produce a good crop. (2) Having responsibility for a private plot of land brought out the natural competitive instincts of each farmer, who, as a result, worked hard to outproduce his fellow entrepreneurs. (3) Each farmer in on the conspiracy was highly motivated by the incentive of having more food for his family. These factors combined to produce not just a better crop but a crop so abnormally large there was no way to conceal their capitalistic subterfuge.

Like the farmers in Rand Paul's true story, people in a capitalist setting tend to be more motivated and ambitious than their socialist counterparts because, first, they are given personal responsibility and are held accountable. They are also attracted to the kinds of incentives inherent in capitalism. What's more, they have a natural instinct for competition, and they feel a sense of ownership. Capitalism harnesses all of the factors that make people more productive. Thus, people tend to work harder, smarter, and longer in a capitalist setting. Socialism, on the other hand, eliminates or undermines the factors causing people to be more productive. Thus, in a social-ist society people tend to approach work from a minimalist perspective—or avoid it altogether.

SOCIALISM REDUCES PERSONAL RESPONSIBILITY

Have you ever noticed how people who own their own homes tend to take better care of them than those who live in government hous-ing or even those who rent their homes? Or how drivers take better care of their own cars than the cars they rent for business trips? Have you noticed that students who are responsible for their own indi-vidual assignments work harder than those who are given group assignments and receive a group grade? The key in all of these examples is personal responsibility. Being personally responsible for something can be a powerful motivator. The obverse of this fact is also true.

Consider government housing as an example. When the govern-ment is the owner, it is responsible for upkeep and improvements. Why, then, put your time and effort into upkeep and improvements when you have no vested interest or responsibility? Doing so amounts to spending your time and money on improving someone else's asset. It's like putting your money in someone else's bank account. The same principle applies to rented property.

There is little incentive to make improvements to or even main-tain rented property. But when you are the owner of a home, or any other asset, you are personally responsible for it. More than that, it is yours. Thus, the time, effort, and money you put into upkeep and improvements results in added value accruing to you, again, like putting money in your own bank account.

Another problem with socialism is the concept of *group respon-sibility*. When the group is responsible, as is the case with socialism, nobody is responsible. One of the veterans surveyed for this book put it this way: For a group to be effective, somebody has to be personally responsible for its performance. This is why the military has officers and noncommissioned officers, or NCOs. It is also why organizations have managers and supervisors. At every level in an organization, be it private, public or military, someone is personally responsible for a group's performance, and that someone is held accountable.

Another veteran we interviewed is a college professor. She explained why group projects—socialism applied to academics—are anathema to good students. According to this veteran, the better college students dread group projects. They prefer individual assignments for which they are personally responsible and accountable. Group responsibility allows the less motivated, less ambitious students to ride on the coattails of the better students, who must work even harder than normal to compensate for the slackers in the group. In the end, the slackers know they will get the same grade as the students who worked hard and carried the weight of the whole group.

This is precisely what happens in any kind of socialist work group. As a result, even the high performers eventually see the futility of working hard, smart, and long. Once this happens, they do what any sane person would do: bow to the inevitable and join the unmotivated slackers in coasting through their work, doing as little as possible. All collectivist strategies, even group projects in college courses, reward underperformers and punish high achievers. This is a formula for failure when it comes to organizational output and human productivity.

Being personally responsible for property, work projects, classroom assignments, or anything else makes one accountable. When you are accountable it means you get the credit when things go well and the blame when they don't. Small wonder, then, that personal responsibility and accountability are such powerful motivators, a fact that concerned one of the veterans we surveyed. This veteran expressed doubt that youngsters today are learning personal responsibility and accountability, two things required to be productive, contributing citizens.

As a police officer, she can cite many examples of parents stepping in to "protect" their children from the consequences of their bad behavior rather than using childhood missteps to teach them personal responsibility and accountability. This veteran was adamant that failing to teach young people personal responsibility and accountability is undermining the character of an entire generation and leaving young people susceptible to the false promises of socialist ideologues. Children who are "protected" from the consequences of their behavior grow up to become adults who expect the same kind of "protection" from a nanny government.

A rapidly growing cultural phenomenon in America is an attitude toward personal responsibility known as the *entitlement mentality*, which we mentioned briefly in earlier chapters. People with an entitlement mentality believe they deserve the benefits of success without having to earn them. Such individuals are easy marks for socialist ideologues who tell them they "deserve" free health care, free college tuition, lifelong welfare with no work requirement, and student-debt forgiveness. Of course, entitled young people never ask the functional question in this situation: *Why do I deserve these things—what have I done to deserve them?*

What socialist snake-oil salesmen are really promising naive Americans is life without responsibility or accountability. Need health care? Let somebody else pay for it. Want to go to college? Make someone else fork over the money for tuition. Buried in student debt? Pawn it off on somebody else. Don't feel like working? Go on welfare and let taxpayers support you. These kinds of propositions appeal to entitled individuals who believe they should have anything they want without any effort or responsibility on their part.

The entitlement mentality manifests in a variety of ways in American society. One of the worst examples can be seen in the attitudes of people of prime working age who want a job but don't want to work. Entitled people expect to enter the workplace at the top and enjoy all the attendant perquisites without having to invest the time and effort necessary to climb the career ladder.

Another example is college students who want a degree but don't want an education; that is, they don't want to do the hard work necessary to become truly educated. Entitled students would be happy if they could simply purchase a diploma to hang on the wall, without having to bother attending classes, studying, completing assignments, passing tests, or conducting research. This is why so many young people now choose to major in made-up, academically anemic disciplines, such as diversity studies, fat studies, women's studies, and queer studies.

After coasting through four years of the mindless drivel and indoctrination associated with these unmarketable programs, they receive a college degree but they don't receive an education. They can now say they are college graduates, but a degree in many college majors these days is worth less than the cost to print the diploma. The real world outside the college campus is looking for people who are educated, not indoctrinated.

One veteran we surveyed is a small business owner. He claimed that the entitlement mentality is a greater threat to American competitiveness than the cheap labor available in Asian nations. He went on to say that a lot of the younger applicants he interviews want to be afforded unrealistic wages and benefits while working as little as possible. People with an entitlement mentality are easily taken in by the false promises of socialist ideologues.

SOCIALISM OFFERS NO INCENTIVES TO EXCEL

Human beings respond to incentives. We are hardwired in this way. It's not something we have to learn; it's in our DNA. Little children can be induced to behave by offering them the incentive of thirty more minutes of play time before going to bed. Teenagers can be induced to wash and wax the family car by offering them the incentive of using it for their date on Saturday night. Athletes can be induced to practice longer and harder by offering them a chance to make the starting lineup.

Military personnel can be motivated to study harder, work longer, and volunteer for extra duty when there is the incentive of a possible promotion. Employees can be induced to do their best and continually improve by offering them such incentives as raises, bonuses, promotions, and recognition. Although it can take time, even entitled employees will eventually respond to incentives. Serious students will study harder if there is the incentive of making a good grade or earning a scholarship.

Socialist ideologues criticize the use of incentives to enhance performance, claiming this practice is grounded in selfishness. They believe people should automatically do their best out of a benevolent commitment to serving the greater good, which to a socialist means serving the government. This particular point of view demonstrates one of the fundamental flaws of socialist thinking. Socialist advocates confuse enlightened self-interest with selfishness. The two are not the same. Confusing them is one of the reasons socialism always underperforms and typically fails.

Selfishness means being exclusively concerned with oneself, without regard for others. Selfish people won't hesitate to deny, inconvenience, or even harm others to get what they want, nor do they share what they have no matter how much they have. The only concern of selfish people is their own self-interest. They serve only themselves and are willing to exploit others' hard work for their own benefit, without properly acknowledging their contributions. Their favorite word is "I," and they use it a lot. Consider the following example.

A baseball team is in the running for the league championship. It's the bottom of the ninth inning, and the score is tied. The bases are loaded, and the team's best hitter, Mark, is at the plate. If Mark can knock in just one run, the game is over and his team will play for the league championship. But the issue is complicated by the fact that Mark needs only one more home run to be the league's home run champion. He has hit a lot of home runs, but there is a problem. Mark often strikes out when going for the fence. On the other hand, he is an excellent bunter, and the opposing team has a poor record of handling bunts.

Weighing his options and the odds, the coach signals Mark to lay down a bunt and bring in the winning run. This is the smart play, the one giving the team the best chance to play in the championship game. But Mark is selfish. He is more interested in winning the home run championship for himself than the league championship for his team. Mark ignores the coach's signal and swings for the fence. He hits a long fly ball easily caught by the opposing team's center fielder, stranding three men on base. The game remains tied. When the opposing team scores in extra innings and his team doesn't, the game is lost along with the chance to play for the championship. Mark was more interested in setting a record for himself than in helping his team play in the league championship. This is selfishness.

Enlightened self-interest, on the other hand, contains an element of helping others. In fact, it often amounts to helping oneself by helping others. For example, work teams are like sports teams in that their members help themselves by helping the team perform better. In the example of the Chinese farmers earlier in this chapter, they weren't being selfish in their desire to raise more crops; they were trying to provide more food for themselves and their families. In helping themselves, they were also helping their wives and children. In fact, these entrepreneurial farmers were also helping the families of other collective farmers by increasing the overall size of the harvest they would eventually share.

In the example of Mark, the selfish batter, enlightened self-interest dictated that he lay down a sacrifice bunt, knocking in the winning run. By doing so he would have helped himself as well as his team. He would have helped his team by putting them in the league championship game. He would have helped himself because he would have gotten several turns at bat in the league championship game. This, in turn, would have given him additional chances to hit the home run he needed. This is the beauty of enlightened self-interest: you help yourself by helping others, a concept socialists seem unable to grasp.

A major advantage of capitalism over socialism is it encourages enlightened self-interest by incentivizing it. Socialism, on the other hand, expects everyone to serve the government without concern for self-interest and without incentives. To a socialist, there is nothing wrong with individuals suffering as long as the larger group—the government—benefits in some way. Sacrificing for the team, something enlightened self-interest encourages, is not the same as suffering for the team, something socialism demands.

On the surface, the socialist principle of serving the group might sounds like the biblical principle of sacrificial love, but this is hardly how it plays out in reality. The harsh reality of socialism is that those who benefit from the labor of the masses are the few at the top of the bureaucratic hierarchy who control the government. These few elite bureaucrats become fat and rich from the labor of socialist minions while the minions endure lives of perpetual scarcity.

SOCIALISM DISCOURAGES COMPETITION

One of the veterans interviewed for this book expressed concern that we are raising a generation of young people who don't know how to compete. He was shocked to find in his grandson's baseball league that everyone made the team, every team got a trophy, and the scoreboard was covered so the players on the losing team wouldn't get their feelings hurt. In other words, decision makers in the league had decided to eliminate the element of competition. By doing this they created a situation at odds with both human nature and the realities of life. The desire to compete grows out of the human instinct for survival. Further, life is full of situations in which competing is essential to success.

This veteran claimed competition was the most important factor in driving him to become successful. He had excelled in his military career and in the private sector after retiring because he'd worked hard and smart to outperform the competition. Competition kept him on his toes and highly motivated. Capitalism rewards the natural human instinct for competition while socialism undermines it. Competition, in turn, enhances performance and productivity.

A VETERAN SPEAKS UP

With their focus on equal results rather than equal opportunity, socialists undermine motivation and competition. Here is what one veteran had to say about the value of competition:

My best friend and I ran track in high school. Our event was the 440-yard dash. We both started out running the 440 in around 54 seconds; not a winning time. However, through self-motivation and healthy competition between the two of us we got our times down to around 50 seconds.

Competition pushed us individually and together to do better. After high school, my friend won acceptance to the U.S. Naval Academy and I earned a college scholarship. Competition helped build our work ethic, discipline, and time management skills.

—Sidney Earl "Skip" Hull, U.S. Marine Corps, 1975–1978

Hull served as battalion supply officer for the Third Battalion, Fourth Marines, and ordnance officer for headquarters and service battalion, Second Marine Division.

Competition and the desire to win are as normal to human beings as breathing. They are also biblical. First Corinthians 9:24 clearly encourages competition: "Do you not know that in a race all the runners run, but only one receives the prize? So run that you may obtain it." The words "run that you may obtain it" mean work hard, practice often, and continually improve so you will be the one who "receives the prize." Clearly, giving every player a trophy and covering the scoreboard is at odds with the teachings of Scripture, the rules of competition, and the basics of human nature.

Competition is in our DNA; it's part of our survival instinct. Human beings are hardwired for it. Little kids who have not yet learned to say the word "competition" try to win at the games they play with other children. They don't have to be coerced to exert themselves to outrun, outclimb, or outscore each other. In addition, even little children feel the sting of losing. Wanting to win is as natural to them as closing their eyes when they sneeze. Consequently, the desire to win can be a powerful motivator. However, when everybody wins, as is supposed to happen in socialist utopias, nobody wins. In fact, everybody loses.

A benefit of capitalism is in harnessing the human desire to win and reinforcing it through the smart application of incentives. As human beings, we are motivated by things that appeal to our enlightened self-interest. In other words, we are motivated by well-thought-out incentives. Our inborn penchant for competition drives us to do what is necessary to win and, in turn, receive the desired incentives. Have you ever met anyone who enjoyed losing? Even people who are well schooled in good sportsmanship will tell you they would rather win than lose. There is a big difference between being a good loser and being good at losing. The former is good sportsmanship; the latter is bad thinking.

One of the veterans we surveyed coaches Little League baseball. He teaches his players that, yes, they should be good sports when they lose, but more important, they should practice, train, and constantly strive to improve so they can win. He also explains that most baseball games are won by the preparation before the game ever starts. Competition, when approached properly, can enhance the performance of individuals and, in turn, organizations, a fact that renders socialism ineffective. Socialism discourages competition and, in so doing, undermines performance. When everyone on both teams gets the same share of the postgame bonus, what does it matter which team scores the most runs?

In socialist countries, employees don't compete against each other for incentives, such as raises, promotions, or bonuses. Rather, they are paid the same regardless of their comparative output or relative performance. Socialists call this principal *equality*, but it's not. Equality exists when people are paid the same amount for the same level of production, not when lesser performers are paid the same as top performers.

Socialism's erroneous view of equality is at odds with human nature and the realities of life. Commenting on the lack of incentives in socialist settings, one of our veteran friends asked, "Why work harder and longer when you will be paid the same as employees who sleep through their shift?" Good question. Another good question is, How long will it be before the harder-working employees see the writing on the wall and start sleeping through *their* shifts?

In capitalist countries, employees who arrive at work early and work late are responding to incentives such as the potential for raises, promotions, and performance bonuses or they are competing with other employees for these things. Take away the incentives encouraging competition and you take away the basis for competition. When this happens, the performance of individuals and, in turn, the team or organization suffers. The socialist ideologue's utopian expectation for voluntary commitment to the group with no individual incentives is wishful thinking at its worse. With socialism, when wishful thinking fails, government coercion usually follows. As history has shown in China, the Soviet Union, Cambodia, Venezuela, and elsewhere, basing citizens' health and welfare on wishful thinking has tragic results.

SOCIALISM DAMPENS AMBITION

Human ambition explains why entrepreneurship is closely associated with capitalism but not socialism. Most human beings have an inherent desire to improve their lives materially, and many harbor a strong desire to be their own bosses. In other words, they have ambition, a concept that violates the most basic tenet of socialism: equality. Ambition is a desire to rise to greater heights. Ambitious people don't want to be equal (read: average or mediocre); they want to be better. Ambition drives them to achieve, improve, and benefit in ways requiring commitment, perseverance, determination, and hard work. Ambitious folks are willing to work hard, smart, and long to achieve their goals and improve their lives.

Socialist ideologues like to portray ambition as a bad thing. When equality is the supposed goal, anyone who wants to do better is considered a rebel. To portray ambition as a bad thing, socialism advocates use the old debating ruse of basing their case on exceptions rather than the rule. They like to point out individuals who let their ambition drive them to behave unethically or even illegally. While it is true that there are people who will lie, cheat, and steal to achieve their ambitions, their despicable deeds are the result of misguided ambition, not well-guided ambition, and selfishness, not enlightened self-interest. Further, they exist in every society, not just capitalist settings. In fact, in socialist settings they tend to rise to the top (e.g., Mao, Stalin, Castro, Chávez, Pol Pot, et al.) Like all human concepts, ambition must be tempered by morality or it can go awry.

In a capitalist system there are safeguards against people who break the rules out of blind ambition. The same cannot be said for socialist systems. In fact, blind ambition is indigenous to socialism. When the only way to fulfill one's ambition to do better is to climb higher in the government bureaucracy, tactics such as bribery, lying, cheating, and stealing become not exceptions but the rule. Never forget how Stalin, Mao Tse-tung, and Pol Pot murdered their way to the top of their socialist "utopias" and then stayed in power by repression, coercion, manipulation, scheming, and additional murders.

Ambition resting on a foundation of morality motivates people to work hard and smart. It can also motivate people to think entrepreneurially. One of our veterans is a small business owner. He explained how the ambition to be his own boss drove him to risk every penny he had in the bank and to mortgage his home to generate the cash needed to start his own business. There were some difficult months during his first three years of operation, but he persevered and became the owner and CEO of a successful, growing business providing jobs for twenty-three other people.

Entrepreneurship involves undertaking the financial risk required to start a business based on a new or innovative product or service. Entrepreneurs attempt to identify specific human needs and then build businesses around the products or services to meet those needs. Rags-to-riches stories of people who rose from poverty by becoming entrepreneurs are common in capitalistic countries. Capitalism encourages entrepreneurship because it is a demand-based economic system. Consumer demand that is not being met or can be better met is an opportunity for an entrepreneur.

Socialism, on the other hand, discourages entrepreneurship because it is a command-based economic system. In such a system, central planners in the government decide what the people need, how the need will be met, and even if it will be met at all. Further, in a socialist country the benefits derived from an innovation or improvement developed by individual entrepreneurs accrue to the government, not the entrepreneurs. Therefore, there is no incentive for citizens of a socialist country to think entrepreneurially. In fact, they might pay a price for doing so. Think back to the entrepreneurial farmers on the Chinese collective farm earlier in this chapter. Thinking entrepreneurially could have cost them their lives.

Because of the lack of incentives and the constraints put on individuals, the best way to satisfy the ambition to improve your life in a socialist country is to seek ever higher positions in government. Not surprisingly, the only way to climb the career ladder within the government bureaucracy of a socialist country is by demonstrating unswerving obeisance to those who hold the reins of power. This is another reason entrepreneurship is lacking in socialist countries. What entrepreneurs are saying when they develop innovations or suggest improvements is "I have identified an unmet need" or "There is a better way to do this." In a socialist setting, either of these messages would be interpreted by central-planning bureaucrats as disloyal criticism.

Socialism's collectivization of private property is another factor dampening ambition. There is no reason to strive, innovate, or improve if the fruits of your labor belong to the government. Ambitious people strive because they hope to enhance their own lives, not the lives of faceless government bureaucrats they don't know and will probably never meet. Further, ambitious people stand out from the crowd. This is not a good idea in a socialist setting, where conformity is the expectation.

One of the veterans we interviewed for this book spent lots of time in socialist countries during his military career. He explained the difference in the attitudes of socialists and capitalists toward those who succeed materially. In a capitalist country, he said, if your neighbor gets a new car, you are likely to react in one of two ways. You will either be pleased for him or you will envy him. If envy is your reaction, you might get a new car yourself. The latter concept is known as "keeping up with the Joneses."

According to this veteran, a socialist would approach the situation differently. If his neighbor got a new car, a socialist would not be pleased or even envious; he would be resentful. A socialist would hope his neighbor wrecks his new car, or he might rally his socialist comrades in the neighborhood and together they might vandalize the car. They would make their neighbor rue the day he bought a new car better than theirs. In a socialist setting, those with the ambition to do better must be knocked down and brought back into line. They must remain on an equal footing with everyone else.

SOCIALISM DAMPENS MOTIVATION

Motivation is the desire of an individual to do something. People who are highly motivated to achieve a given goal will work hard, smart, and long to do so. Motivated people take the initiative in solving problems, and they persevere when the tasks in front of them become difficult. Some people are internally motivated. Such people are said to be self-motivated. They require little or no supervision, nor must they be urged by others to do a good job. It is in their nature to perform well, work hard, and go the extra mile.

Other people must be externally motivated until they learn the value of striving for excellence. Striving for excellence is something learned. It was once taught in public schools by teachers and coaches. In her book, *Time to Remember*, Rose Fitzgerald Kennedy, mother of President John F. Kennedy and senators Robert and Edward Kennedy, speaks to the issue of teaching young people to strive for excellence: "Superior achievement or making the most of one's capabilities is to a very considerable degree a matter of habit. The [Kennedy] children were encouraged by their father to be winners and leaders in whatever they set their hand to, and to develop the habit."[2]

Mrs. Kennedy goes on to write how her children were not allowed to make excuses or to blame anyone else for their failures. Having been taught from a young age to strive for excellence, make no excuses, compete hard, and refuse to blame others for their failures, the Kennedy children became self-motivated achievers. For them excelling became a habit.[3] Whether people have to learn to strive for excellence or are hardwired to do so, the key to keeping them motivated is to offer incentives that appeal to their sense of enlightened self-interest.

According to Mrs. Kennedy, pleasing their parents and winning in competitive activities were incentive enough to keep the Kennedy children motivated.[4] But different people are motivated by different incentives. This is why it is vital for parents to know their children, supervisors their direct reports, teachers their students, and coaches their players. Only by knowing the people they hope to influence can those in leadership positions determine which incentives are most likely to motivate them.

Self-motivated people tend to be achievement-oriented. The primary incentives for them are recognition and the feeling of satisfaction they get from achieving goals. Self-motivated people are easy to spot. They typically have shelves full of trophies and walls full of certificates and plaques. Recognition of their achievements is a powerful incentive for self-motivated people. Externally motivated people, on the other hand, tend to respond well to such incentives as the potential to earn raises, promotions, bonuses, perquisites, and paid vacation time. In both cases, offering the kinds of incentives appealing to their enlightened self-interest is the key to keeping people motivated.

A foundational principle of socialism, first named in chapter 1, is income equality. All members are supposed to contribute equally to the group, and all are supposed to be paid equally for their contribution. But, of course, equality except in the eyes of God is a pipe dream. People are not equal when it comes to talent, ambition, motivation, skills, education, strength, physical stature, or a host of other important factors affecting their productivity. As a result, rarely do people contribute equally to the good of the group.

Think of a baseball, football, basketball, or soccer team. In every case, some players contribute more to the team's success than others. If all players on the team were equal, there would be no product-promotion contracts for athletes, a major source of income for outstanding players. This fact alone demonstrates why the principle of income equality is fatally flawed. The pay of workers in a socialist setting might be equal, but their contributions to the group are not, and people within the group know it.

In any setting—socialist or capitalist—there will be those who outperform the others. There will be those who contribute more to the group, team, or organization's success. Consequently, paying everyone the same regardless of their relative contributions is a formula for failure because it dampens the motivation of even the self-motivated. When everyone must be equal, there is no reason to strive to achieve.

When everyone must be equal, the incentives driving internally and externally motivated individuals are missing. As a result, so is their motivation. Poor motivation inevitably results in poor performance and poor quality. On the other hand, highly motivated people can improve the performance of everyone around them by their examples. The fact that it undermines motivation is one more reason socialism is a bad idea in a globally competitive world.

One of the veterans we surveyed used the analogy of a horse race to demonstrate the flawed nature of the socialist principle of equality and how it dampens motivation. He commented that in a socialist horse race, all of the entrants begin at the same time and place as in any other horse race. But what happens next is what matters. No matter which horse crosses the finish line first, all of the horses' owners are given an equal share of the prize money. All get to stand together in the winner's circle. All of the jockeys get a trophy. As a result, over time the jockeys stop prodding their horses to run faster and faster.

Instead, when the starting gates pop open, the jockeys simply walk their horses slowly around the track, caring little which horse arrives at the finish line first because it doesn't matter. In fact, some of the jockey's don't even bother to circle the track. They just dismount and wait for the others to join them in the winner's circle to collect their equal share of the prize money. After all, why bother when the reward for winning and losing is the same?

The self-motivated jockeys are no longer motivated at all because there is no sense of achievement. Those who once responded to external incentives are no longer motivated because there are no external incentives. Predictably, people eventually stop buying tickets to the races. After all, who would want to watch such a farce, not to mention there would be no reason to bet on the races? As a result, the income the races used to generate for the owners and jockeys dries up and the entire enterprise has to shut down. That's socialism for you in nutshell.

Socialism breeds laziness because it is at odds with human nature. It substitutes group responsibility for personal responsibility, eliminates competition, and offers no performance incentives. As a result, socialism dampens ambition and motivation. These statements are not just pro-capitalism conjecture; they represent facts proven time and again. Because socialists value equality and conformance over achievement and entrepreneurship, socialist countries will always struggle with shortages of essential goods.

In spite of this, a growing number of Americans who have never experienced socialism still claim they prefer it to capitalism. This is foolishness taken to the nth degree. The evidence of socialism's manifest failures and inherent flaws is readily available, yet there are a lot of people who choose to ignore it. Decades of socialist indoctrination in our public schools and colleges is finally paying off for the Left, but it is taking America down a one-way street to disaster.

A VETERAN SPEAKS UP

Socialists don't want equal opportunity; they want equal results, and they think equal results can be achieved by government coercion. Here is what one veteran had to say about this issue:

> *While I believe in and support equal opportunity with regard to fairness in the workplace, I do not support the socialist portrayal of equal opportunity. It's an unrealistic, skewed outlook on fairness, but it is presented in a warm blanket that appeals to many who do not understand it. Many may be swayed by how socialism is presented, but the narrative of the Left is misleading and simply a lie.*

—Shawni Jones, United States Air Force, 1990–2014

Jones began her career in the U.S. Air Force as a pharmacy technician at Sheppard Air Force Base, Texas, and continued in that field until 2006, when she cross-trained and became an emergency actions (EA) controller at Scott Air Force Base, Illinois. Her service as an EA controller took her to duty in Grand Forks, North Dakota, and Hickam Air Force Base, Hawaii. She completed her career in the Air Force as command and control manager for policies and procedures at Joint Base Pearl Harbor–Hickam, Hawaii.

CHAPTER 4

SOCIALISM IS GROUNDED IN ECONOMIC ILLITERACY

After experiencing the complexities of the government's
Payroll Protection Program and the Small Business Admin-
istration's Disaster Loan Program during the COVID-19
shut down of 2020, I wonder how private enterprise might
have handled this crisis. We have seen how Christmas gifts
can be ordered online, paid for, shipped, tracked for deliv-
ery, and placed on the customer's doorstep in a minimum
amount of time. Perhaps the government needs to let a
private company such as Amazon or Wal-Mart handle the
distribution of emergency funds during the next crisis.

—Tom Rice, United States Army, 1969–1996

Rice is a retired first sergeant and a veteran of both Desert Shield and Desert Storm. Among his many military awards and decorations are the Southwest Asia Service Medal with two Bronze Service Stars and the Saudi Arabian Kuwaiti Liberation Medal. In 2017 he was inducted into the Florida Veterans' Hall of Fame. As a civilian, Rice is a restaurant owner who devotes all his free time and energy to supporting veterans, active-duty personnel, and their families. He is a board member of Florida Veterans, Inc., an organization dedicated to making Florida the most veteran-friendly state in the U.S.

Tom Rice, the veteran who provided the introductory quote for this chapter, gives an enlightening example of the inefficiency of government when compared with the private sector. It is an example those who naively think they prefer socialism to capitalism should take to heart. As a small business owner, Rice learned firsthand how inefficient even the most well-intentioned government programs can be.

One of the veterans surveyed for this book commented on taking Economics 101 in college, an elective class for nonmajors. Knowing the students in this class weren't likely to ever become economists, the professor told them that if they remembered nothing else about economics, remember this: nothing is free, everything has a cost, and somebody has to pay it. Our veteran claimed this was one of the best lessons he learned in all of his college studies. Socialist ideologues and those they dupe with false promises of free health care, free college tuition, lifelong welfare, and student-debt forgiveness would do well to learn this lesson.

This same veteran commented on his survey form that not only are those who advocate for socialism illiterate about basic economics; they don't even know what they don't know. With this in mind, we use this chapter to explain some foundational principles of economics that socialist advocates don't know but should or ignore but shouldn't. Bear in mind, as you read about these various principles, they are not the advanced and often arcane theories that interest professional economists. Rather, they are down-to-earth, common-sense principles any thinking person can grasp, and they have proven valid over and over for centuries.

This being the case, socialist advocates who do not understand these principles or, worse, reject them have no excuse. It follows, then, that the only explanation for the economic illiteracy demonstrated by advocates of socialism is ideological hubris: socialist advocates don't understand the basic principles of economics because they don't want to. What's more, they don't want you to.

SPENDING MORE THAN YOU CAN PAY BACK IS A BAD IDEA

There has never been a time in America's history when it is more important to understand that you should never spend more than you can pay back. That applies to nations in the same way it applies to individuals. In the United States, decades of creeping socialism in the form of a burgeoning, bloated bureaucracy and ever-increasing spending on welfare programs has run up a national debt fast becoming untenable, if it's not there already. Even if the United States can continue to service the level of debt it has incurred, your grandchildren and great-grandchildren will spend their lives paying an ever-increasing level of taxes just to keep our country from going bankrupt. The day will eventually come when American citizens cannot be taxed enough to pay our nation's debt.

Government handouts, bailouts, and well-intentioned but not always wise stimulus programs have escalated America's national debt to the point it now exceeds our country's gross national product (GDP). This situation already existed when the government added substantially to the national debt with its COVID-19 rescue programs. As a result of past and present overspending, America now owes more money than it generates. Our nation is like individuals with maxed-out credit cards totaling more than they earn and, in turn, more than they can pay back. What's worse, this situation came about without a socialist in the White House or socialist control of Congress. Imagine what will happen with socialists in control of the federal government.

As things stand now, spending in America is already dangerously out of control. In spite of this, socialist ideologues masquerading as "progressives" are advocating for such budget-busting policies as free health care, free college tuition, student-debt forgiveness, lifelong welfare, and the Green New Deal, to name just a few of their pet projects. These projects of the Left would add at least $40 trillion to the national debt, a debt rapidly approaching $30 trillion. With America's GNP hovering around $21 trillion, socialist ideologues propose to generate a national debt more than three times that size.

Because numbers stated in trillions can be difficult to grasp, let us paint a scenario easier to understand. For a nation with a GNP of $21 trillion to take on more than $60 trillion in debt is the equivalent of an American family earning $100,000 per year running up credit card debt of $300,000. Strapped with this much debt, neither the family in this example nor our country will be able to climb out of the hole they have dug for themselves. This is what one of the veterans surveyed for this book meant when he worried that during his lifetime, the U.S. would become the next Venezuela.

Another veteran asked why socialist ideologues cannot grasp the need for a country to live within its means. That's easy: socialist ideologues don't concern themselves with debt. Their response to burgeoning debt is to print more money. Tyrants all over the world have used this tactic when socialism threatened to bankrupt their nations. But printing more money just leads to hyperinflation, rendering the nation's currency useless. The aforementioned example of Venezuela's 700 and 1,000,000 percent inflation is proof positive. With these rates, a shopping cart full of money would not buy a loaf of bread.

ENLIGHTENED SELF-INTEREST IS GOOD FOR THE ECONOMY

Traditionally, one of the first lessons learned in an economics class has been the principle of the "invisible hand," developed by eighteenth-century economist Adam Smith. In its simplest form, this principle means individuals and economies do better when they operate on the basis of self-interest. In chapter 3, we explained how and why people are motivated by self-interest, which is not the same as selfishness. Think about it. Some of the most charitable people in the history of our country became wealthy and thus able to be charitable because they were motivated by enlightened self-interest.

When people can voluntarily enter economic transactions on the basis of perceived self- interest, everyone is better off. People naturally work harder and smarter when doing so will benefit them. One of our veterans commented about a college professor who told him socialism is just another term for teamwork. This is just one more myth perpetuated by ideologues trying to make socialism more palatable. This professor obviously knew little about socialism or teamwork. If socialism were just another name for teamwork, organizations would not select, recognize, and reward the most valuable players on their teams. Remember, with socialism everyone is equal; nobody is allowed to stand out from the crowd.

Ironically, the best way to get people to be good team players in sports or the workplace is to offer them incentives that appeal to individual self-interest, such as recognition, awards, bonuses, raises, and promotions. But, of course, the only incentive socialists are prepared to offer group members is the knowledge of knowing they are serving the best interests of government elites and their bureaucratic minions.

Imagine how things would change in major-league baseball if all the bonus money for winning the World Series were given to the team's manager and owner instead of the players. The players' motivation level would fall to less than zero.

Consider another scenario. What would happen if the bonus money for winning the World Series were divided equally among all players on the team, including those who'd skipped practice, played poorly, and put forth no effort? How do you think the players who had pitched their hearts out, slammed into the outfield fence chasing long fly balls, hustled to steal bases, got base hits, and slid hard into home to score runs would respond? Highly motivated, talented players who did what was necessary to win could be forgiven in this case for wondering *What's the point?* This is why teams that win the World Series typically vote on who gets how many "shares" of the bonus money. They want to reward players in amounts consistent with their contributions to the victory.

This is why the socialist ideal of serving the group to the detriment of self-interest is a nonstarter. The concept is at odds with human nature. Think back to the story of the Chinese farmers from chapter 3. Their small plots of private land produced considerably more per acre than the collectivized farm they were required to work on. Why? Because the private plots allowed the farmers to satisfy a deeply felt need: feeding their families better. The chance to pursue their self-interest motivated the farmers to work harder, longer, and smarter on their private plots. On the other hand, working harder on the collective farm would not serve their self-interests, so why bother?

A VETERAN SPEAKS OUT

Business leaders and entrepreneurs make important contributions to American exceptionalism. Here is what one veteran had to say about these contributions:

America's business owners make it happen by assuming risk and taking responsibility. These intrepid men and women are routinely judged by employees, clients, customers, bankers, and everyone else in the marketplace. These founders, these imagineers, these leaders of America's business sector represent the very best characteristics of America. They are the power source of American prestige and influence around the globe.

—Robert M. Kirila, United States Army, 1991–2017

Colonel Robert M. Kirila (retired) served in the Special Forces community for almost all of his twenty-six years of military service. Since retiring from the Army, Kirila has run DEFENSWERX, an innovation and technology support company, and Your Grateful Nation, an executive transition foundation, both as the CEO. Kirila is currently the managing director of Black Powder Holdings, a private capital company established to support the transition of ownership of America's highest-performing small businesses.

ECONOMIC GROWTH IS DRIVEN BY INNOVATION

A hard-and-fast rule of socialism is conformity. With socialism, central planners develop the economic plan for the nation, and the people are expected to conform to it. To do otherwise is to risk being labeled a miscreant or a rebel, which in many socialist nations can be bad for one's health. One of the reasons socialist nations tend to have stagnant economies is that economic growth is the result of innovation, not conformity. Innovation, by its very nature, involves breaking the rules and thinking outside the box. Innovators are, in fact, nonconformists. The beauty of capitalism is it encourages positive, creative nonconformity, which, in turn, encourages innovation. Socialism, on the other hand, demands citizens stay inside the box and conform.

Imagine life without the following innovations of the nineteenth and twentieth centuries:

- the automobile
- the light bulb
- air conditioning
- the radio
- the television
- the airplane
- antibiotics
- the personal computer
- alternating current, batteries
- xerography
- the Internet
- cell phones

These innovations and many others have transformed how people work and live. They were not developed by obedient, conforming socialists who viewed innovation as a slap at central planning. They were developed by entrepreneurs who found innovative ways to meet human needs and stood to benefit personally from their innovations. These entrepreneurs were motivated by enlightened self-interest, not conformity, and their inventions were the result of innovation.

To demonstrate this point, let's look at just two entrepreneurial innovators, one from the past and one from the present: Andrew Carnegie and Bill Gates. The innovations of these two visionaries made them fabulously wealthy on a personal level. Their wealth, in turn, allowed them to benefit not just themselves and their families, but society in general through philanthropy and charitable donations. What is even more noteworthy is that stories such as theirs are commonplace in capitalist countries but virtually unheard-of in socialist nations.

Andrew Carnegie started out in life with very little. His family immigrated to America from Scotland. Carnegie is noted for founding the Carnegie Steel Company and developing it into one of the largest, most successful companies in America's history. Although closely associated with the mass production of steel, Carnegie didn't invent steelmaking. Rather, he developed innovative methods for making the process more efficient. These methods included using the open-hearth furnace, which supplanted the old Bessemer process, and overhead cranes and hoists for moving raw materials and finished products more rapidly and efficiently.

Carnegie was so successful that when he died in 1919, his personal net worth exceeded $5 billion in 2020 dollars. Andrew Carnegie used his wealth to invest in and develop other businesses in the critical fields of oil production, automobiles, and communication. He believed wealthy people were obligated to use their money for the betterment of society. To this end, he established the Carnegie Institution to fund scientific research. He also donated $10 million to provide pensions for retired schoolteachers.

Although his philanthropy in a number of fields was legendary, Carnegie is probably best known for funding the construction of public libraries. He built two thousand of them. There is irony in using private funds to build public libraries, but without Carnegie's help these libraries might not have been built. Think about it; just one man built more public libraries than most socialist *nations* build. Carnegie's example demonstrates how one individual, because he was allowed to pursue his own self-interest, was able to benefit not just himself but his fellow citizens and their posterity for generations. Carnegie died in 1919, but Americans who don't even know who he was are still benefiting from his philanthropy.

Another innovator who pursued his self-interest, and in the process became extraordinarily wealthy, is Bill Gates of Microsoft fame. By shaping the personal computer revolution in America, Gates developed Microsoft into a trillion-dollar business. As of this writing, Gates is the second-wealthiest individual in the world. His net worth is approximately $105 billion. Using this wealth, Gates and his wife established the Bill & Melinda Gates Foundation. To date the foundation has donated millions to promote global health, literacy, access to education, and better agriculture, while at the same time working to eliminate disease, famine, and poverty.

Once again, because he was not shackled by the constraints on self-interest and innovation imposed by socialism, one individual was able to generate so much personal wealth he is now able to devote the rest of his life to helping others all over the world. Gates has stated many times this is exactly what he plans to do. Over the course of his lifetime, he intends to invest most of his money in solving problems governments are unable to solve.

One of the reasons we don't associate rags-to-riches stories such as those of Andrew Carnegie and Bill Gates with socialist nations is central planning and forced equality are the antithesis of innovation. Central planners in socialist nations tend to base their decisions concerning what to produce and how much on last year's numbers. Hence, they are always looking backward at the past. Innovators, by their very nature, always look to the future.

Innovators and entrepreneurs are constantly seeking better ways to do things and better products and services to provide for consumers. As the examples of Carnegie and Gates demonstrate, in a capitalist setting, individual entrepreneurs and entrepreneurial organizations can generate substantial wealth for themselves by developing innovations that appeal to consumers. Their wealth can then be voluntarily shared with others through philanthropy. This and not the income redistribution of socialist countries is what Christ had in mind when He gave us the second greatest commandment, in which He told us to love our neighbors as ourselves (Mark 12:30).

There is a reason the computer, Internet, cell phone, and other technologies that have made people more productive were not invented in the Soviet Union, China, Venezuela, or Cuba. Capitalism unleashes and encourages creativity and innovation while socialism discourages these things. Once again, return to the entrepreneurial Chinese farmers from chapter 3. Not only were they not rewarded for finding ways to increase crop production, they might have been killed for daring to challenge the government's set-in-stone collective approach to farming. Any governing philosophy that makes innovation a crime is bound to fail.

YOU GET MORE OF WHAT YOU REWARD

In the previous section, we explained that innovation is associated with capitalism because capitalism rewards it. This leads us to another simple but profound economic principle: with people, organizations, and economies, you get more of what you reward. Want more investment? Reward investment. Want employees to work harder? Reward hard work. Want more innovation? Reward innovation. Want to discourage investment, hard work, and innovation? Take away their rewards by requiring everyone to be equally compensated regardless of their relative contributions. In other words, if you want to squelch investment, hard work, and innovation, adopt socialism.

Because economies grow as a result of innovation, it is crucial to understand how capitalism rewards innovation and socialism doesn't. One of the most important ways capitalism rewards innovation is by protecting intellectual property rights. Protection of private property may be the most fundamental tenet of capitalism, but to socialist ideologues private property is anathema. In a socialist setting, the government, not the individual, is the property owner, whether the property in question is physical or intellectual.

By offering individuals opportunities to patent their inventions and copyright their written work, such as books, songs, poetry, articles, plays, movie scripts, research reports, and so on, capitalism protects the individual's intellectual property. For example, this book is considered intellectual property. To protect our intellectual property, the publisher copyrighted this book. As a result, others—including the government—are prohibited from using any part of this book for their own profit without permission.

Knowing their work will be protected means creative people can be assured they will benefit from their efforts should their ideas pan out. Copyrighted or patented work will not be taken from them by the government. This assurance encourages visionaries to innovate, create, and invent. The obverse is also true. Knowing their intellectual work will belong not to them but to the government discourages creative people. With socialism, the government has the right to take your property at any time and become the new property owner. This decreases the incentive for individuals to create, innovate, or invent.

Why put forth the effort to create anything groundbreaking when the people most likely to benefit are a few elite bureaucrats at the top of the government? Why work to find innovative new production methods? Why invent new and better products and services? Capitalism encourages innovation by protecting private property—physical and intellectual. As a result, capitalism is closely associated with innovation. Socialism, on the other hand, discourages innovation and, as a result, gets less of it.

FREEDOM ENCOURAGES ECONOMIC GROWTH

The freedoms enjoyed in capitalist/democratic countries include the freedom to share information. This is important from an economic perspective because few things encourage innovation more than the free exchange of ideas. When creative people are allowed to interact, share ideas, and consult with other creative people, innovation blossoms. Innovation, in turn, leads to economic growth. Problems that might otherwise inhibit innovation can be solved faster and easier when smart people share information. Conversely, when information is not shared, problems persist.

For example, one of the most persistent stumbling blocks to scientists and medical professionals trying to cope with the COVID-19 pandemic in 2020 was China's refusal to share information. The Chinese Communist Party's clampdown on information was even more of a deterrent to solutions than it otherwise might have been because China was ground zero for the novel coronavirus. Because the laboratory where the virus got its start was in China, that nation could have been a treasure trove of useful information for scientific and medical personnel trying to curb the spread of COVID-19. Unfortunately for the world, China does not afford its citizens the freedom to receive or share information. In fact, Chinese scientists who tried to share useful information about COVID-19 were jailed or otherwise disciplined.

If you are old enough to remember the days before the Internet, think of how much faster you can locate the research reports, articles, white papers, opinion pieces, and other information you need now that we have the World Wide Web. The Internet has ensured individuals anywhere in the world have instant access to almost unlimited information as well as the ability to easily share information. This is a far cry from the days when the information people needed came mostly from newspapers and nightly news programs or required hours of hands-on research in a library.

Because of the Internet, you typically know about breaking news from all over the world before your local newspaper is printed or the nightly news programs are aired. Articles, papers, and research reports that used to take hours to locate, if they could be located at all, can now be found on the Internet in seconds. As one of the veterans we surveyed commented, the Internet is information sharing on steroids, a fact that encourages innovation and, in turn, economic growth. But socialist countries don't always want the world to know what is happening within their borders, nor do they want their citizens to know what is happening in the world outside their borders. China is an example of this phenomenon.

One of the veterans surveyed for this book was a China expert while serving in the Air Force. He claimed that although censorship is common in most socialist countries, China is by far the most aggressive at preventing information sharing. According to this veteran, there is even a name for China's online censorship program: the Great Firewall of China. This government-controlled firewall prevents Chinese citizens from accessing Facebook, Twitter, You-Tube, Instagram, Snapchat, and Google, as well as most other widely used social media sites and Internet services.

It is obvious Communist officials don't want the world to know what is happening in China; nor do they want Chinese citizens to know what is happening in the world. This explains why China must stoop to stealing the technological innovations of other nations. By discouraging information sharing not approved in advance by the Communist Party, Chinese officials deny their own country the innovative advances their citizens could, no doubt, develop if information sharing were encouraged and innovation rewarded.

China may be the worst of the Communist/socialist nations when it comes to banning information sharing, but it's not the only culprit. This kind of censorship is common in socialist countries where hiding the truth protects the ruling elite. Leaders in socialist nations typically find it necessary to keep their citizens and the rest of the world in the dark about their internal goings-on and corresponding problems. This is why any information coming from the government of a socialist nation should be treated with skepticism. It is likely to be propaganda.

Information sharing is good for the economy because it multiplies by orders of magnitude the number of smart people working to solve problems, create new technologies, and improve processes. This is why organizations use group brainstorming as a problem-solving technique. Scientists in laboratories trying to find a cure for some deadly disease are more likely to make a breakthrough if they are able to share ideas with other scientists concerned about the same disease. Knowing what worked and what didn't for other scientists can reduce the time, energy, and money required to make needed breakthroughs.

FREE MARKETS RESPOND MORE RAPIDLY TO CHANGE

Change being one of the few things we can count on in this world, individuals, organizations, and nations must be able to respond quickly and appropriately to change. Something economists of all stripes agree on is free markets driven by consumer demand respond more rapidly to change than socialist economies driven by bureaucratic central planning. One of the many disadvantages of socialism is its slowness in responding to change. This is important because nations responding appropriately and quickly to change prosper while those that don't experience economic stagnation or worse.

The importance of being able to respond to change became apparent during the COVID-19 pandemic of 2020 when a silent, invisible killer was unleashed on the world by a laboratory in Wuhan, China. The single most frightening characteristic of this deadly virus was its hyper-contagiousness. Overnight, people all over the world found themselves in need of personal protective equipment (PPE) and supplies, such as disposable gloves, face masks, hand sanitizer, and disinfectants. Hospitals were suddenly in need of additional ventilators and other equipment for treating respiratory illnesses. Nobody anticipated the pandemic that followed; hence, nobody was prepared for it. Scientists and medical professionals had to learn on the run how to treat the virus. Their challenge was like trying to repair a flat tire on a bicycle while riding it.

Not surprisingly, the sudden increase in demand for certain supplies and equipment created shortages. Further, when government officials issued stay-at-home orders, panic buying set in, as we noted in chapter 1. This intensified the shortages and expanded them to include essential goods, including flour, toilet paper, paper towels, meat, bread, canned goods, milk, and other common grocery items. That was the bad news. The good news was the shortages didn't last long in capitalistic countries because the fundamental benefits of free markets quickly came into play.

As demand for certain items skyrocketed, the manufacturers of these items were unable to keep up. This just stoked the fires of panic buying. But within days, other types of businesses were converting their production lines to manufacture the high-demand items. For example, liquor distillers devoted some of their alcohol stock to producing hand sanitizer. Automobile manufacturers made the adjustments necessary to produce ventilators. Restaurants closed to sit-down customers sold their stocks of toilet paper and paper towels and started preparing take-out meals. Making face masks became a cottage industry, with so many people sewing the masks in their homes that consumers soon had access to all the masks they needed and in their choice of colors, sizes, and patterns.

Now let's look at how government responded during the COVID-19 pandemic. People put out of work by the pandemic had to spend not just hours but days on government Internet sites, trying to apply for unemployment compensation. Small businesses that were promised loans so they could retain their employees had to wait so long for their applications to be processed that many lost their employees anyway. Many of the loans intended for small businesses went to large businesses.

Stimulus checks authorized by Congress for citizens who earned less than a set amount arrived well after the promised date.

Government bureaucracies are notoriously slow in responding to change. This is the point veteran and small business owner Tom Rice made in the opening quote for this chapter. There are just too many layers of bureaucracy in government and too much distance between the bureaucrats and the people they are supposed to serve to expect efficiency.

If the U.S. government was this slow to respond to the challenges imposed by COVID-19, imagine how slow the response would have been in a socialist America. In socialist nations, the normal shortcomings of government are exacerbated by central planning. Central planners far removed from consumers' daily lives have little or no idea what is needed. But in a free-market setting, it's different. Consumers who walk into a grocery store know what they want, and that's what they demand. They also know how much they are willing to pay for what they want, and that's how much they will pay.

Grocery stores, in turn, are in direct and constant contact with their suppliers. Thus, the suppliers know what is needed and how much. Direct consumer feedback updated by the minute allows suppliers to quickly make the adjustments necessary to meet consumer demand. What is even better about free markets is if the traditional manufacturers of high-demand products cannot meet consumer demand, other manufacturers will. In a socialist setting, central planners far removed from the front lines have no idea what consumers need. Worse, they have no incentive to respond to consumer demand. And when essentials are in short supply, the bureaucrats who control the government quickly monopolize the limited supply.

Central planners respond to government directives, not consumer demand. Consequently, their response to consumers facing shortages can be summarized in these words: *You don't tell us what you need; we tell you.* Manufacturers in a free-market setting, on the other hand, have two huge incentives to respond to consumer demand: (1) survival, and (2) prosperity through increased profits. The faster and better they respond to changes in consumer demand, the more money they make. Once again we see the invisible hand of enlightened self-interest at work in free markets.

HIGH TAXES DISCOURAGE PRODUCTIVITY

The more you are able to keep of the money you earn, the more motivated you are to work. Correspondingly, the less you are allowed to keep of the money you earn the less motivated you are to work. Therefore, high taxes on earnings or profits are de-motivators; they discourage work and, in turn, productivity. Think about it. People who are de-motivated by taxes will respond predictably: they will work less, and when they do work, they will put less effort into their jobs. Why work hard to earn more when the government is going to take it from you in taxes?

The more the government keeps of the money you earn, the less motivated you are to work. A child could understand this principle, but advocates of socialism either cannot or don't want to. One of the ways socialist ideologues in the United States are trying to achieve their overarching goal is through ever-increasing taxes. That overarching goal, of course, is transforming America into a socialist utopia in which they control you by controlling the government.

One of the veterans we surveyed asked why socialist ideologues can't understand that overtaxation will eventually lead to serious consequences. Among the consequences he listed in his survey were (1) elimination of the most important motivation people have for working, (2) fewer people willing to work, (3) diminished effort from those who do work, and (4) fewer of the things generating income and profits, including investment, creativity, and innovation. He was right, of course, but socialists don't see things through the eyes of logic or common sense. To socialists your money is not yours in the first place; it belongs to the government; meaning it belongs to them. Money is just one more thing a socialist government doles out to you in amounts it decides you need.

On the subject of taxation, another veteran surveyed for this book commented that since 10 percent is good enough for God, why isn't it good enough for the government?[1] Again, good question. The answer, of course, is the government requires more than 10 percent of your income to finance all the things it is doing not called for in the Constitution; and this is the government of the United States, a nation that still has a quasi-capitalist economy. In socialist countries the question of taxation is reversed. Citizens in these countries don't ask how much the government is going take from them in taxes. Rather, they ask how much the government will allow them to keep after it takes what it wants in taxes.

GOOD INTENTIONS DON'T ALWAYS RESULT IN GOOD POLICIES

One of the veterans we interviewed told of a conversation that took place in a Bible study at his church. One of the younger members of the group, a college student and an advocate of free health care, free college tuition, and student-debt forgiveness, was trying without much success to convince the other members of the viability of socialism. Finally, in a fit of frustration, this young man threw up his hands and stomped out, exclaiming as he left, "At least socialists have good intentions."

This student's supposition about the good intentions of socialists is questionable, but even if true, it wouldn't change anything. Those who use good intentions to justify their actions should be reminded that the road to hell is paved with good intentions. Intending to do good things and actually doing them are two different propositions. A deceived or misinformed person intending to do well can do a lot of damage. As we have demonstrated over and over in this book, the results of socialism are rarely if ever good.

The economic illiteracy indigenous to socialism could be easily cured if Leftist educators were willing to teach the truth to young people and college students. But instead, American students are indoctrinated year after year with the false narrative of the Left. Is it any wonder, then, that so many college students borrow huge sums of money they have little chance of paying back and then hoping the government will rescue them? With socialism the government cannot even rescue itself from debt, much less overextended college students.

A VETERAN SPEAKS UP

In socialist countries, those who take risks that don't work out are often punished. For capitalists, mistakes create opportunities for learning and improvement. Here is what one veteran had to say about this issue:

In the United States companies are built around capitalism and the formula of more success and responsibility = more money and reward. There is also more risk, and the way business leaders have learned to mitigate and manage risk is by taking risks and sometimes failing, but learning from the experience. Then each time they overcome a challenge they are better prepared to work even smarter next time.

—Patrick Byrne, United States Army, 2006–2016

Byrne served as company commander, Headquarters Company, Second Battalion, 501st Parachute Regiment, Fourth Airborne Brigade Combat Team, Eighty-Second Airborne Division.

CHAPTER 5

SOCIALISTS REJECT THE VALUES OF AMERICA'S FOUNDERS

A powerful way to redirect a nation's future is to rewrite its past. America has done some unworthy things, but our country has also done many, many great things. No other nation in the history of the world has had the power or the ability America has, and no other nation has come close to the U.S. in exercising restraint in the exercise of its power. Further, America has been the most benevolent victor in the history of war. Can you name even one nation America defeated in war that we currently own, and that we have not rebuilt so that it is better off now than it was before the war?

—Samuel Nelson, United States Air Force, 1980–1985

Nelson is a distinguished graduate of the United States Air Force Academy (1980) with a master's degree from Air University. His civilian career, spanning nearly four decades, has been spent in the research and development of air-launched weapons for the Air Force. During this time, Nelson has helped develop some of the most sophisticated, effective, and lethal non-nuclear weapons in the history of the U.S. military.

America was built on a foundation of Christian values. Does this mean our founders established America as a nation for Christians only or as a theocracy? Absolutely not. In fact, just the opposite. Early European settlers came to America seeking religious liberty and fleeing religious persecution. They wanted to be able to practice the religion of their choice without being pressured by kings and queens who made the royal religion mandatory and required citizens to support it through taxation.

In the Europe of those days, religions other than the one prescribed by the king or queen were actively and often brutally suppressed. The Founders were determined that this kind of religious coercion would not happen in America, nor did they want a theocracy. Perhaps better said, they knew there could be no theocracy since Jesus had put an end to the Levitical priesthood. Rather, they wanted to ensure the United States was built on a foundation of Christian values. Because of the hard work and determination of our founders, that is exactly what happened.

To claim America was built on a foundation of Christian values is not mere conjecture; it's a fact borne out by the historical record. Unfortunately, it's also a fact many Americans no longer recognize because they have been indoctrinated by socialist ideologues in schools, government, colleges, universities, the mass media, and the entertainment industry. To validate the secularist principles of socialism, its advocates must undermine America's Christian foundation. They must distort, rewrite, and even erase much of America's history in an attempt to eradicate the values that made America great.

Let's look at the American values socialists find so offensive: limited government, self-determination, individual freedom, religious liberty, equal opportunity, personal responsibility, self-reliance, a positive work ethic, fair competition, and the rule of law. Although these are some of the values that made America great, they run counter to the fundamental principles of socialism. Consequently, for socialism to prevail in America, socialist ideologues must ensure our foundational values are invalidated, or better yet, from their perspective, eradicated.

AMERICAN VALUES SOCIALISTS REJECT

Whereas the Founders took a minimalist approach to government, socialists take the opposite approach. To socialists, big government is not just desirable; it is an end unto itself. An all-pervasive, all-powerful government in control of every aspect of your life is the socialist's ideal. Then there is the issue of self-determination. Self-determination means, among other things, that Americans choose who they put in office to govern and are able, through free and open elections, to replace elected officials periodically.

The importance of free and open elections is why so many Americans are still concerned about irregularities in the presidential election of 2020. If the claims of voter fraud and manipulation of the vote count are true, the election was invalid and one of the cornerstones of our constitutional republic was shattered. Even in countries practicing so-called democratic socialism, the citizens don't enjoy self-determination in the true sense of the concept. Once elected, democratic socialists often manipulate the system, suppress opposition, and use the power of government to maintain their power and control. This is precisely the purpose of the Democratic Party's proposals to stack the Supreme Court, eliminate the electoral college, and make Washington, DC, the fifty-first state. These actions would ensure Democrats never have to relinquish control of the government.

Our founders enshrined freedom of religion in the Constitution by including it in the First Amendment. So, Americans can practice any religion they choose without fear of government interference. They can also choose to observe no religion at all or to even oppose the practice of religion. The same cannot be said for citizens of socialist countries. To a socialist, government is god. Therefore, citizens of socialist countries must view government as something resembling a deity. With socialism, religions that do not worship at the altar of government must be suppressed. Socialists understand that anyone who worships the God of Holy Scripture will not worship big government. This is why religion is the first thing to be attacked when socialists take over a nation.

While Americans believe in equal opportunity for all, socialists believe in equal outcomes and use government coercion to achieve this delusional goal. Equal opportunity involves taking appropriate steps to ensure everybody begins the race at the same time and same starting line. It does not mean everybody finishes the race at the same time. Equal opportunity is a worthy goal to pursue but a difficult goal to achieve. Some people are born into situations providing advantages, and some are not. This will always be the case in an imperfect world.

However, in the United States we try to level the playing field as much as possible through passage of equal opportunity laws that apply to employment, housing, bank loans, education, and other areas of life. Even with these measures in place, the only way people are ever really equal is in the eyes of God. However, in the United States we try hard to come as close to ensuring equal opportunity as possible. To a socialist, equal opportunity is not enough. They demand equal outcomes, an impossible goal when you consider the individual differences in people, including differences in motivation, ability, education, ambition, work ethic, perseverance, and so on, as we touched on in chapter 1.

Socialists like to attack capitalism claiming inequality is inherent in the concept. One of the veterans we questioned in preparation for this book pointed out that socialists need to realize life isn't fair, it hasn't been fair since the garden of Eden, and it never will be fair this side of the grave. While it is true inequalities will always exist in a capitalist setting, socialist attacks on capitalism are rendered less credible by the fact that inequalities exist to an even greater extent in socialism. The major difference between capitalism and socialism when it comes to inherent advantages is who enjoys them.

This fact is ironic since equality is touted by socialists as one of their foundational principles. Whereas with capitalism wealth can provide advantages and privileges, with socialism advantages and privileges are determined by one's position in government. The higher one rises in a socialist government, the more powerful one becomes. The more powerful one becomes, the more advantages one gains and the more privileges one has. In the United States we attempt to level the playing field by passing and enforcing equal-opportunity laws. In socialist countries, the government simply claims everyone is equal in spite of their obvious differences, all the while knowing government bureaucrats are more "equal" among supposed equals.

Personal responsibility is another American value that socialists reject. Another veteran we surveyed stated that the America he'd grown up in was one in which people believed individuals are responsible for building their own lives, providing for their own families, and succeeding or failing by dint of their own talent, ambition, motivation, work ethic, and perseverance. He added that people who believe in personal responsibility want government to stay out of their way. Socialists, on the other hand, want people to look to government as the benevolent provider of all their needs. In a socialist country, if the government doesn't provide it, you don't need it and no amount of personal effort, ambition, talent or perseverance will get it for you (although a bribe to a government official might).

Closely related to personal responsibility is the long-standing American value of self-reliance. The commitment of Americans to being self-reliant goes all the way back to the founding of our country, when the Pilgrims and pioneers had to build new lives from scratch on an unfamiliar and sometimes hostile continent. They had to learn to rely on themselves or die. The desire to be self-reliant is one of the reasons some of the most widely sold books in America are self-help books. We want to be able to do things ourselves. Contrast this attitude with how socialists think.

With socialism, self-reliance is considered rebellion against the government. The citizens of socialist countries are supposed to rely on the government, not themselves. To be self-reliant is to be disloyal and to reject a fundamental principle of socialism: government provision and control. In a capitalistic setting, self-reliance can make you less dependent on others. In a socialist setting it can land you in prison or, at the very least, make you an outcast among your peers.

A positive work ethic has traditionally been one of the hallmark values of Americans. The American work ethic, coupled with capitalism and our constitutional freedoms, is why the United States has become the most powerful, most economically advanced nation in all of history. Although creeping socialism is changing things, Americans have traditionally been among the most productive people on earth, willing to put in hard work and long hours to achieve their personal goals. Being called a "hard worker" has long been a compliment in America, but this is not the case in socialist nations. In a socialist setting, it's better to be known as a "conformist."

Being a hard worker in a socialist nation can make one stand out from the crowd—not a smart move in a setting where equality is enforced not just by peer pressure but by government coercion. Anyone who sticks his head up above the crowd in a socialist setting is liable to get it cut off. The socialist expectation of group cooperation and collaboration actually undermines the work ethic of individual members of the group. Since all members of the group are paid the same regardless of their relative contributions to the group's output, there is no incentive to work hard or smart and certainly not long. What would be the point?

Traditionally, Americans have loved competition. We've said it before: striving to win is in our DNA. Even little kids strive to outrun each other, win at Monopoly, make better grades than others, make the varsity team, be in the starting lineup, and so on. But to socialists, competition is a foreign concept. Cooperation, not competition, is the end goal. In a socialist race, everyone is supposed to cross the finish line at the same time.

This is why parents in America should be skeptical about allowing their children to play in kiddie sports leagues where everyone makes the team, everyone wins, and everyone gets a trophy. Intentional or not, this approach to organized sports undermines the competitive instinct of youngsters, encourages an entitlement mentality, leaves kids unprepared to deal with the harsh realities of the world they will live in as adults, and preconditions them to accept socialism.

No thinking person would claim America's justice system is perfect. In truth, it is only as effective and impartial as the imperfect people who run it. However, in spite of the shortcomings of our system of justice, there remains a persistent and powerful expectation among Americans that every person stands equal before the law. Americans frown on a person's relative status in society being a help or a hindrance where justice is concerned. Further, we believe a jury of our peers should decide guilt or innocence. This is not the case in socialist nations.

In socialist nations, guilt and innocence are determined by those who control the government and their minions in the various levels of bureaucracy. Socialist nations are infamous for their forced-labor prisons, reeducation camps, gulags, and other hellhole destinations for people who speak out against the government, get on the wrong side of a powerful bureaucrat, or dare to question socialist orthodoxy. As for a fair trial before a jury of one's peers, don't count on that in a socialist nation. Millions of citizens in socialist nations have been unceremoniously shot, beaten to death, starved, or worked to death without the benefit of a trial. Further, trials in socialist countries are often shams in which the outcome is determined before the proceedings begin.

In his book, *Prisoner of Mao*, Bao Ruo-Wang describes in detail how the criminal justice system works in a socialist setting.[1] In America, those accused of crimes have the right to face their accuser and thoroughly cross-examine that individual. We also have laws prohibiting slander and libel. Contrast this with Mao's China, where anyone could make an anonymous accusation against a neighbor, and all were encouraged to do so, even with no evidence to back up their claims.

In Mao's socialist "utopia," making anonymous claims against fellow citizens was a way to show one's loyalty to the government. Accusing fellow citizens of anti-socialist words, acts, or behavior, even if the accusations were false, was a favorite pastime in Mao's China. As hard as it may be for an American to believe, an anonymous accusation by a fellow citizen was all it took to have the accused charged, brought to trial, convicted, and sent to a forced-labor camp, often for life.

Trials were a sham in which the outcome was usually predetermined. The minute an accusation was made, a Chinese citizen was considered guilty. During the trial, the accused quickly learned the only way he could avoid a life sentence and protect his family from incarceration or worse was to confess his transgressions against the government in great detail, even if this meant making them up.

Because word spreads quickly, even in repressive socialist settings, people accused of crimes against the government understood beforehand how trials worked under Chairman Mao. Accused individuals knew better than to attempt a defense. To do so was to call the government a liar, usually a crime worse than the one you were charged with. The expeditious route was to confess as many misdeeds as possible, even if they were fictional.

In Mao's China, being accused was the same as being convicted. One of the reasons for this was people sent to prison were used as free labor for the Chinese government, which needed all the free labor it could get. Guilt and innocence were irrelevant. Even the few individuals who were sentenced to less than life were told they faced a life sentence and the only way to shorten it was to (1) work hard for the government, and (2) accept the socialist philosophy in its entirety without hesitation. This blatant coercion was referred to by Chinese authorities as "re-education." According to Bao Ruo-wang, this carrot-and-stick method of coercion was very effective.[2] The same methods have been used in other socialist countries.

In America, a convicted person has the right to appeal his sentence without fear of government retribution. In Mao's China, to appeal was to demonstrate rebelliousness. The fastest way to turn a less-than-life sentence into a life sentence was to appeal a conviction. In prison, the fastest way to earn favor with the guards and prison officials was to accuse fellow inmates of thinking bad thoughts against the government, displaying a negative attitude toward their supposedly benevolent minders, or, worse, speaking out against prison conditions. The jobs prisoners were assigned and the amount of food they were given were determined by how fully and enthusiastically they accepted the socialist philosophy, or at least how convincingly they pretended to.[3]

The conditions under Chairman Mao are not exceptions. Similar conditions existed in the Soviet Union under Stalin and his successors, Cambodia under Pol Pot, Venezuela under Hugo Chávez and more recently Nicolas Maduro, as well as in other socialist nations. Anytime allegiance to the government is more important than personal liberty, abuses of power are going to be the norm, not the exception. This is one more reason America's founders were committed to limited government and individual rights. Never forget the Bill of Rights was put in place to protect citizens from the government.

Another traditional American value socialist ideologues reject is maintaining a strong national defense. America's ability to defend itself against threats from rogue nations such as North Korea and Iran, international terrorist groups, and dominance-seeking nations such as China has never been more important. Yet, in spite of the ongoing threats from our enemies, politicians on the extreme Left have an unfortunate tendency to hollow out the military through budget cuts to the Department of Defense (DOD).

Socialist ideologues within the Democratic Party are constantly working to transfer funding away from the Department of Defense and into social programs that will increase the dependence of more Americans on government. Presidents Clinton and Obama both cut military spending during their terms in the White House. The Left has a history of proposing, lobbying for, and actually making cuts to the DOD budget, cuts that leave America weakened in the face of growing threats from Iran, China, North Korea, Russia, and terrorist groups worldwide. History has shown the worst time to serve in the military is during a Democratic administration.

REFUTING THE HISTORICAL REVISIONISM OF SOCIALISTS

Socialism is doomed from the outset in a country subscribing to Christian values. This is why Christianity is always suppressed and often outlawed in socialist nations. Christianity poses a serious problem for ideologues who believe the United States is the place where they can finally prove socialism will work. Advocates of socialism want to convert America into a government-run "paradise" to be held out as a model for the rest of the world, but Christianity is an unyielding obstacle to their plans.

A VETERAN SPEAKS UP

While America's enemies are rapidly increasing their military spending and correspondingly improving their military capabilities, the Left in America continues to lobby for cutting military spending. Here is what one veteran had to say about this issue:

As soon as President Donald Trump was elected, he immediately increased military spending and implemented a policy designed to strengthen our armed forces. Morale in the military improved, aging equipment was upgraded or replaced, and once again Teddy Roosevelt's motto—"Speak softly and carry a big stick"—was revived. Trump's actions could not have been more timely as China flexed its military muscles and became the biggest threat to our country. Our strong military posture ensures China will respect the United States. Unfortunately, fanatical terrorist groups do not share this same respect, but our strong military posture enables us to deal with this threat as well.

—Charles E. "Chuck" Merkel Jr., PhD, United States Army, 1967–1987

Major Merkel (retired) is a professor of history and president of the West Point Society of Northwest Florida. Merkel is a master army aviator with more than 3,000 hours of flying time, including hours in the Air Force T-28 jet trainer. His military decorations include the Legion of Merit, Bronze Star with one oak leaf cluster, Purple Heart, Meritorious Service Medal, Air Medal with eleven oak leaf clusters, Army Commendation Medal with four oak leaf clusters, and an Army Achievement Medal. Dr. Merkel is a member of the Florida Veterans' Hall of Fame (class of 2018).

Few things stand more firmly in the way of socialist ideologues and their heinous agenda than a populace subscribing to the vision of America's founders. That vision rests on a solid base of Christian values, and these values are the polar opposite of the principles of socialism. This is why socialist ideologues work so hard to tear down our Christian foundation, distort America's history, undermine traditional values, ignore the Declaration of Independence, and rewrite the Constitution. By controlling public education at all levels, the Left has made progress in achieving its anti-America, anti-Christianity agenda. But in spite of their efforts to eliminate it, evidence of America's Christian heritage still abounds. Plenty of proof exists that America was founded on Christian values for anyone open to the truth rather than the false narrative of the Left.

EVIDENCE OF AMERICA'S CHRISTIAN HERITAGE

Tour our nation's capital and you will find yourself surrounded by confirmation of America's Christian heritage. In his book, *Rediscovering God in America: Reflections on the Role of Faith in Our Nation's History and Future*,[4] former Speaker of the House of Representatives Newt Gingrich provides an excellent summary of this evidence. Let's take a brief written tour of the Capitol and see what we find.

In the U.S. Capitol Rotunda, several historical paintings are displayed. Three of these paintings in particular have Christian themes. The first is titled *The Embarkation of the Pilgrims*. This painting depicts a day of fasting and prayer by the Pilgrims. The second painting is titled *Discovery of the Mississippi*. It depicts Hernando de Soto seated on a horse. A monk prays as a crucifix is placed in the ground. The third painting shows Pocahantas being baptized and is titled, appropriately, *Baptism of Pocahantas*.[5]

As you walk though the Capitol, references to faith and God abound. For example, in the Cox Corridor you will find this line from "America the Beautiful" carved into the wall: "America! God shed His grace on thee, and crown thy good with brotherhood, from sea to shining sea." Enter the House chamber and you will see "In God We Trust" inscribed on the wall. Visit the Senate chamber and you will find the words *Annuit Coeptis* (Latin for "God has favored our undertakings") inscribed at the east entrance. At the southern entrance you will again see the words "In God We Trust." The chapel contains a stained-glass window showing

George Washington in prayer under the words "In God We Trust." The window also contains the following prayer: "Preserve me, God, for in Thee I put my trust."[6] By the way, don't overlook the fact that America's capitol contains a chapel. If America weren't founded on Christian principles, why would there be a chapel at our seat of government?

The Washington Monument is a veritable treasure trove of evidence relating to America's Christian heritage. The capstone originally placed on top of the monument contained the phrase *Laus Deo*, which is Latin for "Praise be to God." Other inscriptions within the monument include the following: "Holiness to the Lord," "Search the Scriptures," "The memory of the just is blessed," "May Heaven to this union continue its beneficence," and "In God We Trust" to name just a few. The cornerstone of the monument includes a copy of the Bible.[7]

At the Lincoln Memorial you will find yourself surrounded by the sixteenth president's words reflecting an abiding belief in God. Contained within Lincoln's Gettysburg Address inscribed on the walls of the monument are the words, "We here highly resolve that these dead shall not have died in vain, that this nation, under God, shall have a new birth of freedom." Also inscribed on the wall of the monument is Lincoln's second inaugural address, in which he quoted the Bible twice and mentioned God fourteen times.[8]

At the Jefferson Memorial are references to God made by America's third president. This is ironic because Jefferson has long been singled out by the Left as a deist rather than a Christian, in spite of copious evidence suggesting otherwise. A deist believes God created the world but having done so, has no further interest in it. To a deist, God does not involve himself in the lives of people. He leaves the world to itself and whatever happens, happens. The evidence of the Left's perfidy in denying the Christianity of Jefferson is found in the great man's own words, many of which are inscribed on his monument.

For example, the interior dome of the monument contains these words from Jefferson: "I have sworn upon the altar of God, eternal hostility against every form of tyranny over the minds of man." A wall panel contains Jefferson's famous words from the Declaration of Independence: "We hold these truths to be self-evident: That all men are created equal, that they are endowed by their Creator with certain unalienable rights, that among these are life, liberty, and the pursuit of happiness."[9]

Jefferson's words hardly describe a God who takes no interest in His creation. The Left's treatment of Jefferson is just one more example of their penchant for deceiving and distorting in order to divide and destroy. What is even sadder than the Left's distortions concerning Thomas Jefferson is that many Christians have allowed themselves to be duped into accepting the Left's false portrayal of the great man. They have heard the lie about his faith repeated so often they have come to accept it.

Perhaps the best evidence of Jefferson's Christianity can be found in another wall panel in the monument, where you can read these words from Jefferson's *Notes on the State of Virginia*, written in 1785: "God who gave us life gave us liberty. Can the liberties of a nation be secure when we have removed a conviction that these liberties are the gift of God? Indeed I tremble for my country when I reflect that God is just, that His justice cannot sleep forever."[10]

If God is just and His justice will not "sleep forever" it stands to reason that He is, in fact, interested in His creation. These few quotes only scratch the surface of Jefferson's copious writing, but even a cursory examination of his words belies the Leftist claim that Thomas Jefferson wasn't a Christian and that America's founders did not base their work on Christian principles.

A claim often made by Leftist ideologues is that America's founders were either unbelievers or, at best, deists. This is historical revisionism at its worst. Most of the founders who framed the Constitution were members of orthodox Christian churches, and half of the fifty-six founders who signed the Declaration of Independence received degrees from seminaries or Bible colleges.[11] During meetings of the Continental Congress, many of the founders attended services at Christ Church, which is located near Independence Hall in Philadelphia. In fact, several signers of the Declaration of Independence are buried at Christ Church. These luminaries of American history are Benjamin Franklin, Benjamin Rush, James Wilson, Francis Hopkinson, Joseph Hewes, and George Ross.[12]

One of the strongest statements made by a founding father about America's Christian heritage came from John Adams, second president of the United States: "The general principles on which the fathers achieved independence were . . . the general principles of Christianity."[13] America's first chief justice of the Supreme Court, John Jay, who was also president of the Continental Congress and a coauthor of *The Federalist Papers,* made clear his views on Christianity when he proclaimed, "Providence has given to our people the choice of their rulers; and it is the duty—as well as the privilege and interest—of our Christian nation to select and prefer Christians for their rulers."[14] Then there is the father of our country, whom Leftists are fond of portraying as a deist. The most famous of George Washington's public speeches is his "Farewell Address," in which he announced his intention to step down from the presidency at the end of his second term, an act that established a two-term precedent now enshrined in law. In this famous speech, Washington said, "Of all the dispositions and habits which lead to political prosperity, religion and morality are indispensable supports. In vain would that man claim the tribute of patriotism, who should labor to subvert these great pillars."[15]

If God took no interest in the daily affairs of man, religion would not be considered an "indispensable" support. Washington was prescient in knowing there would be people who would attempt to "subvert" the "great pillars" of religion and morality as socialist ideologues are now trying to do with their adherence to secular humanism, agnosticism, and atheism. But to do this they must be willing to uncouple themselves from the historical record and reality.

It would take a book the size of *The Oxford English Dictionary* to catalog all the statements made by America's founders concerning their Christian beliefs. Those summarized herein are just the tip of an immense iceberg. But we cannot end this section without including a few words about the original institutions of higher education in America and the evidence they provide of our Christian heritage.

Today's colleges and universities are ground zero for the historical revisionist movement of the Left. No institution in America demonstrates more blatant bias against Christianity and America's

Christian heritage than the academy. The core values of academic freedom and freedom of speech once prevailing on college campuses have been supplanted by unyielding demands for adherence to the Left's narrative of anti-America, anti-Christianity propaganda. Their fabricated narrative about America is at the center of the socialist agenda. Leftist orthodoxy prevails in higher education, and those who challenge it—whether professors or students—do so at their own risk.

Colleges and universities in America began as Christian institutions but have since devolved into *reeducation camps* dedicated to anti-Christian indoctrination. They now function more as propaganda arms for the Left than organizations dedicated to truth, free speech, and academic freedom. One of the veterans surveyed for this book is a longtime college professor. He claimed today's colleges and universities should place signs at all entrances reading "No Christians Allowed." The signs would apply to professors, students, and guest speakers.

Whereas colleges and universities once prided themselves on exposing students to a wide range of ideas, opinions, and philosophies, they now dedicate themselves to limiting student exposure to just one view of the world: the Leftist view. Institutions that used to teach students how to think now teach them what to think. Once upon a time, they encouraged independent thinking. Now, they demand sheeplike conformance. Whereas the goal of higher education was once to expand the minds of students, the new goal is to control the minds of students. The mind-control ideologues who are in the majority in colleges and universities these days expect students to obediently parrot the views of their Leftist professors, compliantly conform to Leftist orthodoxy, and refrain from asking inconvenient questions.

Let's consider the stated views of just a few of the more prominent leaders of the radical Left concerning God. We selected these individuals because their views are representative of those widely held by the radical Left in America. Richard Dawkins is an atheist and professorial fellow at New College, Oxford University. In his book *The God Delusion*, Dawkins contends a supernatural creator does not exist and belief in a personal god qualifies as a delusion, which he defines, quoting "the dictionary supplied with Microsoft Word," as "a persistent false belief held in the face of strong contradictory evidence."[16]

This definition overflows with irony. If delusions are false beliefs held in the face of strong contradictory evidence—which we agree they are—what does that say about socialist ideologues, whose false beliefs are contradicted by the evidence of America's Christian heritage? One must be blinded by either hubris or ignorance to deny a fact so well-documented as America's Christian heritage.

Another *giant* of the Left, now deceased, was Christopher Hitchens. Though not an academic like Dawkins, Hitchens was widely admired among socialist ideologues, and his book, *God Is Not Great: How Religion Poisons Everything* is still popular with Leftist college professors, many of whom make it required reading in their classes. Hitchens was unique among spokesmen for the Left in that he attacked not just Christianity but all religions. However, his most vitriolic diatribes were always directed against what he called "the three great monotheisms": Christianity, Judaism, and Islam.[17]

One final spokesman whose opinions are representative of how the radical Left views Christianity is Sam Harris, an atheist and philosopher who contends that religion threatens the survival of civilization. In his book *The End of Faith*, Harris states, "Religious faith represents so uncompromising a misuse of the power of our minds that it forms a kind of perverse, cultural singularity—a vanishing point beyond which rational discourse proves impossible."[18]

His statement is straight out of the playbook of secular humanism. It is an example of the humanist principle that God is unnecessary because man's power of reason is sufficient. Harris and his followers have somehow managed to convince themselves the reasoning powers of man are greater than the God who created the universe, including them. How's that for faulty reasoning? With all its supposed reasoning power, humankind has yet to find a way to reason itself out of war, famine, disease, and other forms of destruction, yet Harris and his followers still believe human reason renders God unnecessary.

We chose Dawkins, Hitchens, and Harris as our examples of anti-Christian ideologues because their views are popular with and widely held among Leftist college professors, a sad fact that shows how far institutions of higher education have drifted from their roots. Although it would be difficult to find institutions in America more intent on eradicating all traces of America's Christian heritage, it hasn't always been this way. American colleges weren't always opponents of the Christian religion; in fact, just the opposite. Ironically, America's most well-known universities were originally founded as Christian institutions with the mission of furthering God's kingdom. Consider the religious affiliations of the following old and revered American institutions of higher education:

- Harvard: Puritan congregational
- The College of William and Mary: Anglican
- Yale: Congregational
- Princeton: Presbyterian
- Columbia: Anglican
- Brown: Baptist
- Rutgers: Dutch Reformed
- Dartmouth: Puritan

If America had not been founded by Christian believers whose views of the world were informed and guided by Holy Scripture, these colleges would not have been established as Christian institutions. In fact, they probably would not have been established at all. It is one thing for socialist ideologues to disagree with the Christian principles that formed the foundation of our country. It is quite another for them to deny the key role these principles played in America's founding and then to revise history accordingly. Evidence of America's Christian heritage abounds. We have barely scratched the surface of what is available. There is much more, and it is readily accessible to anyone who values the truth, in spite of efforts by the Left to bury, deny, ignore, and revise it.

CHAPTER 6

SOCIAL DEMOCRACY: "SOFT TYRANNY" IS STILL TYRANNY

The military by its nature has a chain of command which is a critical element to the effective functioning and mission success of military units. The clear lines of authority that flow from the chain of command dictate how the individual and unit function. Without rank, service members would not be responsible to authority, would not follow orders from superiors—since there would be no superiors. The result would be disorder and chaos.

—Bruce J. Host, United States Air Force, 1959–1981

Colonel Host graduated from the Aviation Cadet Program in 1960 and received his navigator wings and the rank of second lieutenant at the age of twenty. During his career, he flew more than 4,000 hours, mainly in the C-130. Missions included troop carrier, photo mapping, and rescue. During the Vietnam War, Host flew as part of the SonTay POW rescue mission. He received a bachelor's degree through Operation Bootstrap and later a master's degree while attending the Navy Command and Staff College. Host is also a graduate of the National War College in Washington, DC. Following his retirement from the military, Colonel Host served for eight years as a county commissioner in Leon County, Florida. He is the founder of the Florida Veterans' Hall of Fame and the Hall of Fame Society.

To succeed in their quest to take over America by taking over the government, socialist ideologues face a vexing problem. Not only do they have to rewrite America's history to disguise the accomplishments and greatness of our country (as shown in chapter 5); they have to ignore the history of socialism to avoid having to answer embarrassing questions about its failures and weaknesses. One of the questions they like to avoid has to do with their principle of universal equality, the concept refuted by Col. Bruce Host in the opening quote of this chapter.

Unable to erase the historical failures of socialism and disassociate it from Stalin, Mao, Pol Pot, Castro, Hugo Chávez, and Nicolas Maduro, its advocates hit upon a clever strategy, one Leftist ideologues have used with success on other fronts: engage in semantic subterfuge by giving socialism a new and appealing name to disguise what it really is. This is one of the favorite tactics of the Left. The more appealing but misleading name they have chosen for socialism is *democratic socialism.*

This ruse makes socialism sound more appealing because Americans hold the concept of democracy in high esteem. To most Americans, a democratic version of anything must be good. But remember: soft tyranny of democratic socialism is still tyranny. Said another way, total government control of your life is still total government control whether accomplished by violence and coercion or high taxation and regulations.

WHAT IS DEMOCRATIC SOCIALISM?

The simplest definition of democratic socialism is: socialism implemented within a democratic framework. This is an accurate definition in theory, but as is often the case with socialism, there are major differences between theory and actual practice. Following are the fundamental principles of democratic socialism:

1. The government allows elections for choosing public officials (this is the *democratic* element of democratic socialism).

2. The government owns much but not all of the means of production (it typically owns such key industries as electricity, water, gas, coal, oil, and telecommunications).
3. The government uses taxation to redistribute income in the name of income equality.
4. The government provides a high minimum wage or universal income levels.
5. The government maintains a high level of taxation to support a large welfare component, universal income levels, and government services.
6. The government imposes onerous regulations on the parts of the economy it does not own.

One of the veterans we surveyed stated quite accurately that the only real difference between democratic socialism and traditional socialism is the means by which socialists control their citizens. Stalin, Mao, and Pol Pot used coercion, mass murder, intimidation, forced labor, and starvation to control their citizens. Leaders of countries practicing democratic socialism are more benevolent in their methods. They use high taxation, onerous regulations, and dependency on the government to control the people. Concerning this difference between democratic socialism and pure socialism, our veteran asked, "Does it really matter how the government controls you? Whether by coercion and intimidation or taxation and regulations, government control is government control. In both cases, the people lose their individual rights and personal liberty."

This veteran's comment brings to mind act 2, scene 2 from Shakespeare's famous play *Romeo and Juliet*. In this scene, Juliet speaks from her balcony. In paraphrase she says a rose by any other name is still a rose. With apologies to the Bard, government control by any other method is still government control. It follows, then, that socialism by any other name is still socialism. Regardless the type of socialism, the bottom-line principle is still government control. With government control, individual rights and personal liberty are either diminished markedly or lost altogether.

Americans got a small taste of how it is to live under complete government control during the COVID-19 lockdown in 2020. American citizens accustomed to personal liberty and the relative autonomy that accompanies it suddenly found themselves hemmed in by government edicts that forced them to stay isolated in their homes and shutter their businesses, schools, and churches. People who lived from paycheck to paycheck were suddenly in the untenable situation of having to violate government edicts to put food on their tables and pay their bills. Some were actually arrested or fined for working to support their families.

The government-imposed lockdown forced millions into unemployment lines; closed colleges, schools, churches, and businesses; forced people to wear masks and gloves; jailed or fined Christians and Jews for attending church and synagogue or conducting services; fined people for exercising in parks; jailed small-business owners for opening their establishments during the lockdown; and in some cases even told citizens what they could and could not purchase at the few retail establishments allowed to remain open.

Granted, these actions were taken in response to a worldwide pandemic, but the point here is they gave Americans a taste of how it is to live under democratic socialism. The fact that tens of thousands of Americans rebelled against the lockdown and risked going to jail by defying it shows what they think of the oppressive control associated with democratic socialism. What made the so-called emergency measures especially difficult to take was the inconsistencies in their application. In some states, bars and nightclubs were allowed to remain open while churches and synagogues were forced to close. This is precisely what happens in social democracies: decisions that should be left to individuals are made and enforced by the government.

Democratic socialists like to point out their concept is not pure socialism and American capitalism is not pure capitalism. Actually, they are right on both counts. In fact, pure forms of either concept are not just rare but probably nonexistent. Even in countries that have come close to practicing pure socialism, there have always been pockets of capitalism (e.g., the black market). In capitalist countries, the free market has never been completely free. It has always been tempered to some extent by government regulations and taxes.

However, the gulf between the quasi socialism championed by democratic socialists and the quasi capitalism practiced in America is still broad and deep. One major difference can be seen in how the two respond to economic downturns. In a quasi-capitalist setting, when the economy slows down, the tendency is to move closer to pure capitalism by cutting taxes, lowering interest rates, and eliminating unnecessary regulations. These actions quickly stimulate entrepreneurship and free enterprise, which, in turn, promote consumer confidence, job growth, and higher wages.

Donald Trump proved the efficacy of this strategy when, immediately after taking office as America's forty-fifth president, he cut taxes and used executive orders to eliminate onerous regulations bogging down the economy. As a result, until it was undermined by the COVID-19 pandemic of 2020, America's economy soared to unprecedented heights. Unemployment in all sectors was lower than it had ever been, the stock market set new records almost daily, and consumer confidence was at an all-time high.

Contrast this strategy with what typically happens when the economy of a socialist democracy slows down: just the opposite of what happens in a quasi-capitalist setting. In a social democracy, the government tightens the reins of control over the economy, increases taxes to cover the revenue shortfalls caused by the downturn, prints more money (which leads to inflation), and becomes increasingly coercive in its attempts to force the economy back on track.

When this approach makes matters worse, as it always does, social democracies are forced to adopt capitalist measures on an emergency basis to stimulate their economies, a fact demonstrating the efficacy of capitalism over socialism. This is one of the many ironies of socialism. History has shown that when socialist countries experience economic downturns, out of desperation they temporarily adopt capitalistic strategies to restore their economies. Common sense begs the question for socialist ideologues, If to rescue your country you temporarily adopt capitalist measures during times of economic distress, why not adopt capitalism all the time?

THE "SOFT TYRANNY" OF DEMOCRATIC SOCIALISM

We must credit French philosopher Alexis de Tocqueville for coin-
ing the term "soft tyranny." He used the term in his landmark book
Democracy in America to describe what is now called democratic
socialism, or *nanny government*.[1] Tocqueville described democratic
socialism as a benevolent but misguided philosophy that is the government version of the "helicopter parent."

The only aspect of Tocqueville's portrayal of democratic socialism
we disagree with is his attribution of the motives of it advocates to ill-
advised good intentions. While this motive may apply to some who
advocate for democratic socialism, it overlooks the more common
motive of socialists: power. Socialists want the power to control your
life, not improve it. Further, they know that the kind of power needed
to control your life comes only from an all-encompassing government.

You may recall that helicopter parents are those who hover over
their children, provide everything they could possibly want or need,
shield them from the consequences of their actions and behavior,
and "protect" them from the sometimes-harsh realities of life. As a
result, their children fail to develop personal responsibility, the
steadfastness needed to face life's difficulties, and a willingness to be
accountable for their actions.

Soft tyranny is the result of government replicating the mistakes
of helicopter parents by attempting to provide everything its citizens
might need and creating a utopia to shield them from the inevitable
trials of life. Those who subscribe to this way of thinking would do
well to remember the following adage from chapter 1: A government big enough to give you everything you want is a government
big enough to take from you everything you have.[2]

With democratic socialism, citizens are turned into adult ver-
sions of helpless children completely dependent on government and
unable to fend for themselves. Viewing democratic socialism
through the lens of helicopter parenting makes for an apt comparison. Tocqueville claimed the false benevolence of nanny government traps people in a perpetual state of childlike dependency.[3]
Think of a nation of citizens who resemble in their helplessness that
thirty-year-old son we described in chapter 1.

Interestingly, Tocqueville pointed out that one of the main reasons people allow themselves to be taken in by the concept of socialism is the promise of equality.[4] This promise always appeals to the poor because they think socialism is going to make them equal to those who are better off financially. Of course, this is just wishful thinking on their part. It never happens, because socialism cannot simply anoint poor people with the assets that allow others to improve their financial status (e.g., education, training, ambition, motivation, a positive work ethic, determination, creativity, entrepreneurship, and perseverance).

In reality, income redistribution doesn't make the poor richer; it makes the rich poorer. This is what Sir Winton Churchill meant when he told the House of Commons on October 22, 1945, "The inherent virtue of Socialism is the equal sharing of miseries."[5] The equality claimed by ideologues as a central virtue of socialism always turns out to be equality of want, need, and misery. Marxist professors who live off of the largesse of capitalism while espousing socialism would do well to face up to this sad fact.

PROBLEMS WITH DEMOCRATIC SOCIALISM SUMMARIZED

There are a number of problems with democratic socialism people should be aware of, particularly those who find themselves being seduced by the false promises of its advocates. The best way to analyze these inherent flaws is to examine the six principles of democratic socialism presented earlier in this chapter. Let's compare socialist theory against reality. As you will see from these comparisons, with democratic socialism, as with all varieties of socialism, there is a major chasm between theory and reality.

Democratic elections

The first principle of democratic socialism that we listed earlier is democratic elections. In theory, this principle is supposed to empower citizens to prevent the other five principles from going awry in the hands of unscrupulous elected officials. This is a valid enough principle, at least in theory. However, the historical record shows there is often a yawning gap between theory and reality when it comes to elections in countries that adopt democratic socialism. It is folly to expect elections to counterbalance the inherent flaws and abuses of democratic socialism because voters, vote counts, and the balloting process can be manipulated.

Americans got a taste of how elections are often conducted in social democracies during the presidential election of 2020. Among the corrupt strategies allegedly used by the Democratic Party were these:

- months of warped public opinion polls aired over and over by the mainstream media, making it appear the Republican incumbent had no chance of winning when, in fact, the race was too close to call
- blatant bias on the part of the mainstream media in favor of the Democratic Party's candidate
- censorship of messages supporting the Republican candidate by the tech companies controlling social media
- millions of unsolicited mail-out ballots sent, allowing Democrats to vote more than once and even allowing dead people to vote
- counting of mail-in ballots only after the walk-in votes were counted, enabling Democratic elections supervisors to know how many of the mail-in ballots would be needed to give their candidate the win
- refusal of Democratic elections supervisors to follow the laws of their own states concerning observers monitoring the polling stations
- too few absentee ballots sent to military bases to allow all military personnel to vote, enabling Democratic elections supervisors to limit the number of votes the Republican candidate received from military personnel (typically, a much higher percentage of military personnel vote for Republican candidates than for Democrats)
- Democratic elections supervisors violating state laws pertaining to how ballots are to be handled (e.g., requiring no

identification and counting ballots received after the legally posted deadline)
- mainstream media outlets calling states for the Democratic candidate well before the vote count was complete
- Democrats loudly demanding all votes be counted instead of all legal votes.

When these types of corrupt practices can be perpetrated on the public in an America not yet run by socialists, imagine how embedded they will become if social democrats are able to gain complete control of the government. Then there is the economy. When the government controls a nation's economy—either by owning the means of production, through regulation and taxation, or by a combination of these—elected officials can use the power of government to suppress political opposition.

Then there is the media. An all-powerful government can also transform media outlets into propaganda organs that support a given political party while providing the opposition little or no media coverage, or worse yet, only bad coverage. This has already happened in America without government coercion. Conservative politicians are either attacked or ignored by the mainstream media every day and censored by social media giants.

The social-democratic principle of turning ineffective elected officials out of office assumes citizens will be well-informed about their government, closely monitor the actions of elected officials and their bureaucratic minions, and turn out in high percentages to remove from office those who abuse their power. The problems with these assumptions will be obvious to anyone familiar with Democratic politics.

First, when media outlets, including social media, are little more than propaganda organs for the Left, how do citizens stay informed and how do they monitor the actions of government officials? Second, when citizens believe systematic voter fraud makes turning out to vote a waste of time, how many will turn out to cast ballots? Finally, when the party in power is willing to use intimidation and threats, the number of ballots cast by the opposition is not likely to be sufficient to turn despots out of office. Because of these inherent flaws, coupled with the predictable scheming of elected officials, democratic socialists, once in office, tend to stay in office. Further, in actual practice, democratic socialism has an unfortunate tendency to become less democratic and more dogmatic over time.

Economic downturns and national emergencies almost always cause democratic-socialist governments to assume even tighter and broader controls, and in the process, become more authoritarian and less democratic. Again recall how Leftist governors and mayors shut down major cities during the COVID-19 pandemic. As reasonable elected officials worked hard to find the proper balance between fighting the coronavirus and protecting jobs and Americans' mental health, far-Left officials used the crisis to gain more control over citizens. This is and always has been a favorite tactic of the Left. Worse yet, when the crisis of the moment is over, rather than relax its emergency controls, a Left-wing government maintains them. Because of this tendency, democratic socialism is particularly susceptible to tyranny and despotism. For socialist ideologues who crave total government control, national emergencies and crises are welcome events. Instilling fear in citizens while touting the need for more security is a favorite tactic of democratic socialists for increasing government control and reducing individual liberty.

Social democrats who seek high office are often corrupt demagogues already. However, even in those cases where they aren't, elected social democrats are often corrupted by power. The adage that power corrupts and absolute power corrupts absolutely could have been written for socialist governments, even those starting out as democratic. Think about it. Elected demagogues who are corrupted by power are not likely to give up power willingly. Rather, they are more likely to use the power of government to manipulate elections in ways to keep them in office. For an example of this, consider the case of Hugo Chávez in Venezuela and his successor, Nicolas Maduro.

Hugo Chávez was originally elected president of Venezuela through a democratic process. But once in office, he used coercion, manipulation, intimidation, and other disreputable means to win future elections and stay in office. Even when the once-booming economy of Venezuela lay in tatters and its citizens were living in abject poverty because of the failure of his socialist programs, Chávez managed to remain in office by using the power of government to manipulate elections. Nearing the end of his life, Chávez used the same unscrupulous practices to transfer power to his crony, Nicolas Maduro, who picked up where Chávez left off.

Because of the abuses of power associated with Chávez and Maduro, Venezuela has been labeled an "authoritarian regime" by the Economist Intelligence Unit (EIU), a London-based organization that conducts economic research, forecasting, and analysis.[6] Companies considering doing business in Venezuela look to the EIU in making their decisions. The label of "authoritarian regime" for Venezuela is accurate, but verification by the EIU is redundant since socialist regimes tend to be authoritarian by their very nature. As one of the veterans surveyed for this book commented, any government that is long on bureaucratic control and short on individual liberty is an authoritarian government.

Government ownership of key industries

The second characteristic of democratic socialism is government ownership of key industries, such as electricity, water, gas, coal, oil, and telecommunications, the most essential industries in citizens' everyday lives. There are two obvious problems with government ownership of these essential services: (1) government inefficiency, and (2) the government's ability to use control of such services to manipulate and coerce citizens. Multiple layers of bureaucracy, the fact that government enterprises are monopolies, and the distance between decision makers and the people who need the services all contribute to inefficiency and at the same time give government officials almost unlimited power over citizens.

This is why shortages of essential services are common in social countries. It is also why the government is slower to respond than private-sector providers when natural disasters interrupt essential services. Once again, consider the example of Venezuela. Although it has the largest oil deposits in South America, citizens of that country are often without power for weeks at a time. This is like a family with a storeroom full of food starving because nobody knows how to access the food and prepare it.

This kind of inefficiency is characteristic of government-run enterprises. In addition, shutting off the power is one more weapon the government of Venezuela has to keep dissidents in line. If disgruntled citizens in a given region rise up against the government, bureaucrats can simply turn off the power to that region until the dissidents agree to get back in line. If you think this is too drastic a tactic ever to be used in America, think again. During the COVID-19 pandemic, the governor of California threatened to cut off power to any organization that refused to comply with the government-mandated lockdown.

Income equality

The third principle of democratic socialism is income equality. The term "income equality" is yet another example of semantic subterfuge. What the term really means is redistribution of income through taxation, that is, taking money from wealthy and middle-class citizens through onerous taxes and using it to "equalize" the income levels of lesser wage earners. It typically amounts to taking money from people who earn it and businesses that create jobs and giving it to people who do neither.

Some socialist ideologues smugly refer to income redistribution as their *Robin Hood principle*. Most people know the story of Robin Hood. He robbed from the rich and gave to the poor. The problem with the analogy as used by socialist ideologues is Robin Hood took from the rich only what they had illegitimately taken from the poor. He simply returned to the poor what was already theirs but had been taken by the king's minions, typically in the form of oppressive taxes. Robin Hood administered justice, not coerced income equality.

A VETERAN SPEAKS UP

Socialist ideologues use the concept of wealth to create class envy they can then exploit. Here is what one veteran had to say about this issue:

Democratic socialists envy the so-called top 1 percent while ignoring the fact that most wealthy people in America are entrepreneurs who earned their economic status by providing better, less expensive, and higher-quality goods and services to the public. Democratic socialists slander the wealthy as exploiters of their employees while at the same time exploiting the public at large through high taxes and inflation of the currency.

—Archie Jones, PhD, United States Marine Corps, 1960–1964

Dr. Jones is the author and coauthor of several books, including *The Gateway to Liberty* and *Liberal Tyranny in Higher Education.*

The socialist principle of income equality demonstrates one of the more serious flaws of socialism, an ironic failing that applies to all varieties of the concept. On the one hand socialism in all of its forms runs counter to human nature. On the other hand it simultaneously appeals to the worst aspects of human nature. Anyone with an ounce of insight into human nature knows people don't want to be equal; they want to be better, wealthier, faster, stronger, handsomer, prettier, more influential, more powerful, and so on. People who argue for equality do so only until they achieve that status, then they want more.

Another blatant flaw in this principle is that socialist ideologues advocate for income equality on the basis of fairness. They question the fairness of some people being wealthy while others are poor, but in doing so they make two major mistakes. First, they assume people are poor because of unfairness. While this may be true for some, there are also a lot of other reasons people are poor, such as bad choices, lack of ambition, dropping out of school, and a poor work ethic.

Second, socialists only consider the fairness question from the perspective of the poor. What about fairness to the wealthier members of society? How is it "fair" to take money from people who earned it—whether by hard work or by smart investing—and give it to people who neither worked for it nor risked losing it by investing? Fairness, to the extent it can exist in the first place in a fallen world, is not a one-way street. People who are better off financially have just as much right to fairness as do those at the lower end of the economic spectrum.

Listening to socialist ideologues, one gets the impression the wealthy in society are all evil people who came by their money by iniquitious means and, thus, don't deserve to be wealthy. Ironically, many of the Leftist politicians who make these claims are wealthy themselves. Granted, some members of the wealthy elite inherited the money they enjoy, but they are a minority. Upward mobility is one of the most attractive aspects of capitalism, and it is how most wealthy people in America became wealthy. Even in the case of inherited wealth, money handed down through generations was earned by someone somewhere along the line.

The highest percentage of wealthy people in the United States earned their money by dint of working hard, smart, and long while thinking entrepreneurially. Typically, they also invested in education, training, and other self-improvement activities that increased their earning potential. Now, having done the difficult things necessary to generate personal wealth, they are attacked by socialist ideologues who think they should be required, in the name of equality, to give much of their wealth to those who have not worked equally hard and long or invested equally wisely to improve their earning potential. How is that fair?

Let's look at an example of why income equality is not just misguided but unfair. Consider two brothers who work in the same engineering firm. One studied hard so he could get into a good college and earn an engineering degree. He is now the firm's star engineer. His work is one of the main reasons the firm is successful. His brother, on the other hand, partied his way through high school, barely graduating. He did not go to college or complete any kind of specialized training. He is employed as the office gofer at the engineering firm, a job his brother got for him. In a country where democratic socialism is the governing principle, the brother who worked hard to become an engineer and whose work is so important to the success of the firm would have his income highly taxed and redistributed to his less qualified, less motivated brother, a low-level employee who contributes little to the firm's success and who could be easily replaced. This is the reality of the socialist principle of income equality—and socialist ideologues call it "fair."

This example demonstrates why income redistribution to achieve income equality is a bad idea. It undermines the motivation, ambition, entrepreneurship, and work ethic of the most productive members of society, those who work hard and smart as well as those who create jobs through entrepreneurship. Productive people and entrepreneurs are not fools. One of the veterans we surveyed wondered, *Why should people work hard and smart when most of what they earn is going to be taken away by the government and given to people who don't?* Productive people respond to incentives. Income redistribution to achieve income equality is a disincentive. In fact, it is worse than a disincentive; it's is an incentive to avoid working hard and smart.

High minimum wage

Minimum-wage jobs have provided a lot of successful people in America with a start in the workforce and the experience they need to climb the career ladder. While they can provide people with a good start, minimum-wage jobs were never intended to be lifelong jobs. Nor were they meant to provide the principal income for individuals or families. However, minimum-wage jobs are fast becoming lifelong endeavors and the main source of income for a lot of Americans as more and more people fail to do what's necessary to obtain better, higher-paying jobs. Viewing minimum-wage jobs as anything but starter jobs is a serious mistake that can have lifelong consequences for individuals, communities, and our country.

Paying a high minimum wage that only goes up reinforces this mistake, yet a high and ever-increasing minimum wage is a fundamental principle of democratic socialism. In a capitalist setting, when the minimum wage is increased, the number of minimum-wage jobs is decreased. To avoid having their profits reduced by increases in personnel costs, businesses find innovative ways to operate more efficiently with fewer employees. This is not conjecture but a fact proven over and over. Yet democratic socialists still maintain a high minimum wage as one of their sacrosanct principles.

Another flaw with paying a high and ever-increasing minimum wage is it rewards the wrong things. No nation is wise to reward people for failing to do what is necessary to be upwardly mobile. Further, it is unwise and hardly benevolent to encourage people to remain in the most economically vulnerable jobs in our society. No employee is easier to replace than a minimum-wage employee. The training required for most minimum-wage jobs can be completed in hours, not months or years. Worse, minimum-wage employees are the ones most likely to be replaced by technologies designed to reduce labor costs. Thus, a principle that encourages people to remain in minimum-wage jobs does a disservice to the very people it purports to help.

A high minimum wage eliminates a major incentive for self-improvement. For example, in a capitalistic setting there are many people who started out working in minimum-wage jobs while pursuing the education, skills training, or mentoring necessary to secure better jobs. This is the concept of upward mobility based on personal effort and ambition. But upward mobility is undermined when providing a high minimum wage is adopted as government policy. This dangerous practice encourages people to remain at the bottom of the economic ladder and rely on the government to improve their economic status.

There is one final, important note about providing a high minimum wage. Socialist ideologues argue the minimum wage should be a "living wage." So, who decides what constitutes a living wage? After all, a "living wage" for one person may not suffice for another person. People have different levels of ambition and taste when it comes to how they live. Some are content to live simply, while others desire extravagance. Thus, the question arises, Who decides how citizens should live? This kind of decision should be made by individuals, not government bureaucrats.

With capitalism, individual citizens decide how they want to live and whether they are willing to do what is necessary to achieve that status. The desire for a better standard of living motivates people to pursue additional education and training, work harder and smarter, save money, and spend wisely. With democratic socialism, the government decides what a living wage will be. By extension, this means the government also decides how people who work for the minimum wage will live. This is governmental overreach at its intrusive worst.

High level of welfare

Welfare was originally envisioned as a temporary safety net to tide people over until they could do better. It was never intended to be a multigenerational way of life. On the surface, the aim of welfare sounds reasonable enough. However, there has always been a glaring enigma welfare advocates have no answer for. How does a nation provide a financial safety net for its citizens without that net becoming a comfortable hammock, a permanent way of life passed along from generation to generation?

Unable to deny welfare's tendency to become a permanent way of life, socialist ideologues have adopted a different tactic. Rather than debate the issue, they simply claim lifelong welfare is acceptable. After all, nothing gives bureaucrats more control than having its citizens dependent on government for their sustenance. The desire for complete government control is why providing a high level of welfare is one of the fundamental principles of democratic socialism. It's one of the ways socialists maintain control of the people so they can, in turn, maintain control of the government. When your daily sustenance comes from the government, you will vote for the party promising to continue the handouts whether you agree with their politics or not.

Few would oppose providing a hand up to those who are too old or infirm to work. But that cohort of welfare recipients is not the one raising eyebrows. The ongoing debate over welfare is about able-bodied people who can work but don't. As we have stated many times already in this book, people respond to incentives. This leads us into another major problem with welfare: it eliminates the incentive to work, or more accurately, it incentivizes not working. When the amount of money and the number of benefits provided by welfare exceed the minimum wage—as they do in every state in the U.S.[7]—why would people on welfare go to work? Welfare actually creates a situation in which idleness pays better than working.

Another problem is the welfare system is susceptible to fraud and abuse. An instructive example is the case of Linda Taylor (aka "the Welfare Queen"), who managed to cheat the system out of more than $150,000 a year.[8] Another welfare recipient, Iris Swift, stated honestly there are "a lot of advantages to staying on welfare."[9] Said another way, there can be serious disadvantages to getting off welfare.

For example, taking a job that increases family income even one point above the poverty line can subject welfare recipients to taxes that cause them to net less income each month even though they earn more.[10] This ill-advised government policy is one more factor incentivizing idleness. Welfare reform is one of those political hot potatoes talked about a lot in Congress, although little is ever done. If socialists control the government, the issue won't even be discussed.

Perhaps the biggest problem with welfare is it creates a culture of dependence often passed along from generation to generation.[11] To a capitalist, being dependent on the government is unacceptable. However, to a democratic socialist total dependence on the government is not just acceptable; it's desirable. What socialists cannot seem to understand is that little truism we discussed at length in chapter 4: with people you get more of what you reward and less of what you discourage. Providing lifelong welfare rewards idleness. This is one of the reasons idleness is rampant among able-bodied people.

By liberally providing welfare, democratic socialists create a never-ending, always-increasing drag on the economies of their countries. The math is simple. The fewer people working, the less productive the country. It's a matter of how many people are pulling the wagon versus how many are riding in it. Those who pull the wagon have to work harder and longer to make up for those who ride in it (i.e., those who choose welfare as a way of life). Not only do the productive few have to do the work their idle counterparts should be doing; they have to pay higher taxes to finance the idleness of those who choose to ride in the wagon.

The best commentary we have ever read on welfare was written by one of America's wisest founders, Benjamin Franklin. Therefore, we will give him the last word on this subject. Franklin wrote:

> *I am for doing good to the poor, but I differ in opinion about the means. I think the best way of doing good to the poor is, not making them easy in poverty, but leading or driving them out of it . . . I travelled much, and I observed in different countries, that the more public provisions were made for the poor, the less they provided for themselves, and of course became poorer. And, on the contrary, the less was done for them, the more they did for themselves, and became richer.*[12]

Government regulations

Few would argue against regulations in general. Rather, what hurts the economy is overregulation, the unending promulgation of unnecessary regulations. Government regulatory agencies are just like other bureaucratic organizations: they tend to grow bigger and more powerful over time. Growing bigger is how they justify their existence. In the case of regulatory agencies, they increase their size and power by continually developing more and more regulations.

For example, between 2001 and 2015 the federal government issued almost fifty thousand new regulations.[13] The proliferation of unnecessary regulations slowed considerably when Donald Trump was elected president in 2016. However, Joe Biden has promised that as president he will reintroduce many of the regulations Trump got rid of. The annual cost of regulatory compliance now approaches $2 trillion.[14] Every penny spent on complying with regulations is money that could have been invested in innovation, expansion, and job creation.

Government regulatory agencies don't get smaller, at least not voluntarily. Can you name even one regulatory agency in the federal government that voluntarily reduced regulations and, in turn, its size? As one of our veterans commented, the worst fear of a bureaucratic agency is that someone might question if it is needed. Consequently, regulatory agencies make a point of showing they are needed by becoming too big to eliminate. In the minds of socialist bureaucrats, the bigger their agency, the more it is needed.

Up to a point, certain selected regulations can help the economy run more smoothly and predictably, provided they are well-thought-out and reasonably applied. Unfortunately, government regulatory agencies are more interested in survival than in boosting the economy. This is the *why* behind the ongoing proliferation of government regulations, many of which are unnecessary. Adopting and enforcing unnecessary regulations is like throwing sand in the gears of business and industry. This is why the gears of business and industry are so sluggish in countries that have adopted democratic socialism.

Writing for the Heritage Foundation, David W. Kreutzer[15] summarized the problems with overregulation succinctly and accurately: "Wages and incomes grow when the demand for labor grows. The demand for labor grows when the rewards for starting and expanding businesses grow. . . . More regulations penalize expansion and start-ups. The costs are passed on to workers in the form of fewer jobs and lower wages."[16] Burdensome regulations are one of many reasons entrepreneurs don't gravitate to socialist countries.

America's founders envisioned a relatively small federal government limiting itself to the responsibilities prescribed for it in the Constitution. They would be appalled to see how huge the federal government has grown over the years. They would be even more appalled to hear American politicians openly advocating for democratic socialism, a concept at odds with everything they believed and risked their lives to establish. Do not let the word *democratic* in "democratic socialism" distract you from the fact that socialism is still socialism no matter what starry-eyed advocates and unscrupulous politicians choose to call it.

CHAPTER 7

SOCIALISTS DON'T EDUCATE; THEY INDOCTRINATE

Like many veterans, I often remember my time in uniform, particularly after 9/11, as being more than just honorable service, but as participating in the events of history. It is easy to look back on our collective history and highlight only those events that make us feel proud rather than uncomfortable. But we must be willing to look at the unpleasant and dark parts of America's past as well the good parts. A complete and accurate remembrance of history is critical for any society to not only learn from its mistakes but to also celebrate and champion its successes. Historical revisionists attempt to present a reinterpretation of historical events that challenges the traditional or accepted view of them. It is proper to correct the historical record based on recent research or newly discovered evidence, but recently we have seen a move toward historical revisionism based on political correctness rather than scholarship. This is often done to reinterpret the moral meaning of the historical record.

The very real danger in this practice is that revisionist history presents an incomplete, and often false presentation of historical events, thereby depriving the American people of a true accounting of our shared history.

—John R. "Jack" Capra, United States Navy, 1993–2014

Captain Capra (retired) earned his undergraduate degree from Florida State University in 1989 and went on to earn his law degree (JD) in 1992 from St. Thomas University School of Law. Following law school Capra continued his education, earning four master's degrees, and is a currently a PhD candidate. Capra served on active duty with the Navy from 1992 to 1997, during which time his service included being assistant force judge advocate for the Fifth Fleet at Bahrain and force judge advocate for Operation Deep Freeze in Antarctica. He transitioned to the Naval Reserves in 1997. However, he was called back to active service on six occasions following the terrorist attacks on September 11, 2001. While serving in Basra, Iraq, in 2004, Capra was wounded when enemy insurgents detonated a radio-controlled IED under his military convoy. He was awarded the Purple Heart and a Combat Action Ribbon for his service in Basra. As a civilian, Capra has enjoyed a successful career serving as a practicing attorney, an elected official, general counsel for a state college, and counsel for a government agency.

If you want to shape people's thinking and instill in them a particular worldview, start while they are young. This is what Horace Mann meant when he said, "Men are cast-iron, but children are wax."[1] Mann claimed to view education as a tool for instilling morality and responsibility, a challenge he misguidedly thought should be left to government, not parents. Since Mann's time, socialist ideologues have taken up his banner and are working hard to turn unwitting children into compliant sheep who obediently conform to Leftist orthodoxy.

When it comes to public education, things have changed over the years, and not for the better. Although there are still teachers, principals, and school districts that reject socialist indoctrination in favor of teaching the truth about America, they are fast becoming minorities in public education. It has become increasingly difficult for educators who believe in academic integrity to stand up to the avalanche of socialist propaganda pervading public education at all levels. God bless these good stewards of true education, but more and more like someone in a sinking ship trying to bail out water with a teaspoon

The American Left has transformed our public schools and colleges from institutions of learning into centers of socialist indoctrination. All too often today's public schools are characterized by:

- dumbed-down curricula
- an emphasis on inclusion rather than excellence
- worship of diversity (except, of course, diversity of thought, opinion, and beliefs)
- demands for tolerance of all beliefs (except those of Christians and conservatives)
- a portrayal of America as an evil nation
- distortion of history to fit the false narrative of the Left
- refusal to give parents a say in what their children are taught.

Before getting into how the Left has accomplished this transformation of public education, three important questions must be answered. First, what is the purpose of education? Second, how does indoctrination differ from education? Finally, who is responsible for the education of America's children? A necessary first step in stopping the socialist onslaught in America is learning the answers to these three questions. Only then will we be able to restore control of public education to the citizens who pay for it. Only then will we be able to restore academic integrity in public education at all levels.

WHAT IS THE PURPOSE OF EDUCATION?

Public education is funded by taxes paid by American citizens, including those who opt out of public education by sending their children to private schools or who homeschool them. In other words, even if you don't send you children to public schools, you still pay for these schools. Therefore, not only do you have a vested interest in what takes place in them; you should have a voice in what takes place in them. It stands to reason public education should benefit the entire public who pays for it.

To this end, the purpose of K–12 education has traditionally been "to provide for the fullest possible development of each learner for living morally, creatively, and productively in a democratic society."[2] We have traditionally expected young people to graduate from high school prepared to take care of themselves in a responsible manner while contributing to the good of their communities and our country. We have also expected them to be prepared to enter the workplace, college, or the military and succeed.

Colleges and universities have long held that the purpose of higher education is "the pursuit of truth, the discovery of new knowledge through scholarship and research, the study and reasoned criticism of intellectual and cultural traditions, the teaching and general development of students to help them become creative individuals and productive citizens of a pluralistic democracy, and the transmission of knowledge and learning to society at large."[3] Though their actions often belie their commitment to achieving this purpose, most institutes of higher learning still claim this or something similar as their purpose.

HOW DOES INDOCTRINATION DIFFER FROM EDUCATION?

"The philosophy of the schoolroom in one generation will be the philosophy of government in the next."[4] This maxim, usually, whether accurately or inaccurately, attributed to Abraham Lincoln, explains in succinct terms why the Left has put so much effort into transforming public schools and colleges into centers of indoctrination. Indoctrination has a much different purpose than education. While education develops intellectual breadth and depth, indoctrination limits both. Education expands; indoctrination constricts. Education feeds growth and development; indoctrination inhibits them.

Indoctrination involves forcing ideas and beliefs on people, who are then not allowed to question them. Education is about teaching people how to think and then letting them draw their own conclusions. Indoctrination is about teaching people what to think and discouraging nonconforming conclusions. Disagreement, alternative opinions, and different beliefs have no place in a setting where indoctrination is the goal. In short, education is thought and mind development; indoctrination is thought and mind control.

Whereas education seeks to expand people's ability to think independently, indoctrination discourages independent thinking. The former expands one's intellectual horizons and encourages creativity, innovation, and critical thinking. The latter limits one's intellectual horizons and dissuades these things. Education broadens one's views while indoctrination restrains them. Education encourages debate, informed disagreement, openness to new ideas, and exposure to a wide range of opinions, worldviews, and perspectives. Indoctrination suppresses all of these things and, instead, demands intellectual submission, obedience, and conformity.

Considering these differences, should anyone be surprised socialism has failed wherever it has been tried? Any nation that seeks to curb the thinking, creativity, and intellectual development of its citizens will not thrive in a globally competitive world. If its government controls and manipulates its citizens rather than serving and protecting them, that nation will to eventually fail. As one of our esteemed veterans noted, any nation that has to force its governing philosophy on its citizens has adopted the wrong philosophy.

WHO IS RESPONSIBLE FOR THE EDUCATION OF AMERICA'S CHILDREN?

One of the biggest frauds ever perpetrated on the American public is the claim by Leftist ideologues that the government, not parents, is responsible for the education of children. This is like saying the neighborhood mechanic is responsible for the maintenance of your car. The mechanic may be the person you pay to perform maintenance on your car, but you are responsible for taking the car in for work and ensuring the car is properly maintained. In his Gettysburg Address, Abraham Lincoln spoke of America as a nation "of the people, by the people, and for the people."[5] With apologies to

President Lincoln, socialist ideologues are intent on transforming America into a nation of the government, by the government, and for the government.

A VETERAN SPEAKS UP

Socialist ideologues are determined to marginalize parents when it comes to the education of America's children. Here is what one veteran had to say on this subject:

At one time parents took responsibility for the education of their children, but in today's modern family too many parents abdicate their responsibility and allow the state, social media, the Internet, culture, and the entertainment industry to indoctrinate their children.

—Sean Aland, United States Air Force, 1982–2003

Lieutenant Colonel Aland was a copilot and weapons systems officer (WSO) in the F4-E and before retiring, also had flights in the F-16, F-18, and AC-130 aircraft. In the immediate aftermath of the 9/11 attacks on the World Trade Center Twin Towers and the Pentagon, Aland served as director of manpower and personnel (J-1) for the Continental U.S. NORAD region.

A key strategy in any socialist's takeover plan is to make government, not parents, responsible for the education of children. When government controls the people and socialists control the government, then socialists control the people. This is and always has been the ultimate goal of socialist ideologues. People are easier to manipulate if you gain control of their minds at an early age, but there is a problem with this for Leftists who worship government: thinking parents might object. This is why advocates of socialism want parents to cede their responsibility for the education of their children to the government. Responsible parents are more likely to "interfere" with the Left's efforts to indoctrinate children in their failed philosophy.

Leftist faculty members and administrators don't welcome input from parents because thinking mothers and fathers might ask inopportune questions. To fend off parents who might not approve of what they are doing, the Left claims that matters of curriculum, content, and methodology should be left to education professionals. This is like saying you should leave decisions concerning your children's clothing to the retail professionals at Walmart and you should have no say in the matter. What nonsense. Your children belong to you, not the government, just as they don't belong to Walmart. Further, just as you pay for the clothing purchased at Walmart, you pay for public education. Therefore, the public schools are supposed to be servants of parents, not of the government.

THE SOCIALIST AGENDA IN PUBLIC EDUCATION

We have already pulled the curtain back on the socialist agenda in public education. When it comes to students, Leftist ideologues want to gain control of their minds while they are children so it will be easier to manipulate them as adults. Here are several specific tactics they are using in our public schools and colleges to accomplish this goal:

- emphasizing inclusion instead of excellence and entitlement instead of merit
- demanding conformance rather than free thought
- espousing tolerance while being intolerant of any views other than those of the Left
- distorting America's history
- dumbing down the curriculum so schools graduate compliant sheep who are easy to manipulate rather than informed thinkers who might challenge Leftist orthodoxy

Let's examine these tactics one by one.

Emphasizing inclusion instead of excellence and entitlement instead of merit

Life is by its very nature an exclusive enterprise. If this were not the case, we would all be wealthy and successful. Some people are wealthy and successful while others are not. Then there are varying degrees of wealth and success. This is because people typically succeed on the basis of merit, not entitlement. In any endeavor, some people do better than others: many succeed; others fail. Since a major part of the purpose of education is to prepare people for successful, productive lives, it stands to reason education should mirror life to the extent possible. In other words, like life, education should reward excellence rather than mediocrity and operate on the principle of merit, not of entitlement.

In the past, education came closer to mirroring life in that it rewarded excellence. In our day, students actually failed if they did not perform at the required level. Students in times past had to earn their distinctions; there were no entitlements. This is why schools once maintained honor rolls and colleges had dean's lists. Some students made the team, while others didn't. Some graduated cum laude; others didn't.

When education mirrored life—meaning failure was a possibility—students had incentives to study hard, attend their classes, participate to the fullest, and do their best. But all of this is changing. Wherever Leftists control public education, the goal is no longer excellence but inclusion. When inclusion is the goal, everybody is entitled to make the team or get a trophy; there is no need to earn these distinctions. The world outside the classroom operates on the basis of merit, but Leftist classrooms operate on the basis of inclusion.

If inclusion meant leveling the playing field and giving everybody an equal chance, it would be a laudable concept. But as practiced by the radical Left, inclusion quickly becomes exclusion, and it is the top performers and high achievers who are excluded or at least discouraged by this confused practice. One of the veterans we surveyed was thankful that in his day the schools he had attended had emphasized excellence rather than inclusiveness.

This veteran went on to describe how hard he had worked to improve his fitness and pass-receiving skills to earn a place on his high school's football team. Because of his hard work and continual improvement, he not only made the team but was part of the starting lineup. Had he been able to make the team on the basis of inclusion instead of hard work, he wouldn't have bothered to invest so much effort and would have been a mediocre player at best.

The experience of succeeding through hard work taught this veteran a valuable lesson that carried over into all aspects of his life. From that point on, he made the pursuit of excellence a lifelong endeavor in everything he did, an approach that paid off in his Navy career as well as in his subsequent private-sector career after retiring from the military. This veteran was certain had his high school emphasized inclusion over excellence, he would never have learned the value of striving for excellence and, in turn, would not have enjoyed the same level of success in life.

The Left uses the term "inclusion" because it appeals to those who don't take the time to find out what it really means. Inclusion, as defined by the Left, doesn't mean everybody gets a chance. Rather, it means everybody makes the team, everybody passes, nobody fails, everybody gets a trophy, and above all, unmotivated and low-performing students don't get their feelings hurt. The obvious problem with this approach is that after graduation, these *included* students enter a world where people do fail and do get their feelings hurt.

To ensure that low performers are not made to feel bad as the result of refusing to apply themselves more energetically, exclusive practices such as maintaining honor rolls and dean's lists are done away with, exclusive clubs with merit-based membership requirements are discontinued, and high-performing students are no longer lauded or allowed to stand out from the crowd. Remember, in a socialist setting everything is about the group, not the individual. Standing out from the crowd is not tolerated. As practiced by Leftist ideologues, inclusiveness amounts to promoting mediocrity over excellence, a formula for disaster in the globally competitive world students will enter after leaving school.

On the subject of inclusiveness, Bret Stephens wrote in the *New York Times*: "It's a revolt of the mediocre many against the excellent few. And it is being undertaken for the sake of a radical egalitarianism in which all are included, all are equal, all are special."[6] The list of problems with inclusiveness is a long one. For example, while it is true all people are equal in the eyes of God, it's also true His eyes are the only place they are equal. People are not equal in talent, intelligence, physical size, motivation, knowledge, perseverance, or any other asset.

Striving to provide equal opportunity is a laudable endeavor, but demanding equal results is blatant foolishness. Including everyone, regardless of effort, relative contribution, and other meritorious factors, deludes students into believing the world they will enter after school will be equally inclusive. It won't, not even in a socialist setting. Consequently, inclusiveness as practiced by the Left just sets young people up for discouragement, disillusionment, and, ultimately, failure.

Human beings are driven by incentives. Take away the incentives associated with excellence and people will stop striving for excellence. *Inclusion* is one of those terms with the comfortable appeal of a warm blanket. It sounds good to the uninformed ear, but the good feelings it evokes are an illusion. The real world rewards excellence, not inclusion. In a globally competitive world, inclusion as practiced by the Left can create a culture of entitlement. This kind of culture can, in turn, be the death knell for a country. As one of our veteran friends commented, any country emphasizing inclusion to the detriment of excellence has embarked on a journey that will end in disaster.

Conformance instead of free thought

Socialism requires conformance to a government-prescribed worldview, a false narrative certain to be questioned by thinking people. To socialists, free thought and free speech are dangerous enterprises that, if allowed, might upset their applecart. But to Americans, freedom of speech and freedom of thought are fundamental rights so ingrained in our thinking that it is easy to take them for granted. Don't make this mistake. If socialist ideologues have their way, freedom of speech and thought will wind up on the dust heap of American history.

The process of suppressing free speech and thought in America has already begun. This is why we see conservative and Christian speakers shouted down on college campuses or not invited to speak in the first place. Ironically, ideologues who proudly carry the banner of inclusion openly and vigorously exclude conservatives and Christians. Hence, the kind of inclusion practiced by the Left is not just a distortion; it's an outright lie. A better description of what they advocate is *selective inclusion.*

Thoroughly indoctrinated college students cannot handle hearing opinions that differ from the ones they have been deluded into believing. Worse yet, they have heard only one opinion for so long they are ill-equipped to deal with differing opinions and are offended when they are offered. This is why they attack conservative and Christian speakers rather than doing what educated, intelligent people are supposed to do: listen to the differing opinions, show the speakers due respect, consider with an open mind what they have to say, and then make up their own minds. It is also why they are unable to disagree without being disagreeable. The ability to disagree without becoming offensive is one of the hallmarks of an educated, intelligent person and, therefore, should be something a college student can do. But for college students who are indoctrinated rather than educated, disagreeing without being rude is not possible.

Socialist ideologues use several tactics to suppress free speech and free thought, including political correctness and censorship. The latter is occurring more and more frequently on social media platforms owned and staffed by Leftist ideologues. But their most effective tactic is teaching students in public schools and colleges what to think rather than how to think. Students who don't know how to think are more easily manipulated and less likely to ask embarrassing questions. Socialists need the masses to be compliant sheep, not independent thinkers and they are getting their wish.

To succeed in today's world, students need to develop curiosity, creativity, critical thinking, analytical thinking, and problem-solving skills. In other words, they need to know how to think. To learn how to think, students must be encouraged to establish a set of principles to live by; question the ideas, opinions, and perspectives of others; make their own choices within the framework of their beliefs based on logic, reason, and facts; and be open to considering opposing views. But students who do these things represent the socialist's worse nightmare.

To a thinking person, the inherent failings of socialism are easy to identify. They are simply too obvious to hide from someone who is rational and inquisitive. Therefore, socialist ideologues long ago determined that teaching students what to think rather than how to think was the best strategy for their cause. Moreover, to encourage a herd mentality, it is also necessary to instill in them a willingness to conform to the socialist worldview without questioning it. This is why socialists need students to be obedient conformists, not independent thinkers.

Socialism doesn't fare well under careful scrutiny. Nor does it stand up well to probing questions. This is why socialist ideologues insist that society simply "go along to get along." To ensure this, they must begin the indoctrination process when students are young and malleable. This explains their focus on taking over public education at all levels. Young people whose teachers and peers pressure them to blindly accept what they are taught become the kind of adults who allow others to do their thinking for them. Then they will listen to the evening news—on a blatantly biased network—and accept what is said without questioning it. They will also believe anything they read on social media.

Intolerance masquerading as tolerance

Socialist ideologues use the term *tolerance* the way gunslingers in the Old West used their pistols. Tolerance is a weapon used by the Left to discourage opposition, quell dissent, quash differing opinions, and avoid inopportune questions. The fastest way to get yourself labeled an intolerant bigot these days is to disagree with a Leftist on anything. The moment you disagree with the Left's narrative, you become a target, an enemy who must be destroyed.

Attacking, vilifying, and withdrawing support from a dissenter has led to what is now called the "cancel culture." If the individual who disagrees with a Leftist owns a business, boycott that business. If the person is well-known, vilify him or her on social media. If the individual is employed, get him fired. The cancel culture is a cult of personal destruction and the epitome of intolerance, yet it is a methodology established and used by Leftists who claim to be "tolerant." If you believe the myth of tolerance espoused by the Left, try this test: go on social media and state your opposition to abortion, the Green New Deal, global warming, or any other plank in the Left's political platform and see what happens.

Tolerance is supposed to be a willingness to open-mindedly abide differences in others, including differences in race, sex, worldview, religion, politics, and opinions. Three marks of the truly tolerant are their ability to (1) interact positively with people they consider different, (2) disagree with people who hold different views without being disagreeable, and (3) acknowledge others' right to hold differing views. Intolerant people, on the other hand, are typically narrow-minded, prejudiced, and bigoted because they reject others on the basis of race, sex, worldview, religion, politics, ethics or opinions. This is where socialist ideologues get tripped up.

Although they portray themselves as the embodiment of tolerance, Leftists are often the most intolerant people you will ever meet when it comes to differences in worldviews, religion, politics, and opinions. Not only are Leftists unwilling to abide differences in these areas; they quickly become quarrelsome disagreeable when they disagree. In fact, they often become downright hostile toward those who disagree with them. Say something a socialist ideologue disagrees with and your words will be labeled "hate speech." Question the actions of a minority politician and you will be labeled a racist. Oppose abortion and you will be attacked as a misogynist and woman hater. Profess Christianity and you will be labeled narrow-minded, bigoted, and hateful.

Do any of these things on social media and your messages will be censored. The tech giants who control social media are similar to the mainstream media: they have become purveyors of the false narrative of the Left. Because they can control what is and isn't published on social media, they have the power to eliminate any messages challenging the Left's agenda or question its narrative. This is precisely what they are doing. Posts from conservatives and Christians are regularly taken down by the social-media giants while those supportive of the Left are given the front-and-center treatment.

The problem became so acute in the run-up to the presidential election of 2020 that Congress held hearings on the matter in which tech company executives were questioned about their biased practices. These executives almost uniformly hid behind the protections Congress granted them in Section 230 of the Communications Decency Act (Title V of the Telecommunications Act), which states, "No provider or user of an interactive computer service shall be treated as the publisher or speaker of any information provided by another information content provider." Section 230 was originally intended to protect social-media giants from being sued over what is posted on their platforms but it is now being used to justify censorship.

Section 230 sounded like a good idea when it was passed, but, as is often the case, Congress failed to consider the unintended consequences of its actions. One of those unintended consequences is Section 230 can be twisted to empower the tech giants who control social media to selectively censor the material uploaded on their platforms. A law passed to promote free speech and protect social-media companies from lawsuits for giving people a free-speech platform has been turned on its head and is now being used to censor free speech. As a result, in October 2020 there arose an outcry to repeal Section 230. On September 23, 2020, the U.S. Justice Department sent draft legislation to Congress to reform Section 230.

Perhaps the most telling demonstration of Leftist intolerance can be found on college campuses, where conservatives have become an endangered species. Writing for the *New York Times*, Nicholas Kristof reported, "Four studies found that the proportion of professors in the humanities who are Republicans ranges between 6 and 11 percent, and in the social sciences between 7 and 9 percent. Conservatives can be spotted in the sciences and economics, but they are virtually an endangered species in fields like anthropology, sociology, history, and literature. One study found only 2 percent of English professors are Republicans."[7] With their faculties so lopsidedly Leftist, how can colleges and universities claim they expose students to a variety of opinions and ideas? The fact is, they can't, don't, and do not intend to.

While conservative professors are "an endangered species" on college faculties, conservative and Christian speakers are practically extinct. The few Christians or conservatives who are invited to speak at higher education institutions accept at their own risk. Not only are Christian and conservative scholars, authors, and newsmakers who challenge Leftist orthodoxy not welcomed when they speak at these institutions; they are often shouted down, harassed, and even physically assaulted.

To college students indoctrinated by the Left, free speech is a good thing only if they agree with what is said. They are offended by differing opinions, and the worse crime you can commit on a college campus these days is offending the fragile sensibilities of indoctrinated snowflakes masquerading as college students. The irony of blatant suppression of this sort happening at institutions that are supposed to be bastions of free speech is apparently lost on the Leftist zealots who dominate college and university faculties, administrations, and student bodies. So much for tolerance.

Distorting America's history

Even a cursory examination of the historical record will show America is both good and great, and no other country has been more compassionate or giving toward its neighbors in the community of nations. Nor has any other nation provided more freedom, self-determination, or prosperity for its citizens. This being the case, why do we need socialism? After all, it looks as if America has done just fine without it. Thinking Americans might reasonably tell socialist ideologues, "If it's not broken, don't fix it." That America is doing splendidly without socialism makes it difficult for Leftist ideologues to justify the changes they say America needs to make.

Their difficulty in finding an acceptable justification for their cause leaves socialist ideologues just one option: rewrite and distort the historical record in ways that portray America as the opposite of good and great. If people can be convinced the United States is neither good nor great, it becomes easier to make a case for adopting socialism. Consequently, distorting the historical record has become not just a strategy but a necessity for advocates of socialism, a strategy they are applying with vigor.

This nefarious strategy consists of two tactics. The first involves making false claims about America's history and then repeating the lies over and over until people accept them as fact. This was a favorite tactic of Adolf Hitler's propaganda minister, Joseph Goebbels, who is often credited with developing it,[8] although the same tactic is sometimes attributed to Vladimir Lenin, the father of Soviet Communism. It is sad, indeed, to see a shameful tactic favored by Nazis and Communists also used by Leftist politicians, the mainstream media, educators, and the entertainment industry in America.

The second tactic in the Left's grand strategy for portraying America as an evil nation involves omitting from the historical record any evidence of America's greatness or goodness. This is the easier and more effective of the two tactics. Information left out of books, lectures, essays, and articles is never learned in the first place, so it doesn't have to be rewritten or distorted. The Left's favorite and most blatant historical distortions and omissions have to do with America's Christian heritage, which we examined in chapter 5.

As we reiterate throughout this book, the god of socialism is government. Therefore, socialism's advocates can abide no god except government. For this reason, socialist ideologues go to great lengths to remove from the historical record any trace of Christianity's influence on America. Two of their favorite claims are that the U.S. Constitution is a "Godless document" and that the Founders intended there to be a "wall of separation" between church and state. The first claim is simply made-up and cannot be substantiated by the facts. The second is a distortion that turns the historical record on its head, making it mean the opposite of what the Founders intended.

A veteran we surveyed for this book wrote of how her grandson, a history major, was taught in a college class that the Constitution is a Godless document. This veteran, a history major herself, knew better and made sure that before her grandson went to college that he was well-versed in America's Christian heritage as well as the biblical principles the majority of our nation's founders embraced. When her grandson challenged the professor's claim, he was ridiculed in front of his fellow students.

Notice the professor didn't offer any evidence to support his claim. Instead, he simply belittled the student who had challenged it. This ad hominem approach is standard practice among Leftist educators bent on indoctrinating their students. Leftists often use ad hominem attacks in the classroom, during debates, and in the public square as a smoke screen to disguise the weakness of their positions. Unable to substantiate their claims with data or reason, they simply attack anyone who questions them.

Undeterred, our veteran's grandson told the professor his unfounded claim revealed an appalling ignorance of both the Constitution and the Bible. When several students chuckled at this comment, the ill-equipped professor became enraged and demanded the student leave the room. Not surprisingly, the young man wound up dropping the class and taking it from another instructor, but what of the biased professor's claim? Is the U.S. Constitution really a Godless document? This is an easy enough lie to tell a class full of students who have never read the Constitution or the Bible and who have been conditioned to simply accept their professors' opinions without validation.

The first thing you need to know is why the professor chose the Constitution as the subject for his distortion rather than the Declaration of Independence. Simple: the Declaration makes too many direct references to God to be susceptible to such a claim. Consequently, those who endeavor to rewrite the historical record concerning America's Christian heritage employ the tactic of omission: they simply omit any reference to the Declaration as a founding document. Thus, the Declaration's obvious references to God—there are five of them—never come up for discussion.

The Constitution was written primarily by men who were well versed concerning the teachings of Scripture. They used the Bible as one of their primary sources of reference when writing the Constitution—and most other documents they wrote, for that matter. A study by political scientists of the writings of the Founders revealed that by far the Bible was their most frequently referenced source.⁹ The reason references to God are less obvious in the Constitution than in the Declaration is explained by the differing natures and purposes of the two documents.

The Declaration of Independence is a philosophical document setting forth the rights of human beings and where those rights come from. This is why it contains overt references to God. The majority of America's founders believed God—not government—to be the source of all human rights. The Constitution, on the other hand, is a technical document—a user's manual on how Americans are to implement the concept of self-government and protect the God-given rights of citizens. This is why scriptural references are less overt in the Constitution.

Nonetheless, students of the Bible will recognize several obvious references to Scripture in the Constitution. They are more subtle than those in the Declaration, but they are easy to recognize if one knows the Bible, as the Founders did. Here are just a few examples of how the Bible influenced the Constitution and how biblical principles are incorporated into the document:¹⁰

- The requirement in Article II, Section 1 that the president be a natural-born citizen is based on Deuteronomy 17:15. Bible students will recall that this verse prohibits a foreigner from serving as a ruler over the people
- The requirement for witnesses in trials found in Article III, Section 3 is based on Deuteronomy 17:6, a verse that requires the testimony of two or three witnesses in order for someone to be put to death for a crime
- The Republican form of government set forth in Article IV, Section 4 is based on Exodus 18:21, which establishes the concept of representative government and of choosing leaders to oversee the various sizes of citizen groups.

With just this surface-level treatment of the subject, it should be obvious that to claim the U.S. Constitution is a Godless document is evidence of either ignorance or dishonesty. But this invalid claim is just one example of how the Left alters the historical record through commission and omission. It would require a book the size of an encyclopedia to capture all of the historical distortions and omissions perpetrated by the Left to justify socialism.

Perhaps the favorite historical distortion of Leftist ideologues is the claim that the Founders intended there to be a wall of separation between church and state. This supposed wall, according to Leftist revisionists, was meant to ensure the church would have no influence on government, or said another way, to protect the government from religion. As you will see, this is exactly the opposite of what the Founders intended. They were concerned in the First Amendment with protecting the church from government, not government from the church.

The first and subsequent amendments that make up the Bill of Rights were intended to protect American citizens from their own government because the Founders had been suppressed, manipulated, controlled, and coerced by the British government. In fact, the Founders hoped and prayed the Bible would influence all who served in government just as it influenced them in developing the Declaration of Independence and the Constitution. This is a far cry from expecting there to be a wall of separation protecting government from religion.

The Founder's concerns about church and state harked back to the pre-independence days, when the King of England designated the Church of England as the official denomination for Christians. This designation allowed the church to collect taxes from the citizens of the American colonies, even citizens of other denominations. It also discouraged participation in other Christian denominations. This interference of government in religion is why the Founders developed the religion clause of the First Amendment. They were determined to ensure that the American government could not establish an official religion so Americans would be free to practice the religion of their choice, or even no religion.

Before getting into how the Left came up with their distorted allegation concerning church and state, hear what Supreme Court justice John Marshall had to say about Christianity's intended influence in our nation: "One great object of the colonial charters was avowedly the propagation of the Christian faith."[11]

Many years later, President Harry Truman, while lighting the national Christmas tree on the White House lawn, stated, "In this great country of ours has been demonstrated the fundamental unity of Christianity and democracy."[12]

Perhaps the best-known observer of the American character was the French philosopher, Alexis de Tocqueville. In his landmark book, *Democracy in America,* he wrote, "There is no country in the whole world in which the Christian religion retains a greater influence over the souls of men than in America."[13]

These are just a few representative observations illustrating that the intent of those who drafted the religion clause of the First Amendment was to protect the church from government, not vice versa. The Founders were not concerned that Christianity might influence government; they were concerned it wouldn't. In fact, they intended that Christianity would positively influence those who govern our country. To the Founders, a government that operated according to biblical principles was the best form of government.

One more thing you should know is how the so-called wall of separation was inaccurately foisted on the American public. Read through the entire Constitution and all of the amendments. You will not find the words "wall of separation" or "separation of church and state" anywhere in the document. Read through the records of the Founders. Again, you will find no reference to separating church and state. So, where did this misinterpreted concept originate?

The origin of the "wall of separation" can be found in a letter written by President Thomas Jefferson to the Danbury Baptist Association in response to a letter they had sent him. These Baptists had written to Jefferson to express their concern that the government might try to regulate the religious activities of the church, as had been done for centuries in Europe. Worried that the government might establish a state religion, as the king of England had done, thereby outlawing the Baptist denomination, they hoped to pin the president down on this subject.

Jefferson obliged them. He wrote back to assure the Danbury Baptists they need not worry; the First Amendment protected them from just the kind of governmental overreach and interference they feared. His exact words—and the origin of the "wall of separation" distortion—were: "Believing with you that religion is a matter which lies solely between Man & his God, . . . I contemplate with sovereign reverence that act of the whole American people [the First Amendment] which declared that their legislature should 'make no law respecting an establishment of religion or prohibiting the free exercise thereof,' thus building a wall of separation between Church & State."[14]

The wall Jefferson referenced was intended to protect the church from the government, not the reverse. He meant to relieve the Danbury Baptists of their anxiety about government regulation of the religious activities of the church, not to protect the government from the influence of religion. What is ironic about Jefferson's letter being used to justify fencing in religion is that in early court cases such as *Reynolds v. United States* (1878), the court cited the same letter to reiterate the Founders' intent to protect the church from government coercion and interference.

Later court rulings clarified how the government had the authority to intercede on behalf of common decency should churches undertake such practices as human sacrifice, incest, polygamy, or child abuse. However, the decisions rendered in these cases strictly limited government "intrusion" into the church's activity to these few specified prohibitions.[15] For more than sixty years, the court's decisions upheld the original intent of the Founders and of Jefferson's letter concerning the meaning of the First Amendment.

In 1947 everything changed.

An activist court, engaging in what has come to be known as legislating from the bench, ignored the historical record and the court's own precedents to turn the interpretation of the First Amendment upside down. In *Everson v. Board of Education*, the Supreme Court ruled for the first time that the First Amendment limited religious expression rather than government intrusion. To justify their ruling, the Court ignored the historical record and quoted out of context eight words from Jefferson's letter to the Danbury Baptists: "a wall of separation between church and state."[16] The justices were clearly motivated by politics and their personal worldviews.

The ruling in *Everson* was blatant and intentional revisionism on the part of the highest court in the land. The court knowingly produced a ruling at odds with both precedent and the historical record to advance a political agenda held by the majority of the justices serving at that time. Since 1947, piling distortion upon distortion, the Left has used the ruling from *Everson v. Board of Education* as their foundation for chipping away at religious freedom in America.

It is ironic that the court would choose to justify its glaring bias on the basis of just eight words taken out of context from a letter written by Thomas Jefferson. After all, Jefferson himself played no role in drafting the First Amendment. He was representing the United States in France when the amendment was written. But the justices in *Everson* had no choice if they were going to advance their Leftist agenda through historical revisionism. Research into the intent of the men who did write the First Amendment would have pulled the rug out from under the court's abominable scheme and purposely faulty legal reasoning.

Dumbing down the curriculum

The headline from a report by the Pew Research Center practically leaps off the page: "U.S. students' academic achievement still lags that of their peers in many countries."[17] Unfortunately, poor academic achievement is not a new problem for American students. They have lagged behind their global counterparts for decades. Since the 1960s, Left-leaning ideologues have continually dumbed down the K–12 curriculum in America's public schools. Why? As we stated earlier in the chapter, "the philosophy of the schoolroom in one generation will be the philosophy of government in the next."[18]

By shifting the focus of schooling from education to indoctrination, excellence to inclusion, and thinking to compliance, socialist advocates have produced several generations of students who are not only disinclined to question Leftist orthodoxy but wouldn't know how to go about it if they wanted to. At the same time, they have diminished America's ability to compete in a global marketplace driven by technological innovation and requiring a high level of math and science ability. Sadly, the performance of American students on international assessments is most deficient in these two areas.

As a result of dumbing down education in America, employers complain that high school and even some college graduates cannot read, write, speak, listen or compute at an acceptable level; for community colleges, remedial courses in English and mathematics are big business; and high-tech firms struggle to fill key positions in such critical fields as engineering, math, science, and technology. Writing for the Edvocate website, Matthew Lynch claimed the problem of dumbing down is so critical as to pose a national security risk for our country.[19]

The traditional focus of public schools on achievement in English, math, science, history, geography, and other core academic disciplines has been supplanted by a focus on inclusion, feelings, self-esteem, and fitting in, all under the umbrella of social-emotional learning (SEL). As one of the veterans we interviewed stated, we are producing an entire generation of young people who cannot read, write, or compute at an acceptable level but who are taught to feel good about themselves regardless of their deficiencies. It is now acceptable for students to be deficient in the basic academic disciplines as long as they feel good about themselves and are included.

Perhaps the best way to illustrate just how dumbed down the K–12 curriculum has become is to look back at what was expected of schoolchildren in times past. Writing for the *Washington Post*, Valerie Strauss reproduced a test given in 1895 to eighth graders in Kansas. Here are just a few of the questions from that test:[20]

GRAMMAR

- Name the Parts of Speech and define those that have no modifications
- What are the Principal Parts of a verb? Give Principal Parts of do, lie, lay, and run
- What is Punctuation? Give rules for principal marks of Punctuation
- Write a composition of about 150 words and show therein that you understand the practical use of the rules of grammar.

ARITHMETIC

- Name and define the Fundamental Rules of Arithmetic
- A wagon box is 2 ft. deep, 10 ft. long, and 3 ft. wide. How many bushels of wheat will it hold?
- If a load of wheat weighs 3,942 lbs., what is it worth at 50 cts. Per bu., deducting 1,050 lbs for tare?
- Find the interest of $512.60 for eight months and 18 days at 7 per cent.

U.S. HISTORY

- Give the epochs into which U.S. History is divided
- Relate the causes and results of the Revolutionary War
- Describe three of the most prominent battles of the Rebellion
- Who were the following: Morse, Whitney, Fulton, Bell, Lincoln, Penn, and Howe?

ORTHOGRAPHY

- What is meant by the following: Alphabet, phonetic orthography, etymology, syllabication?
- What are the following, and give examples of each: Trigraph, subvocals, diphthong, cognate letters, linguals?
- Mark diacritically and divide into syllables the following, and name the sign that indicates the sound: Card, ball, mercy, sir, odd, cell, rise, blood, fare, last
- Write 10 words frequently mispronounced and indicate pronunciation by use of diacritical marks and by syllabication.

GEOGRAPHY

- Name and describe the following: Monrovia, Odessa, Denver, Manitoba, Hecla, Yukon, St. Helena, Juan Fernandez, Aspinwall, and Orinoco
- Name and locate the principal trade centers of the U.S.
- Name all the republics of Europe and give [the] capital of each
- Why is the Atlantic Coast colder than the Pacific in the same latitude?

PHYSIOLOGY

- Where are the saliva, gastric juice, and bile secreted? What is the use of each in digestion?
- What is the function of the liver? Of the kidneys?
- How would you stop the flow of blood from an artery in the case of laceration?
- Give some general directions that you think would be beneficial to preserve the human body in a state of health.

Few of today's college graduates could pass this test, yet this is the type of material eighth graders were expected to know in 1895. The same kind of dumbing down has occurred at the college level. In the early days of our country, it was not uncommon for young people to start college at age thirteen. However, regardless their age, students back then had to demonstrate mastery of Latin and Greek to win admission to college. Today you can forget about Latin and Greek. A substantial number of college students born and raised in America have not even mastered the English language. Many freshmen must be remediated in the basics of English before they can enroll in college-level classes.

One of the veterans surveyed for this book wrote about an incident that occurred at a book signing. He was standing in line, waiting for the author to sign his book. There was a woman ahead of him in line who seemed agitated. When her turn came, the woman loudly berated the author, criticizing everything about the book. But her most ironic claim was that she had a master's degree but could not read more than two pages in the book without consulting a dictionary or thesaurus. She also claimed the book was too long (it was two hundred pages).

As it turned out, the book was written at the tenth-grade level. This means an individual with a master's degree from an American university could not read at the tenth-grade level. Further, she suffered from what we call the *Twitter syndrome*: the inability to read anything longer than 140 characters. This woman was obviously a victim of the dumbing down of the curriculum at all levels of education. Unfortunately, she is not an exception.

What is even more concerning than the decline of public education into a state of mediocrity is that the decline has been intentionally orchestrated by the Left. In her book, *The Deliberate Dumbing Down of America*, Charlotte Thomson Iserbyt describes the "deliberate, malicious intent to achieve behavioral changes in students/ parents/society which have nothing to do with commonly understood educational objectives."[21] She tells of returning to the United States after living abroad for eighteen years, some of those years in socialist countries. From her experience abroad, Iserbyt knew America's transformation from a sovereign constitutional republic into a socialist democracy would occur not as a result of armed combat but through a war of ideas, a war that would take place in our public schools.[22]

When she returned to the United States, that war was well underway. Here is how she described the public education system she found: "I was shocked to find public education had become a warm, fuzzy, soft, mushy, touchy-feely experience, with its purpose being socialization, not learning."[23] Academic achievement and educational excellence had been supplanted by "brainwashing" and "values clarification."[24] Instead of focusing on English, math, science, history, geography, and other traditional academic disciplines, students were being instructed in "health education, sex education, drug and alcohol education, . . ."[25] Worse, parents like Iserbyt, who objected to the dumbing down, were labeled "resisters," and education officials took great pains to marginalize them and deflect their criticism.[26]

In a speech given on September 11, 1973, Aleksandr Solzhenitsyn said, "Coexistence on this tightly knit earth should be viewed as an existence not only without wars . . . but also without [the government] telling us how to live, what to say, what to think, what to know, and what not to know."[27] Socialist ideologues disagree, and they are working hard to create a society in which the government does tell citizens "how to live, what to say, what to think, what to know, and what not to know."[28] Their efforts are focused in large measure on America's public schools and colleges.

CHAPTER 8

SOCIALISTS DEMAND TOLERANCE BUT ARE THEMSELVES INTOLERANT

*As we lead, we do so with a view toward soliciting input,
thought, and opinions from others. It is the fool who thinks
his ideas are the only ones worth considering, or worse, the
only correct ones. There are few things more meaningful
than recognizing and valuing the contributions others make
to our world. Leading through such a contributory posture
works to the benefit of all involved."*

—Robb Schiefer, United States Air Force, 1978–1982

Schiefer served in the Air Force as a munitions specialist, loading ordnance
on F-4, F-106, and F-101 aircraft. After leaving the Air Force, he became
a successful businessman, entrepreneur, restaurant owner/operator, leadership trainer, and professional career coach.

In the above quotation, Robb Schiefer comments on the importance of being open to differing points of view and opinions. In a
pluralistic society, this kind of openness is essential. It's why we have
the First Amendment. Political debate and dissent have long been
two of America's favorite pastimes. In the United States, we are

accustomed to people speaking out, often loudly and stridently. Although the "noise" of public debate can be off-putting at times, silence in the public square would be much worse.

Criticizing government officials at all levels is practically a sport in America, a sport every American plays. We have a long and hallowed tradition of not just tolerating but encouraging free speech, dissent, and debate in the political arena, the public square, and the classroom, but things are changing—and not for the better. Our tradition of free speech is being undermined by two of the Left's more contemptible but effective tools: political correctness and the cancel culture. As America continues to move farther to the Left, we become more and more like socialist countries, where dissenting speech can land you in hot water.

A noted example of how socialist governments treat dissenters is the case of Aleksandr Solzhenitsyn. Best known as the Nobel Prize–winning author of the book *The Gulag Archipelago*, in 1945 Solzhenitsyn was a loyal soldier who served long and well in the Soviet Union's Red Army. Just as the Red Army was poised to overrun Berlin in the last major European battle of World War II, Solzhenitsyn—a highly decorated officer—was arrested and sent to Moscow for trial, accused of anti-Soviet propaganda.

The outcome of his show trial was a foregone conclusion. Solzhenitsyn was sentenced to hard labor in a Siberian prison for eight years. What was the substance of his "anti-Soviet propaganda"? Solzhenitsyn had questioned Stalin's conduct of the war in letters to a friend. In other words, he did something virtually every American does from time to time: criticize the government. It is hard for Americans to imagine a head of state could be so paranoid and insecure as to be threatened by the criticism of one lone soldier, but socialist leaders have a long and ugly history of paranoia and insecurity. Heads of state who hold on to power only through coercion and manipulation are bound to be paranoid and insecure.

Americans find it difficult to believe someone would be sent to prison for doing what we do all the time: criticize national leaders. As one of the veterans in our survey claimed, almost every soldier, sailor, airman, and marine who ever served has questioned the conduct of his or her leaders at one time or another. It happened in General Washington's time, and it still happens today. Speaking out against government leaders is an American pastime protected by the First Amendment, a right exercised openly, freely, and frequently.

One can understand why Americans who have long been protected by the First Amendment find it difficult to imagine being punished for speaking their minds about the government. But in the America of today, we should beware complacency. Our country has already taken the first steps down a path leading to this kind of intolerance. Political dissent, freedom of speech, academic freedom, and honest debate are all under attack, and these attacks are all being perpetrated in the name of tolerance. For a preview of coming events in America, one need only look at what is happening on our college campuses or to conservative posts on social media sites. But before getting into these sad scenarios, a few words about the concept of *tolerance* are in order.

INTOLERANCE MASQUERADING AS TOLERANCE

For socialists, the term *tolerance* is practically sacred. Unfortunately, they have done with tolerance what they often do with sensitive subjects: engage in word warping by adopting an appealing name for an unappealing concept. The name chosen, of course, distorts the true meaning of the concept. One of the veterans we surveyed for this book questioned, "Why should I trust anything said by people who have to resort to deception to disguise what they really mean? Why should I trust people who call censorship 'tolerance'?"

Coerced conformance to Leftist ideology is what the Left now calls *tolerance*. Although rife with hypocrisy, this feat of semantic subterfuge was a devious move on the part of socialist ideologues. To be tolerant of others with whom we differ is a sign of intelligence and maturity. It is the opposite of being a bigot, a label few people want to wear, even those who deserve it. This is precisely why socialist ideologues chose the term "tolerance." With this background, let's look at what tolerance really means compared with what it means to socialist ideologues and their fellow travelers on the left.

Two definitions of tolerance

Tolerance does not mean you accept opposing views, only that you treat those who hold them with grace and respect. This is what the concept has long meant and still means in spite of the distortions of the Left. Tolerant people are able to disagree without being disagreeable. Doing so is a mark of intelligence. But socialist ideologues have turned the concept of tolerance on its head. Although they refuse to admit it, to socialist ideologues *tolerance* is a code word.

Today, socialist wordsmiths have cleverly co-opted the term *tolerance* and changed its meaning to *a willingness not only to put up with Leftist views, but to agree with and accept them.* In other words, to socialists, "tolerance" means adopting their perspective on any given issue. Anyone who refuses to accept the socialist view of the world—regardless how respectfully or open-mindedly this view is treated—is labeled an intolerant bigot. Speech that does not conform to Leftist orthodoxy is quickly labeled "hate speech."

The Left's perspective on tolerance is disturbing because the socialist worldview rejects conservative principles, capitalism, Christianity, and the values that made the United States exceptional in the community of nations. Consequently, socialist ideologues are quick to label conservatives, Christians, and anyone else who holds traditional American values as "intolerant bigots" and their words as "hate speech." Even Christ's words from the second greatest commandment, encouraging us to love our neighbors as ourselves, are viewed as hate speech by socialist ideologues.

Why? Because love requires us to tell our neighbors the truth—for instance, there is such a thing as sin, certain lifestyles are sinful, and sin carries a penalty. Just try telling your neighbor his or her lifestyle is sinful and see how quickly you are accused of "hate speech."

Professor Paul Kengor had this to say about how the Left views tolerance: "Liberals tolerate only what they want to tolerate. They tolerate things they agree with—which, of course, isn't tolerance. Tolerance is about accepting the often-difficult differences between you and someone you strongly disagree with, and respecting that person's right to an opposing point of view."[1] Once again, this is why we have a First Amendment. It is also why the First Amendment is under attack from the Left. The views espoused by socialist ideologues are too weak to stand up to opposing points of view. Therefore, those views must not be allowed to be raised.

Kengor goes on to say that Leftists are "relentless in denouncing, demonizing, boycotting, attacking, picketing, prosecuting, suing, fining, and even threatening to jail people who disagree with them on same-sex marriage."[2] He gives several examples of liberal intolerance toward people of faith: A family in New York was fined $13,000 for refusing to rent their barn to a gay couple for a same-sex wedding ceremony. A wedding photographer in New Mexico was sued because she refused to photograph a same-sex wedding on religious grounds. And a baker in Colorado and florists in several other states were harassed, picketed, and brought before state commissioners for declining to participate in same-sex weddings.[3]

These are just a few representative examples of the kinds of Leftist intolerance occurring all the time. According to Kengor, these types of travesties demonstrate the "phoniness" of the Left's claims of tolerance and reveal, instead, "selective tolerance."[4] Worse, only those on the extreme Left get to decide what should be tolerated and what shouldn't. The rest of us have no say in the matter.

LEFTIST INTOLERANCE ON COLLEGE CAMPUSES AND IN SOCIAL MEDIA

Nowhere is intolerance of those who reject Leftist orthodoxy more apparent than on college and university campuses. A Gallup study revealed a disturbing attitude toward free speech among today's college students.[5] Writing for the *Washington Post*, Jeffrey J. Selingo summarized this attitude in these words: "College students support free speech—unless it offends them."[6] This hardly qualifies as tolerance, especially since today's hypersensitive college students seem to be offended by anything and everything they disagree with.

What kind of speech offends college students who have been thoroughly indoctrinated by the Left? Specifics are difficult to pin down because the views of college students tend to be vaporous and transitory, but suffice it to say they are offended by anything they don't agree with at the moment, especially pro-Christianity and pro-conservative comments. One of our veterans remarked that the authors of the First Amendment must be rolling over in their graves. Speech that offends was precisely the kind of speech the First Amendment was written to protect. Speech that does not offend needs no protection. Further, it is only those who have no confidence in their own views who are afraid to listen to opposing views.

One of the most blatant ways the Left's intolerance of free speech reveals itself is in what happens on the rare occasion when a conservative is invited to speak at a college campus. Consider just one representative example. When conservative Ben Shapiro was asked to speak at the University of California, Berkeley, security measures to protect him from irate college students who might find his message offensive cost more than $600,000 and included police in riot gear and the installation of physical barriers.[7]

Attendance at Shapiro's lecture was voluntary; students were not required to attend. They could have just ignored it and gone on about their business. Instead, they turned into a rabid mob that had to be restrained by the police. Several students were arrested. In today's college environment, some indoctrinated students are so insecure in their views that they would rather go to jail than hear an opposing view.

The irony of students at UC Berkeley trying to suppress free speech might be lost on anyone too young to remember the sixties. During that era, UC Berkeley was the epicenter of the Free Speech Movement (FSM), in which college students spoke out, demonstrated, and rioted against the Vietnam War, anyone over the age of forty, and America in general. Students demanded that their voices and the voices of anyone opposed to the Vietnam War be heard. Nowhere were the demands for giving dissenters a fair hearing louder or more strident than at UC Berkeley .

In the 1960s, police had to don riot gear, use tear gas, and erect barriers to prevent irate college students from acting out their free-speech rights in destructive ways. It was not uncommon for college students to express their right of free speech by bombing, burning down, or taking over college buildings. Fast-forward to the present and, oh, how the tables have turned.

Today on college campuses police still have to don riot gear, use tear gas, and erect barriers, but not to protect campus buildings. Rather, they now have to protect speakers trying to exercise the same free-speech rights that students in the 1960s demanded. College students then demanded that free speech be protected. College students now demand that they be protected from free speech.

One of the rationales offered for the intolerant attitudes of today's college students toward free speech is they were raised during an era in which bullying was prevalent, and they equate speech that offends them to bullying.[8] What nonsense. This is not a rationale; it's an excuse, and a lame one at that. When did stating an opposing point of view on politics, religion, or culture become "bullying"? In times past, this was known as *discussion* or *debate*, both of which were encouraged on college campuses. Bullying, on the other hand, is the use of force or coercion to intimidate or abuse others. Voicing a dissenting opinion hardly amounts to intimidation or abuse.

Besides, if college students are so opposed to bullying, why do they so quickly become bullies when conservatives or Christians are invited to speak on their campuses? When campus police must don riot gear and erect barriers to protect speakers from being accosted and even attacked by hypersensitive students, those students are not just bullies, but thugs. Unfortunately, today's college students are insufficiently educated to grasp the irony of this situation.

Another example of Leftist intolerance on college campuses is the establishment of so-called free-speech zones. Calling these designated areas "free-speech zones" takes semantic subterfuge to a new level. In the first place, every square inch of a college campus should be a free-speech zone. Academic freedom, freedom of speech, and freedom of thought have long been cornerstone principles of higher education. Consequently, restricting free speech to a designated area on campus is an obvious ploy for limiting free speech. This, in fact, is what free-speech zones on college campuses do.

Institutions of higher education with free-speech zones typically implement processes to control access to them. For example, it is not uncommon for free-speech zones to be available for use only during specified times, on specified days, and by appointment only. It is also common for the specified times and days to be those when the fewest students are on campus. Another tactic used to limit free speech is requiring those who want to use a free-speech zone to complete a comprehensive formal application in which the potential user must provide specifics about content as well as personal information about the speaker, in some cases including his or her social security number. Demanding that speakers provide such information is an obvious ploy to discourage them. College students of today were raised on computers and smartphones. They know better than to give anyone their social security number.

One final limiting tactic is to locate free-speech zones in secluded, lightly trafficked corners of campuses to minimize students' exposure to views that don't comport with socialist ideology. Restricting free speech to locations where it won't be heard is a tactic unworthy of colleges and universities. Rather, it is the kind that socialist despots like to use.

The Foundation for Individual Rights conducted a survey of nearly 350 institutions of higher learning. The survey revealed that 75 percent of these institutions maintained practices and policies limiting free speech.[9] Such policies applied during the turbulent 1960s would have resulted in college buildings being burned down. Finally, when it became clear free-speech zones were being used by colleges and universities to suppress free speech rather than enable it, concerned groups began to file lawsuits.

One such suit, filed by the Foundation for Individual Rights in Education, was actually supported in a friend-of-the-court brief by the ACLU, an organization more commonly associated with Leftist causes.[10] The plaintiff in the lawsuit was a campus organization at Arkansas State University known as Peace & Love, a group of students dedicated to using random acts of kindness to promote harmony and understanding.[11] That the university would want to limit acts of kindness aimed at promoting harmony and understanding just shows how foolish weak-kneed Leftist administrators can be.

Not surprisingly, the majority of the lawsuits opposing free-speech zones were filed on behalf of Christians and conservatives.

Preventing these two groups from having a voice on campus seems to be one of the main reasons for establishing restricted-speech zones. ACLU attorneys stated in their friend-of-the-court brief "We oppose government attempts to impose excessive restrictions on speakers, regardless of their ideological viewpoint—in large part because we know that, if given such power, the government will inevitably use it to silence those who criticize them or push for societal change."[12]

What the ACLU feared is precisely what happens when socialists control the government. So-called free-speech zones give Americans an opportunity to peek behind the curtain and see how it would be to live under an authoritarian socialist regime that claims tolerance is one of its highest priorities. Because of lawsuits filed on behalf of Christian and conservative students, some colleges and universities have backed away from free-speech zones. But there are still plenty that haven't. Until tolerance includes not just the views of socialist ideologues and their fellow travelers on the Left, it is little more than intolerance masquerading as tolerance. Colleges and universities suppressing free speech are not worthy of their membership in the academy.

Another way the intolerance of the Left reveals itself is in censorship of conservative posts on social media. The tech giants who own the most prominent social media sites are blatantly anti-conservative in their political views, a fact borne out by what they post and refuse to post on their sites. For example, during the 2020 presidential election, certain social media sites took down or refused to post messages from Republican politicians, supporters of President Donald Trump, and the president himself. Bear in mind these same sites had, in the past, posted the angry diatribes of such terrorist mass murderers as Osama bin Laden.

Censorship on social media became so blatant and so common during the election season of 2020 that calls for regulating the industry, dismantling the big tech companies, and other even harsher remedies were discussed. It is entirely possible measures will have to be taken to protect against the obvious bias of the big tech companies that control social media. Bear in mind, though, that money drives politics, and the big tech companies are willing to spend a lot of it to protect their perceived right to censor conservative politicians while supporting Leftists. Consequently, a more effective solution than government regulation would be the establishment of alternative social media sites controlled by conservative owners. Eat far enough into their market, watch their stock value decline, and then let's see how wedded to socialist causes and politicians the social media giants are.

POLITICAL CORRECTNESS, FREE SPEECH, AND TOLERANCE

A socialist ideologue will tell you political correctness means choosing words carefully so as not to offend others or hurt their feelings. Don't believe it. Speaking carefully to avoid unnecessarily hurt feelings is known as "tact;" a concept that has nothing to do with politics. In reality, "political correctness" means *speech control.* Few more deviously destructive concepts have ever been foisted on the American public. Political correctness is one more tactic dreamed up by the Left to suppress free speech and free thought without appearing to do so.

In a recent protest march, one snowflake carried a sign that read, "We condemn free speech that hurts feelings." Heaven forbid people get their feelings hurt. The sign might as well have read, "We condemn all speech." Frankly, in today's hypersensitive, feel-good society, any speech is going to offend somebody. Second, the whole point of the First Amendment was to protect speech that might hurt feelings. Potentially offensive speech is precisely what the Founders were trying to protect.

A VETERAN SPEAKS UP

Calling statements with which they disagree "hate speech" and labeling those who make them racists, bigots, and misogynists is a favorite tactic of the Left. Here is what one veteran had to say about this malicious practice:

It is important to counteract the false information being put out by the Left. I think some of the statements they are making are unbelievable and I wonder how anyone can believe them. I worry about the world my two grandsons are going to inherit."

—Charles E. "Chuck" Merkel Jr., PhD, United States
Army, 1967–1987

Major Merkel (retired) is a professor of history and president of the West Point Society of Northwest Florida. Merkel is a master Army aviator with more than 3,000 hours of flying time, including hours in the Air Force T-28 jet trainer. His military decorations include the Legion of Merit, Bronze Star with one oak leaf cluster, Purple Heart, Meritorious Service Medal, Air Medal with eleven oak leaf clusters, Army Commendation Medal with four oak leaf clusters, and an Army Achievement Medal. Dr. Merkel is a member of the Florida Veterans' Hall of Fame (class of 2018).

When you advocate for a philosophy that cannot be defended on its own merits, one with a long and tragic history of failure, how do you handle questions, challenges, and expressions of doubt? If you are a socialist ideologue, you don't allow questions to be asked in the first place. How do you prevent people from raising questions or objections? We can answer this question in just two words: political correctness.

As we have stated, political correctness is not just another term for tact. Rather, it is an underhanded method used to suppress dissent, disagreement, rational objections, and embarrassing questions. So, what is politically incorrect speech? What constitutes politically correct speech is a moving target, but we can say for certain what constitutes politically incorrect speech. Any speech that challenges, disagrees with, or questions Leftist orthodoxy is deemed politically incorrect by the Left. If a socialist ideologue disagrees with or simply doesn't like what you say, you are politically incorrect, but not only that. You are also a bigot, hate-monger, and all-around bad person.

The idea behind political correctness is to influence what is considered acceptable in everyday discourse. Anything disapproved of by the Left becomes politically incorrect and, therefore, unacceptable. This allows the Left to use peer pressure and social convention to intimidate people who might hold an "unacceptable" view. It is like using the term "racist" to prevent people from challenging the views of a minority politician, or "misogynist" to ward off challenges to a female politician. The idea is to render people afraid to state their true opinions for fear of being painted with these kinds of pejorative labels.

Another tactic of those who use political correctness to intimidate is labeling dissenting views as "hate speech," as we discussed earlier. This is semantic subterfuge at its worst. The goal of those who wield the term "hate speech" like a sword is to ward off challenges by intimidating anyone who dares to differ with them. People are intimidated because they don't want to be viewed as hateful, biased, prejudiced, or racist. To avoid the label, they simply cave to the pressure and remain silent. Silencing the opposition is the goal of today's cancel culture.

Americans have historically subscribed to a statement attributed to Voltaire: "I wholly disapprove of what you say—and will defend to the death your right to say it."[13] Voltaire's statement is the essence of the First Amendment. Several of the veterans we surveyed for this book paraphrased this statement without knowing its origin, a fact that demonstrates how ingrained in the American psyche Voltaire's sentiment is. The First Amendment might have been based on Voltaire's statement. Both are powerful defenses of freedom of speech.

A VETERAN SPEAKS UP

Censorship of conservative messages by the tech giants who control social media is another way the Left suppresses free speech. Here is what one veteran had to say about this practice:

I was listening to a podcast when a well-known liberal being interviewed announced he planned to vote for Donald

Trump in 2020. The podcast went viral receiving more than two million views on social media. The social-media platform promptly deleted the podcast without explanation. This is one more example of how the Left silences the free speech of anyone who doesn't conform to their false narrative.

—George Fountas, United States Air Force, 1974–1983

Fountas spent most of his time in the Air Force serving in the Strategic Air Command (SAC). He completed his service as an NCO and immediately went to work in aircraft maintenance and refueling, a field in which he served for thirty years.

CHAPTER 9

SOCIALISM IS ALREADY MAKING INROADS IN AMERICA

It seems socialism's practice of taking things from one person and giving them to another is just too strong to resist for unthinking people. When the truth becomes clear about what is really happening and shortages and violence become the norm, it's too late to do anything but sit in a corner and whimper. It is at this point that duped citizens see the truth in the maxim that mice die in mouse traps because they do not understand why the cheese is free.

—Erik Stoer, PhD, United States Air Force, 1973–2003

Dr. Stoer is an Air Force veteran who served in uniform for thirty years, including his active-duty and reserve service. In addition, as a civilian, Dr. Stoer served the Air Force for thirty-four years as a civil servant managing armament development programs. He served an additional eleven years as a defense contractor in armament development. In addition to holding a PhD from Florida State University, Dr. Stoer is a graduate of the Defense Systems Management College.

Since its founding, the United States has been a bastion of freedom, liberty, enterprise, and entrepreneurship—the very antithesis of socialism. For nearly 250 years, our country has stood firm against the spread of socialist tyranny throughout the world. America's steadfastness, coupled with the inherent flaws of socialism, is why this failed concept is in retreat worldwide. How ironic, then, just when socialism is declining on the world stage, that it is gaining ground in the United States, a fact made clear by the 2020 presidential election.

The United States is not a socialist nation, at least not yet. That's the good news. The bad news is we have started down a slippery slope that leads to socialism, and many Americans don't even realize it. The national elections of 2020 pushed us farther down that slope. The reason more Americans don't recognize the progress socialist ideologues have made in America is socialism's use of a long-term strategy known as *boiling the frog*. Another name for this strategy is *gradualism*, that is, slowly introducing new ideas and policies little by little, always giving the public time to become accustomed to the changes, never going so far at any one time as to create a backlash, and never admitting socialism is the goal.

This is what is meant by boiling the frog. You drop a frog in a pot of water and begin heating it ever so slowly. Because the increases in heat are gradual, the frog grows accustomed to the changes in temperature. The incremental increases and the frog's corresponding adaptation continue until, eventually, the unsuspecting victim is boiled alive.[1] This has been happening for decades in America when it comes to socialism. Too many Americans are behaving like the fabled frog that ends up boiled. By ignoring socialist incursions into their lives and simply adapting to them, a lot of Americans are running the risk of being "boiled" by socialism. The 2020 presidential election showed just how many Americans are already boiling.

A BRIEF HISTORY OF SOCIALISM IN AMERICA

Socialism is not new to the United States, although it has historically been little more than a fringe element in American politics and culture. The Socialist Party of America was founded in 1901 by Eugene Debs, a labor organizer and politician, and Victor Berger, an Austrian American journalist and politician from Milwaukee. Many of the party's earliest members were union workers from various industries, particularly the garment industry.

Victor Berger won election to the U.S. House of Representatives in 1910, making him the first socialist elected to Congress. However, it was the more charismatic Eugene Debs who became the national voice of socialism in America. Debs ran for president five times, garnering an insignificant number of votes in his first four tries. Then, in 1920, he made his fifth run for the presidency while incarcerated and managed to receive one million votes. Although this was a record high for Debs, his showing wasn't nearly strong enough to make him a viable candidate.

The high point for socialism in America, until the present day, occurred in the years leading up to World War I. But interest in and support for socialism quickly ebbed when the Socialist Party of America refused to support America's entry into World War I, instead supporting the Russian Revolution. In 1917, Lenin and his Communist cronies led a civil war in a Russia already depleted by World War I. They not only overthrew the government and installed a socialist/Communist state, but they took Russia's ruling family captive and brutally murdered Tsar Nicolas, his wife, and their five children (four daughters and a son). From that point on, Americans associated socialism with the despotism of the Soviet Union, and interest in it waned.

Then, more than seventy years later, when the Soviet Union imploded (in 1991), the association of socialism with Soviet Communism began to fade. Socialism, at least in the eyes of a growing number of Americans, regained some of its lost luster. Proving that Americans have short memories when it comes to history and, in many cases, no knowledge of history at all, socialism's popularity increased, particularly among college students and Americans at the bottom of the socioeconomic ladder. Whereas interest in socialism on the part of Americans in past decades grew out of knowledge of the concept, interest in it today grows out of ignorance. This ignorance of socialism by those who claim to prefer it to capitalism is the result of the indoctrination that takes place in public schools and colleges controlled by socialist ideologues and Marxist professors.

The political-interest group Democratic Socialists of America, has seen a dramatic increase in its membership, but the best evidence of the rising tide of socialism can be found in the number of people who supported Bernie Sanders in both his bids for the Democratic nomination for president and in Joe Biden's questionable election as president in 2020. In 2016, Sanders, an avowed socialist, eventually lost the Democratic primary to Hillary Clinton, but not before garnering 43.1 percent of the votes cast (more than 13 million votes).

Sanders ran again in the 2020 Democratic primary and came in second to Joe Biden with numbers similar to those he received in 2016. Biden then adopted most of Sanders's socialist platform and prevailed in his run against Donald Trump. We do not claim that Biden "won" the election in 2020 because if only legal ballots had been counted, he might have lost. Nonetheless, even if you subtract all of the illegal ballots cast for him, Biden still received a lot of votes from Americans who were attracted to his socialist platform. Biden refused to admit that he is a socialist, but his platform certainly was, and his vice-presidential running mate has a voting record in the U.S. Senate farther to the Left than even that of Bernie Sanders.

In the 2020 Democratic primary, Joe Biden began his campaign as a middle-of-the-road moderate. His plan was to hold the Democratic base while appealing to moderate Democrats and uncommitted, independent voters. But the popularity of Bernie Sanders forced him to take a sharp turn to the Left to avoid losing a substantial portion of the Democratic base—the socialist portion. Joe Biden emerged as the eventual winner in the 2020 Democratic primary, but the most influential candidate in that race was Bernie Sanders, and the real winner was the extreme Left of the Democratic Party. In 2020, socialists finally wrested control of the Democratic Party from the centrists and moderates who had held it for decades.

THE GROWTH OF SOCIALISM IN AMERICA

Socialism in the form of greater and more onerous government control has been steadily making its way into the American mainstream for many years. In fact, for socialist ideologues, that's the plan. Consider this quote, usually attributed to socialist activist Norman Thomas: "The American people will never knowingly adopt socialism. But, under the name of 'liberalism,' they will adopt every fragment of the Socialist program, until one day America will be a socialist nation without knowing how it happened."[2] While we find the devious machinations of the Left odious, one must admit, at the very least, Thomas was prescient. What he claimed would happen is precisely what is happening, as can be seen from the national elections of 2020.

The only thing Thomas got wrong was the name Democrats have chosen to call themselves. Instead of "liberals," they call themselves "progressives." This is one more example of the Left engaging in semantic subterfuge. There is nothing progressive about transforming the United States into a socialist hellhole like Venezuela. For the sake of accuracy, let us state for the record that those who now control the Democratic Party today are neither liberals nor progressives; they are socialists.

Bernie Sanders is the only prominent Democrat forthright enough to admit he is a socialist, but make no mistake about it: his views are shared by many Democrats. Because more than seventy million Americans stand steadfastly opposed to socialism, Joe Biden and Kamala Harris go to great lengths to avoid the label. However, when you adopt a socialist platform and advocate for socialist programs, you are a socialist whether you want to be called one or not. There is a sense in which Biden can legitimately claim he is not a socialist. Socialists have very specific views and beliefs, while Biden has no firm beliefs or principles of any kind. He isn't a liberal, a progressive, a moderate, or a conservative, but at times in his checkered career, Biden has been all of these. What Joe Biden really is can best be described as a chameleon. His record suggests he will claim to be anything at any given moment in time if it will garner him votes. Joe Biden has switched positions on the issues so many times over the course of his career that it takes a scorecard to keep up with him. However, whether he wants to admit to being a socialist or not, he ran for the democratic nomination in 2020 on a socialist platform, invited a socialist to be his running mate, and advocates for socialist programs. If that's not a socialist, we don't know what is.

So, how have socialist ideologues made so much progress in foisting their defective and failed concept on Americans? As we have shown throughout this book, one of their tactics has been the use of semantic subterfuge. It is an essential element of a gradualist strategy because it makes adapting to new concepts easier for people who might otherwise reject them. We want to ensure Americans are not fooled by semantic subterfuge and caught unsuspecting, like the metaphorical frog in the boiling pot. Therefore, the following section will document the steady increase in government control over the lives of American citizens and, in turn, the rising tide of socialism. Never forget that when the government controls the people and socialists control the government, socialists control the people.

The Overton Window and the rising tide of socialism

We have already explained the boiling-the-frog phenomenon. A close cousin of this strategy is a political concept known as the *Overton window*, a nefarious approach used effectively by the Left. It contains five steps and was developed by Joseph Overton of the Mackinac Center for Public Policy to explain how people's hearts and minds can be gradually changed to accept the unacceptable:[3]

Step 1: From unthinkable to radical.

Step 2: From radical to acceptable.

Step 3: From acceptable to sensible.

Step 4: From sensible to popular.

Step 5: From popular to policy.

These steps represent a favorite strategy of the extreme Left for effecting cultural and political change. With the assistance of their fellow travelers in the mainstream media, higher education, and the entertainment industry, socialists are leading oblivious Americans from one step to the next in their policymaking to slowly gain control over every aspect of American life. Americans who still share the vision of the Founding Fathers and who still accept the values that made America good and great must recognize the rising tide of socialism before it's too late. But how?

The key to recognizing the rising tide of socialism is to watch carefully for increases in government control over citizens' lives. This is critical. Opponents of socialism often get bogged down by attacking Social Security and the progressive income tax. While these are certainly issues worthy of every American's attention, we must not focus so intently on the trees that we overlook the forest. A better way to identify socialism's ever-tightening grip is to (1) compare the government described in the U.S. Constitution against the government that now exists, and (2) be on guard against proposals for expanding the federal government even further beyond its constitutional limits.

One of the problems with debates about socialism in American is the parties on both sides of the issue are often unaware of what the Constitution actually says. You cannot understand just how faulty a concept socialism is or how much progress its advocates have made without a thorough knowledge of the Constitution. We should constantly contrast what is written in the Constitution with what exists now in government as well as what is being proposed.

The Constitution, as written by the Founders, limits the power of government and protects citizens from government intrusion into their lives. Unfortunately, you wouldn't know this by observing what the federal government has become in America. Elected officials, unelected bureaucrats, and federal judges are constantly trying to expand their powers over the people, and they have enjoyed much success over the years.

Sadly, politicians on both sides of the aisle have contributed to the progress socialists have made in America. The contributions of those on the Left have been intentional. The contributions of those on the right and in the middle can be attributed to, among other factors, a lack of attention, an unwillingness to fight for their professed beliefs, fear of negative media coverage, and ignorance of the Constitution. This last one is the worst of all.

Therefore, it is imperative that Americans understand the constitutional limits of government and recognize and oppose every attempt by Congress, the executive branch, or the judiciary to overstep these limits. If Americans who believe in the sanctity of the Constitution fail in this regard, Norman Thomas's prediction will become reality. In fact, it is already becoming reality. Unless Americans wake up and say "Enough is enough" our country will become the late, great United States. In the remainder of this chapter, we will demonstrate how the federal government has grown far beyond the limits of the Constitution. We will also uncover how America's ever-burgeoning government is controlling our lives.

THE EXECUTIVE BRANCH AND THE RISING TIDE OF SOCIALISM

The powers of the president are set forth in Article II, Section 2 of the U.S. Constitution. They include: (1) the power to serve as commander-in-chief of the military; (2) the power to make treaties with other countries; (3) the power to appoint ambassadors, public ministers, consuls, judges, and any other officers of the United States whose appointments are not provided for elsewhere in the Constitution; and (4) the power to fill vacancies that occur during the recess of the Senate.

Taking these powers and duties into account, one might reasonably expect the executive branch to consist of the Department of Defense, the Department of State, the Department of Justice, the Treasury Department, and the Executive Office of the President. The Founders, who wrote the Constitution, would be shocked to learn that as of this writing, the executive branch consists of the Executive Office of the President, fifteen separate departments—each with numerous subunits—and a long list of extra-constitutional agencies, bureaus, commissions, and boards.[4]

The biggest danger posed by the executive branch when it comes to socialist intrusion, other than its sheer size, is the proliferation of regulations by unelected bureaucrats in an ever-growing list of departments, agencies, bureaus, commissions, and boards. The executive branch of government now employs more than four million people, many of whom are engaged in the constant creation of onerous, unnecessary regulations. To give you an idea of the size of the overregulation problem, consider that in the ten years before Donald Trump's election as president, government organizations enacted more than fifty thousand new regulations.

In this section, we summarize all the components and subunits of the executive branch that exist as of this writing to demonstrate the extra-constitutional growth that has occurred since America's founding. Fair warning: what follows can make for mind-numbing reading. Nevertheless, it is important for Americans to grasp the burgeoning nature of a government grown so far beyond its constitutional boundaries as to be unrecognizable by the Founders. Of course, this extra-constitutional growth is precisely the aim of socialist advocates for whom government is god.

- *Executive Office of the President (EOP).* The EOP consists of four major subunits: Office of Management and Budget (OMB), Office of the Director of National Intelligence, Office of the United States Trade Representative (USTR), and the White House
- *Department of Agriculture (USDA).* The USDA consists of eight major subunits: Agricultural Research Service, Animal and Plant Health Inspection Service, Economic Research Service, Farm Service Agency, Forest Service, National Agricultural Library, Natural Resources Conservation Service, and Rural Development
- *Department of Commerce (DOC).* The DOC consists of eleven major subunits: Bureau of Economic Analysis, Census Bureau, International Trade Administration, NOAA Fisheries, National Institute of Standards and Technology, National Oceanic & Atmospheric Administration, National Ocean Service, National Technical Information Service, National Telecommunications and Information Administration, National Weather Service, and the Patent and Trademark Office
- *Department of Defense (DOD).* The DOD consists of seven major subunits: Air Force, Army, Defense Logistics Agency, Marine Corps, National Security Agency, Navy, and Space Force

- *Department of Education.* The Department of Education consists of three units: Educational Resources Information Center, Institute of Educational Sciences, and the National Library of Education
- *Department of Energy (DOE).* The DOE consists of nine major subunits: Lawrence Livermore National Laboratory, Los Alamos National Laboratory, National Nuclear Security Administration, Office of Science, Pantex Plant, Sandia National Laboratories, Savannah River Site, Southwestern Power Administration, Y-12 National Security Complex
- *Department of Health and Human Services (HHS)* has two components: the National Institutes of Health and the National Library of Medicine
- *Department of Homeland Security (DHS)* consists of Citizenship and Immigration Services, Coast Guard, Federal Emergency Management Agency, Federal Law Enforcement Training Centers, Intelligence Careers, and the Secret Service
- *Department of Housing and Urban Development (HUD).* This department consists of the Government National Mortgage Association, Office of Lead Hazard Control and Healthy Homes, and Public and Indian Housing
- *Department of the Interior (DOI).* The DOI consists of the Bureau of Land Management, Bureau of Reclamation, Fish and Wildlife Service, Indian Affairs, National Park Service, Office of Surface Mining Reclamation and Enforcement, and the U.S. Geology Survey
- *Department of Justice (DOJ).* Bureau of Alcohol, Tobacco, Firearms, and Explosives, Drug Enforcement Administration, Federal Bureau of Investigation, Federal Bureau of Prisons, Office of Justice Programs, and U.S. Marshals Service
- *Department of Labor (DOL).* The DOL includes the Bureau of Labor Statistics, Mine Safety and Health Administration, and Occupational Safety & Health Administration
- *Department of State (DOS).* The DOS consists of the Bureau of International Security and Nonproliferation and the Department of State Library

- *Department of Transportation (DOT).* The DOT is made up of the Bureau of Transportation Statistics and the Federal Aviation Administration
- *Department of the Treasury.* This department includes the Alcohol and Tobacco Tax and Trade Bureau, Bureau of Engraving and Printing, Bureau of the Fiscal Service, Financial Crimes Enforcement Network, Internal Revenue Service, Office of the Comptroller of the Currency, and United Stated Mint
- *Department of Veterans Affairs.* The VA stands alone
- *Quasi-independent agencies include the Broadcast Board of Governors (Radio Free Asia, Radio Free Europe/Radio Liberty, and voice of America),* Central Intelligence Agency, Consumer Financial Protection Bureau, Corporation of National & Community Service, Environmental Protection Agency, Farm Credit Administration, Federal Deposit Insurance Corporation, Federal Housing Finance Agency, Federal Labor Relations Authority, General Services Administration, Institute of Museum and Library Services, National Aeronautics and Space Administration, National Archives and Records Administration, National Credit Union Administration, National Endowment for the Arts, National Endowment for the Humanities, National Railroad Passenger Corporation (AMTRAK), National Science Foundation, Office of Government Ethics, Office of Personnel Management, Overseas Private Investment Corporation, Peace Corps, Pension Benefit Guaranty Corporation, Selective Service System, Small Business Administration, Tennessee Valley Authority, Thrift Savings Plan, United States Agency for International Development, United States Postal Service, United States Postal Inspection Service, United States Trade and Development Agency, Advisory Council on Historic Preservation, American Battle Monuments Commission, Board of Governors of the Federal Reserve System, Commodity Futures Trading Commission, Consumer Products Safety Commission, Equal Employment Opportunity Commission, Federal Communications Commission, Federal Election Commission, Federal

Energy Regulatory Commission, Federal Laboratory Consortium for technology Transfer, Federal Maritime Commission, Federal Retirement Thrift Investment Board, Federal Trade Commission, International Boundary and Water Commission, Merit Systems Production Board, National Capital Planning Commission, National Council on Disability, National Indian Gaming Commissions, National Labor Relations Board, National Mediation Board, National Transportation Safety Board, Nuclear Regulatory Commission, Nuclear Waste Technical Review Board, Occupational Safety & Health Review Commission, Postal Regulatory Commission, Railroad Retirement Board, Securities and Exchange Commission, United States International Trade Commission, and Interactive Tariff and Trade DataWeb

- *Quasi-Official Agencies.* There is only one: the Smithsonian.[5]

Federal regulations and the rising tide of socialism

We understand if you nodded off while reading our summary of the various departments and agencies of the executive branch. This was a stultifying exercise to go through, but we had a purpose in providing the summary. If your mind gets bogged down just reading about all these departments, imagine how difficult it is to manage them, and that's the point. The executive branch of the U.S. government has grown so large, unwieldy, and cumbersome it is unmanageable. Worse yet, it has become so large it cannot operate without intruding in the lives and freedom of everyday citizens, a characteristic of socialist governments.

Of the four million people currently employed by the executive branch, only two are elected by the people. This means four million nameless, faceless bureaucrats exercise enormous power over the lives of American citizens who have no say in selecting them and, in reality, can do little or nothing to have them removed. What is even more striking than the number of groups that are part of the executive branch is that many of these bureaucratic organizations promulgate federal regulations that govern how Americans work and live. This is not the Republican form of government envisioned by the Founders.

Writing for *Forbes* magazine, Clyde Wayne Crews Jr., policy director at the Competitive Enterprise Institute, had this to say about federal regulations: "Since the federal government is so pervasive, it can regulate private activity without waiting for Congress to pass a law."[6] Crews goes on to underscore what we have already pointed out: most government rules and regulations come from unelected bureaucrats rather than elected officials.[7] Rather than being the government of the governed (the people), as envisioned by the Founders, we are becoming a government of the *government*, and it operates for the sake of its elected officials and bureaucrats rather than the people they serve.

The purpose of regulations is supposed to be to interpret in practical language the laws passed by Congress. However, the number of regulations promulgated by federal-government bureaucrats every year far surpasses the number of laws passed by our elected officials in Congress. The ratio of regulations developed for every law passed by Congress over the past ten years has been twenty-seven to one.[8] This disproportionate ratio is important because of the compliance costs regulations generate and the fact that regulations almost always produce unintended consequences that can generate costs exceeding even the known compliance costs.

Writing for the *Business Insider* about the costs, roadblocks, and burdens associated with regulations, Michael Snyder observed:

> *Small business in the United States is literally suffocated by red tape. We like to think that we live in "the land of the free," but the truth is our lives and our businesses are actually tightly constrained by millions of rules and regulations. . . . It is a wonder that anyone in America is still willing to start a business from scratch and hire employees. The truth is that the business environment in the United States is now so incredibly toxic that millions of Americans have simply given up and don't even try to work within the system anymore.*[9]

Snyder cites several examples of absurdly intrusive and unnecessarily restrictive government regulations (some of what follows are federal regulations, while others come from state and local governments).[10]

- The city of Philadelphia requires bloggers to purchase a $300 business license even if the blog is just a hobby that generates no income
- The state of Louisiana requires monks to be fully licensed as funeral directors in order to sell the wooden caskets they make by hand
- The state of Massachusetts requires all children in day care centers to brush their teeth after lunch (enforcing this must be an interesting challenge)
- In Washington, DC you can be put in jail for ninety days for giving your friends a tour of our nation's capital without a tour-guide license
- It is a violation of federal law to sell raw milk
- In Lake Elmo, Minnesota, farmers can be fined $1,000 and put in jail for ninety days for selling pumpkins or Christmas trees grown outside the city limits
- A Massachusetts fisherman was fined $500 by a federal judge for untangling a giant whale that got caught in his nets and setting it free (he was supposed to call government authorities to untangle the whale although the animal would probably have died before the government officials arrived)
- The food service industry has to spend an additional fourteen million hours annually to comply with federal regulations requiring them to label all products in vending machines and chain restaurants with a clearly visible calorie-count display (as if someone who purchases junk food from a vending machine is concerned about calories).

Now that you know all of the departments, agencies, bureaus, boards, and commissions that come under the umbrella of the executive branch, and now that you know how burdensome the regulatory process is, try to reconcile this knowledge with the duties and responsibilities of the executive branch as spelled out in Article II, Section 2 of the Constitution. Even taking into account the growth of our country since its founding and the complexities of globalization, the size and intrusiveness of the executive branch are difficult to justify.

Can you imagine the looks on the Founders' faces if they knew that an extreme-Left mayor (New York City) had proposed to limit the size of soft drinks citizens were allowed to purchase? This absurd ban on large soft drinks would have gone into effect had a judge not struck down the regulation. This example of government overreach demonstrates just how much control socialist ideologues want to have over your life. With socialists in control of the government, how long do you think it would be before the government tells you, as it did in China, how many children you are allowed to have?

LEGISLATIVE BRANCH AND THE RISING TIDE OF SOCIALISM

As we demonstrated in the previous section, the danger of socialist intrusion from the executive branch comes primarily from *regulatory overreach*. With Congress, American citizens face a different threat. The contributions the legislative branch makes to socialist intrusion comes from the proliferation of programs that turn American citizens into helpless dependents, thereby creating a culture in which depending on the government for one's sustenance becomes not just a way of life but the socialist way of life.

One of the veterans we surveyed reminded us of the maxim "A government which robs Peter to pay Paul can always depend on the support of Paul."[11] Members of Congress, particularly those on the Left, have taken this maxim to heart and are using it effectively to gain and retain power. The plan of Leftist Congresspersons is to steadily increase the number of American citizens who are dependent on the federal government for their sustenance and income. Dependent citizens will, of course, always vote for the representative or senator who promises to retain and expand their government handouts. Unfortunately, this devious strategy is working.

With encouragement from socialist ideologues, a growing number of Americans are developing an entitlement mentality, looking to government to provide them with an income, benefits, and security from cradle to grave. It is no coincidence this is precisely what socialist ideologues promise to do. Commenting on this situation, former U.S. senator Jim DeMint wrote, "By the next election, the majority of Americans will be dependent on the federal government for their healthcare, education, income, or retirement."[12] DeMint was prophetic. As of this writing, half of all American families receive at least part of their income and benefits from the federal government.

You have probably heard the old maxim "Give a man a fish and you feed him for a day, but teach a man to fish and you feed him for a lifetime." We might add, "Give a man a fish today and he will ask you for two fish tomorrow, three the next day, four the next, and on and on forever." Opponents of socialism believe government interventions on behalf of the poor should focus on teaching people to fish rather than giving them a fish. Unfortunately, this is not happening.

The federal government's approach is to give a man a fish and, thereby, create a culture of dependency. This false benevolence on the part of Leftist politicians demonstrates a key point all Americans should understand about socialists: their actions never match their aspirations, or, better said, supposed aspirations. For example, they claim to support ever-increasing levels of welfare out of compassion, but where is the compassion in turning people into lifelong dependent wards of the state? Or in robbing people of their dignity, self-worth, personal responsibility, and work ethic?

The nonpartisan Congressional Research Service (CRS) has identified a total of eighty-three separate federal welfare programs funded by American taxpayers.[13] Annual spending on these programs totals more than $1 trillion, and these eighty-three programs do not include Social Security or Medicare, the latter two being contributory programs.[14] The amount spent on these eighty-three noncontributory programs—the give-a-man-a-fish kind—is more than the total spent on Social Security, Medicare, and national defense combined.[15] In other words, the United States was already well down the path leading to socialism even before Biden and Harris weaseled their way into office.

These numbers are disturbing enough by themselves, but they become even more disturbing when you realize their larger meaning. They mean socialist ideologues are steadily achieving exactly what they hope for: a citizenry wholly dependent on the government. This is a good place to remind readers of the socialist's three-step plan for controlling the lives of American citizens:

Step 1: The government controls the people.

Step 2: Socialists control the government.

Step 3: Socialists control the people.

Even worse than the enormous amount of money spent on welfare programs is that this spending is on the rise and has been for a long time. Spending on the ten largest federal welfare programs has increased by 378 percent over the past thirty years.[16] These programs are as follows:[17]

- Supplemental Nutrition Assistance Program (SNAP)
- Health Insurance Marketplace
- Medicaid
- Child's Health Insurance Program (CHIP)
- Housing
- Supplementary Security Income Program (SSI)
- Temporary Assistance for Needy Families (TANF)
- Earned Income Tax Credit
- Head Start
- Pell Grant.

This is just ten programs out of a total of eighty-three. By giving people a fish instead of teaching them to fish, the federal government is turning generations of Americans into what President Reagan called "helpless children . . . forever dependent."[18]

Former U.S. senator Jim DeMint identified four pillars of freedom he believes, when taken together, are the foundation of America's success: social responsibility, limited government, economic freedom, and spiritual faith.[19] These four pillars, combined with the American work ethic, personal responsibility, entrepreneurship, and individual liberty, made America great. Welfare programs that create a culture of dependency are undermining these foundational

American values and turning America into what Dinesh D'Souza called "the United States of Socialism."[20]

THE JUDICIAL BRANCH AND THE RISING TIDE OF SOCIALISM

The danger posed by the judicial branch when it comes to socialist intrusion is judicial usurpation—activist judges who overstep their constitutional powers and legislate from the bench. These judges *make* laws instead of ruling on their constitutionality. Every time this happens, Americans are handed edicts from on high by unelected judges who for all practical purposes serve for life and are, therefore, unaccountable to the people. History has proven over and over that government officials who are unaccountable to you have no qualms about trampling on your freedom.

Article III of the Constitution established the judiciary. It is shorter than either Article I (Congress) or Article II (the executive branch). The reason for this brevity is the Founders viewed the judiciary, or the Supreme Court, as the weakest of the three branches of government. The Founders gave the Supreme Court the following powers: (1) to rule on cases between the government and American citizens, (2) to reopen old cases and have them retried, (3) to rule on the rights of citizens, and (4) to rule on punishments for people who violate the Constitution.

In the landmark case of *Marbury v. Madison*, the Court assumed a power not granted to it in the Constitution but one that has become its most important power: judicial review. This allows the court to strike down as unconstitutional laws passed by Congress and acts of the executive branch. Judicial review opened the door to judicial activism and, over time, transformed the judiciary into the most powerful branch of the federal government, a clear violation of the Founders' intentions.

Judicial activism occurs when judges arrive at rulings guided by their personal and political views rather than the Constitution. This abuse of power has led to the unconstitutional practice of *legislating from the bench*. This form of judicial usurpation occurs when judges ignore both the Constitution and legal precedent in arriving at their decisions, typically decisions advancing a partisan agenda or their personal views, or both. When this happens, we have unelected judges who serve ostensibly for life handing down edicts governing the lives of American citizens who have no recourse when they disagree with those edicts.

Conservative judges who serve in accordance with Article III of the Constitution are known as *originalists*. They correctly view their job as applying the Constitution to laws in ways reflecting the original meaning of the document or the original intent of it authors. Originalism allows the Constitution to be what the Founders intended it to be: a permanent anchor holding our country firmly in place no matter how much it is buffeted by the ever-shifting winds of cultural change.

Activist judges, on the other hand, subscribe to a concept they call the *living Constitution,* a favorite assertion of the Left. Claiming they subscribe to a living Constitution implies that conservatives subscribe to a *dead Constitution.* By "living" Leftists mean the Constitution changes with the times. This view, of course, makes it susceptible to the vaporous whims of cultural fads and the nefarious machinations of judicial activists, precisely what socialist ideologues want. A living Constitution turns our country into an anchorless ship cast adrift on a stormy sea. Worse, in actual practice the concept allows the Constitution to be twisted to mean whatever activist judges want it to mean. It is easy to see why socialist ideologues are vocal advocates of a living-Constitution camp.

The ability to permanently turn the Constitution into a so-called living document is why a major goal of the socialist-controlled Democratic Party is to "stack the court." This involves increasing the number of seats on the Supreme Court and then filling the new seats with activist judges. The number of new seats is determined by how many are needed to guarantee a comfortable socialist majority. Both Joe Biden and Kamala Harris subscribed to court stacking during the 2020 presidential election.

According to the Founders, judges are to be neutral, objective interpreters of the Constitution. Writing in *Federalist* no. 78, Alexander Hamilton claimed that whereas Congress has the power of the purse and the president the power of the sword, the judiciary has only the power of judgment.[21] This is hardly the case in today's activist environment. Judicial activists are now able to take the power of the purse out of the hands of Congress and the power of the sword out of the hands of the president. Activist Supreme Court justices have become judicial magicians who pull their rulings out of thin air as if the Constitution did not even exist.

A VETERAN SPEAKS UP

Judicial usurpation and legislating from the bench have become common practices in the federal courts, practices in clear violation of the Constitution. Here is what one veteran had to say about this issue:

One would hope that the Supreme Court would be nonpartisan but over time this has become less and less the case. The court should rule on issues in accordance with the law, not their personal biases. It has been disappointing to see hearings on judicial nominations turn into circuses based on political prejudices and defamation. Judges should be nominated and affirmed based on their knowledge of the law and the Constitution.

—Thomas G. Gates, United States Air Force, 1966–1975

Thomas Gates is a Vietnam combat veteran with two tours of duty in Southeast Asia. Gates subsequently spent his civilian career in the Federal Bureau of Investigation (FBI), retiring after twenty years of service. He is a graduate of the University of South Florida. For the past several years, he has supported veterans through various nonprofit organizations. Gates is a member of the Florida Veterans' Hall of Fame, a recipient of the Patriot Award (the highest civilian award given by the United States Special Operations Command), and a member of the Florida Veterans' Hall of Fame society.

This is why the Left engages in such destructive machinations to prevent conservative federal court nominees from surviving the Senate's approval process. The Left cannot abide originalist judges who view the Constitution through the eyes of the Founders who wrote it. Rather, they want activist judges, who are willing to ignore legal precedent as well as the original intent of the Founders. The Left cannot bear the thought having conservative judges who might objectively interpret the Constitution according to the original meaning or original intent while also respecting the concept of legal precedent.

Of course, those who suffer at the hands of unscrupulous activist judges are the American people who are dictated to by their rulings. Americans understand that the Supreme Court has become the most powerful of the three supposedly coequal branches of the federal government. One of our veterans said he didn't care so much who is president or which party controls Congress as long as conservatives have a majority on the Supreme Court. Even socialist ideologues agree with this veteran's notion—provided, of course, there is a Leftist majority on the court. Guaranteeing a Leftist majority is the goal of the Democratic Party's plan to stack the court.

CHAPTER 10

SOCIALISM IN AMERICA: CAN THE RISING TIDE BE STOPPED?

All who wear a Special Forces tab have to demonstrate,
through experience and performance, an ability to persevere
and achieve the remarkable outcomes their nation depends
on them for. Recently I was told of a discussion whereby a
three-star general, while pinning Bronze Star medals on
conventional soldiers, told a Green Beret colonel that what
is considered extraordinary heroism for regular soldiers is a
day-to-day expectation for Green Berets. Therefore, the two
should not be measured in the same manner.

—Robert M. Kirila, United States Army, 1991–2017

Colonel Kirila (retired), whom we also highlighted in chapter 4, served in the U.S. Army for twenty-six years. Today he serves as managing director of Black Powder Holdings, whose mission is "to rebuild America's infrastructure by partnering with America's most elite cadre of leaders from the special operations community and impact investors seeking alternative asset strategies."[1]

As Colonel Robert Kirila suggested in the above statement, America truly is a nation that must be judged by a higher standard than others. We agree, but will this still be the case if socialists continue to gain ground in our country? America has arrived at a critical juncture in its history. We can either continue on our current path toward socialism or reverse course and once again be guided by the Founders' vision, which made America the greatest, most prosperous, most benevolent nation in world history.

As it has always been, maintaining the Founders' vision is the responsibility of the American people. Colonel Kirila spoke of the importance of perseverance. We have arrived at a point in our nation's history when Americans who believe in the vision of our Founders must be willing to persevere if America is going to remain a nation above all others. America's future is in our hands. This is what George Washington meant when he said, "The preservation of the sacred fire of liberty, and the destiny of the Republican model of government, are justly considered as deeply, perhaps as finally staked, on the experiment entrusted into the hands of the American people."[2]

The "experiment" Washington spoke of was an America built on a foundation of Christian values and characterized by such principles as limited government, low taxation, a free-market economy, individual liberty, personal responsibility, freedom of speech and thought, a strong national defense, the Christian work ethic, rule of law, and constitutional sovereignty. These first principles made our country both good and great, and they are the ideologies that America's veterans fought for. But they are all under attack from socialist ideologues and their fellow travelers on the Left, who reject them out of hand.

The key to restoring the America envisioned by the Founders is to restore our founding values and principles. Socialist ideologues envision an America characterized by unlimited government, high taxes, a collective economy, government control of speech and thought, minimal national defense, a dependency culture, and constitutional fluidity. Further, they are willing to deceive, distort, divide, and destroy to achieve their vision.

Restoring the America envisioned by our founders—the America our military heroes fought for—is not a Republican issue or a Democratic issue. Rather, it is an issue for all Americans. People of all stripes who want to see America remain the bastion of freedom, liberty, and prosperity it has been for almost two and a half centuries must speak up. The alternative is to continue down a path leading to socialism and, invariably, to tyranny and despotism. It is a path that ends with total dependence on a government that cannot make good on its promises to provide for the needs of citizens.

We are far down this path already, and the national elections of 2020 pushed us yet farther. If America continues on its present course, even those who claimed to prefer socialism to capitalism and government control to individual liberty will eventually come to regret their choice. If you don't believe this, ask the citizens of Venezuela, who now rue the day they turned to socialism.

Consider the words of Matthew Spalding of the Heritage Foundation concerning America's movement toward socialism: "Where we are tending is a government that does more, spends more, and regulates more and more. . . . As a result, growing numbers are dependent on government benefits and entitlements. The American people are becoming more subjects of the state than self-governing citizens."[3] America was established because our Founders grew weary of being subjects of a tyrannical state: King George's England. Do we really want to return to being helpless subjects of a despotic government?

It's time for Americans of all stripes to do what the veterans in this book did: speak up on behalf of freedom, liberty, and self-government. The message our heroes have conveyed in this book is the same message conveyed by a veteran of the Battle of Concord 245 years ago. When asked what motivated him to go in harm's way to fight against the biggest, best-equipped army in the world, American colonist Levi Preston replied, "What we meant in going after those redcoats was simple. You see, we had always governed ourselves, we always intended to govern ourselves, and they didn't mean that we should."[4] Preston's homespun logic was simple but powerful. Even the most eloquent orator could not have stated the case any better.

If, like Levi Preston, you are committed to freedom, liberty, and self-government, here are some things you can do:

1. Acknowledge the source of the rights Americans have long enjoyed.
2. Advocate for self-determination and limited government.
3. Support initiatives to reduce regulations and taxes.
4. Advocate for a free-market economy and private property.
5. Demand individual liberty and personal responsibility.
6. Restore integrity and truth to public education at all levels.
7. Support a strong national defense.
8. Promote the Christian work ethic over the entitlement mentality.
9. Restore constitutional sovereignty and integrity.
10. Stand up to the "cancel culture."
11. Reject mob violence and support the police.
12. Demand that state legislatures take the steps necessary to ensure fair and transparent elections in which only legal votes are counted and counted on time.

Let's examine each of these actions.

ACKNOWLEDGE THE SOURCE OF THE RIGHTS AMERICANS HAVE LONG ENJOYED

The freedoms guaranteed to all Americans in the Bill of Rights come not from government but from God. The Founders, who drafted the Constitution and the first ten amendments, did not grant the freedoms contained therein to American citizens, nor did they claim to. Rather, the Bill of Rights simply summarized the freedoms and conveyed that they were granted by God—a fact the Founders understood and acknowledged many times but socialists deny. To a socialist, all rights come from government.

We read in the preamble to the Declaration of Independence, "We hold these truths to be self-evident, that all men are created equal, that they are endowed by their Creator with certain unalienable rights, that among these are Life, Liberty and the Pursuit of happiness." Thomas Jefferson made clear what his fellow founders believed: that our rights come not from government but from our "Creator." This is what George Washington meant when he said, "No people can be bound to acknowledge the invisible hand which conducts the affairs of men more than the people of the United States."[5] The "invisible hand" Washington referred to is God's.

Americans who wish to restore the Founders' vision for our country must understand and accept that God is the source of the rights and freedoms we enjoy. This is why Jefferson called them "unalienable." If all men are created equal in the eyes of God and if our rights and freedoms come from Him, no man and no government can take them from us except by force. This simple fact more than anything else is why America is the only nation in the world to have the Emancipation Proclamation and to have fought a civil war over the issue of slavery. Understanding the real source of our rights will checkmate socialist ideologues in their efforts to transform America into something the Founders would neither recognize nor approve of.

ADVOCATE FOR SELF-DETERMINATION AND LIMITED GOVERNMENT

The concepts of self-determination and limited government go hand in hand: As the government grows larger, the voice of the people grows smaller. Correspondingly, the closer the government comes to staying within its constitutional limits, the stronger the voice of the people becomes. A large, centralized federal government is the antithesis of self-determination and limited government. Our republican form of government was intentionally designed to keep government as close to the people as possible. It was never intended to become an out-of-control monstrosity overflowing the banks of the Potomac River.

Keeping government decisions close to the people is the point of the Tenth Amendment, which states, "The powers not delegated to the United States by the Constitution, nor prohibited to it by the states, are reserved to the states respectively, or to the people." The Founders knew keeping government as close to the people as possible would make it more responsive and more accountable. This is why each state has its own legislature, as well as county and municipal governments. These levels of government were instated to fulfill the responsibilities not given to the federal government in the Constitution.

Since a large federal government is less responsive and less accountable, the functional question is this: When is a government too large? In America's case, government is too large when, allowing for growth and the complexities of the modern world, it extends beyond the limits established for it in the Constitution. This, of course, has already happened, as we demonstrated in chapter 9. Over the years, the federal government has assumed more and more powers, leaving fewer and fewer to the states, the municipal governments, and the people.

We recommend that Americans who are concerned about the burgeoning size of the federal government demand that candidates in every presidential election justify every department, agency, bureau, commission, and board that comes under the executive branch with the exceptions of those justified by the Constitution (i.e., the Executive Office of the President, the Department of State, the Department of Defense, the Justice Department, and the Treasury Department). We also recommend citizens pressure Congress to establish a system for regularly reviewing the federal bureaucracy so all departments, agencies, bureaus, commissions, and boards are required to periodically justify themselves to the American people.

In addition to these two broad recommendations, we offer the following specific recommendations for restoring the constitutional limits on the executive branch: Collapse the Department of Agriculture, Department of Commerce, Department of Energy, Department of Health and Human Services, Department of Housing and Urban Development, Department of Labor, and Department of Transportation into one omnibus department with each former department becoming a much scaled-down office.

Reduce all subsidies and grants provided by these offices, and cap the amounts they are allowed to provide in the future so they don't grow back into full-fledged departments. As for the Department of Education, eliminate it. Education is intended to be a state and local enterprise, and that is what it should be. Nothing good comes from allowing the federal government into local classrooms. Unless citizens make limited government part of the political conversation in America, government will continue to grow and self-determination will be replaced by bureaucratic control.

SUPPORT INITIATIVES TO REDUCE REGULATIONS AND TAXES

One of the favorite activities of socialists and their fellow travelers on the Left is spending other people's money. This is why it has been said that "the problem with socialism is that you eventually run out of other people's money."[6] Socialist ideologues view the public treasury as an open purse to be refilled when it runs low by simply printing more money or raising taxes. They are wrong. Printing more money causes inflation, making the currency less and less valuable. In addition, higher tax rates can actually reduce the amount of revenue collected by the government. Here are some reasons why:

- The way the tax code is currently written encourages people to avoid the taxable economy. For example, in May 2012, Facebook cofounder Eduardo Saverin renounced his U.S. citizenship and moved to Singapore to avoid America's capital gains taxes on the estimated $4 billion he was going to receive from Facebook's IPO. Since that time it has become common for moneyed individuals to renounce their citizenship to avoid being subjected to America's tax code
- High taxes reduce the amount of money businesses have to invest in technology, innovation, and expansion. This, in turn, undermines job creation and global competitiveness, meaning fewer people are paying taxes
- The current tax code is so huge, complex, confusing, and ever-changing that individuals and businesses have to spend additional dollars just trying to interpret the code and comply with

it. Tax compliance and administrative costs add twenty cents
to every dollar businesses are required to pay the government
in taxes
- The tax code is inherently unfair in that some citizens pay too
  much while others pay nothing at all. Under the current tax
  code, the top 5 percent of taxpayers pay more than 60 percent
  of all taxes collected by the government. The tax code is especially hard on small businesses, a fact that undermines job
  creation. Small businesses account for more than 80 percent
  of the new jobs created in America, yet they are hurt worst by
  the convoluted tax code
- High taxes reduce the incentive for working. Why work more
  when you have to turn a high percentage of your income over
  to the government? As tax rates increase, the incentive to work
  decreases
- Because of over taxation, Americans now spend more in taxes
  than they do on food, clothing, or medical care.

President John F. Kennedy once summarized the problem of
high taxation: "An economy hampered by restrictive tax rates will
never produce enough revenue to balance our budget—just as it
will never produce enough jobs or profits."[7] Clearly, Americans
who value the vision of the Founders must speak up constantly
for lower taxes. Americans must also speak up on the subject of
overregulation.

We demonstrated in chapter 9 how burdensome the regulatory
process has become in America. Continuing to enact onerous and
unnecessary regulations is like pouring water in the gas tank of business and industry. Government regulations affect all Americans
directly or indirectly by increasing the cost of everything purchased
and undermining the ability of businesses—particularly small
businesses—to compete. This, in turn, undermines job growth and
wage increases.

Shortly after taking office in January, 2017, President Donald
Trump demonstrated why it is important for Americans to speak
up and demand an end to overregulation. Reducing burdensome
government regulations was part of Trump's campaign platform in

his race for the presidency. Trump followed through on his promise to reduce regulations by signing Executive Order 13771, which required two regulations to be eliminated for every new regulation enacted. This and other regulatory cuts made by the Trump administration were projected to reduce regulatory compliance costs by as much as $340 billion.

To grasp how important the Trump deregulation efforts have been, consider that during the Obama administration regulatory costs increased by $122 billion.[8] Every dollar saved in regulatory costs is a dollar that can be invested in innovation, technological development, and improvements to productivity. These things, in turn, lead to job growth and increased wages. Americans who want to stop our country's downhill slide into socialism can help by supporting only those elected officials who will commit to lower taxes and regulatory reform.

ADVOCATE FOR A FREE-MARKET ECONOMY AND PRIVATE PROPERTY

A free-market economy exists when people can freely buy and sell goods and services without interference from outside sources—such as government agencies—concerning value and price. Based on this definition, America has a quasi–free market economy, "quasi" because there *is* interference from an outside source—again, the government—on almost everything that is bought and sold in America. Don't get us wrong; we are not condemning regulations per se. After all, some regulations are helpful and even laudatory. It is not regulations in general that gum up the gears of the free market but unnecessary regulations.

Here is an example of where regulations can be helpful. The Occupational Health and Safety Administration (OSHA), which is part of the Department of Labor, develops and enforces regulations to keep the workplace safe. There are many cases in which OSHA regulations have protected workers from unscrupulous employers who otherwise might pressure them to take life-threatening shortcuts. Like any government agency, OSHA can overdo it when it comes to regulations, but some of their regulations are invaluable in maintaining worker safety.

As you interact with elected officials, political candidates, and other Americans, you must be able to articulate the benefits of a free-market economy. To help in this regard, we offer the following list of benefits:[9]

- A free market gives individuals and organizations freedom, flexibility, and variety in buying and selling goods and services
- A free market allows companies to quickly and effectively adapt to changing market conditions. This is what happened when the COVID-19 pandemic induced panic buying, creating temporary shortages of selected products. These shortages were quickly remedied when private companies began manufacturing new and different products to eliminate backlogs
- In a free market, individuals may buy and sell what they want at prices they deem appropriate, thus encouraging production, commerce, and entrepreneurship
- In a free market, individuals and organizations are more willing to risk capital on research, development, and innovation because they have greater control over their own success. This is important because the key to competing with the cheap labor offered by China and other countries is technological innovation
- In a free market, individuals and organizations can maximize their profits because they are not burdened by excessive or unnecessary regulations
- A free market encourages healthy, productive competition, which in turn benefits consumers by increasing choices while decreasing prices
- A free market encourages maximum efficiency, which in turn makes the best possible use of a nation's resources
- A free market allows decisions to be made on the basis of supply and demand, which is fairer and more efficient than the sluggish, politically motivated central-planning decisions of government.

There is one essential ingredient that must be present if citizens are to enjoy the benefits of a free market: private property. It is the most essential component of a free-market economy.

Without private property protected by law, there can be no free market. Private property is the polar opposite of the mainstay principles of socialism: collectivism and government ownership.

One of the principal issues leading to America's War for Independence from Great Britain was private property. The king of England and Parliament repeatedly violated the private property rights of Americans. For example, before armed conflict broke out, colonists were required to board British soldiers in their homes or to pay for boarding them elsewhere. Try to imagine being required to provide room and board to soldiers who aren't welcome in the community, much less your home. Small wonder this infringement of their private property rights was too much for many colonists.

Private property was a high priority for America's Founders. We know this from reading the *Federalist Papers*, the most authoritative source for learning the intentions of the framers of the Constitution. *Federalist* no. 10 makes clear that the government of the United States was supposed to protect justice and liberty by protecting private property against the unjust actions of a ruling majority or a vocal minority.[10]

Protecting private property was important when America was founded, and it is important now. Private property is the cornerstone of capitalism. It is what allows people to benefit from their own ideas, entrepreneurship, and labor and to work, produce, consume, own, trade, and invest based on their own personal choices. This is why we recommend Americans who believe in the vision of the Founders support only those political candidates who are free-market and private property advocates.

DEMAND INDIVIDUAL LIBERTY AND PERSONAL RESPONSIBILITY

Individual liberty is the antithesis of socialism. It means you have the right to peaceably pursue your own personal, family, and commercial interests and relationships. Here is how French philosopher Benjamin Constant explained individual liberty:

> *It is the right to be subjected to the laws, and to be neither arrested, detained, put to death nor maltreated in any way by*

the arbitrary will of one or more individuals. It is the right of everyone to express their opinion, choose a profession and practice it, dispose of property, . . . to come and go without permission, and without having to account for their motives or undertakings. It is everyone's right to associate with other individuals to discuss their interests or to profess the religion which they and their associates prefer.[11]

A caveat is in order here. Individual liberty does not give people the right to do anything they want, anytime they want, or in any way they want. This is because in a moral society—the kind envisioned by the Founders—for every right there is a corresponding responsibility. One overarching responsibility always present is exercising one's rights in ways peaceful, ethical, and respectful of the rights of others. America's founders were adamant that the republican form of self-government they envisioned had to rest firmly on a moral foundation or it would eventually devolve into chaos, the kind of mob violence that has become common in large American cities anytime the Left becomes angry about anything.

Americans have a right to express their anger and frustration by demonstrating, but they also have a responsibility to keep their demonstrations peaceful. Unfortunately, this is not happening in our larger cities. Demonstrations that begin as peaceful protests are soon hijacked by outside agitators. These demonstrations quickly morph into riots by violent mobs behaving in ways that have nothing to do with the issue that started the demonstrations. These riots soon devolve into looting, arson, and anarchy. Sadly, weak-kneed Democratic mayors and governors not only refuse to do what is necessary to stop the violence; they often condone it.

The riots that have become so common in America's larger cities are led by agitators bent on advancing a destructive agenda aimed not at making improvements but at tearing down the America envisioned by the Founders. They are then encouraged by Leftist mayors and governors who make excuses for the violence. This is why the motto of rioters has become "Defund the police." Fewer police on the streets provides a welcome advantage for criminals. To make matters worse, spineless, Left-leaning city officials have actually sided with the rioters by condemning the police and reducing law enforcement budgets, a mistake some now regret.

Memorize the following benefits of individual liberty tempered by personal responsibility and be ready to articulate them. This knowledge is indispensable if you are to convince elected officials, political candidates, and other Americans to defend the freedoms we hold dear:[12]

- Individual liberty allows people to manage their own lives and pursue their own dreams unencumbered by government interference or coercion
- Individual liberty allows people to enter relationships, contracts, exchanges, and other interactions voluntarily and without government interference
- Individual liberty allows people to freely choose their professions, religions, church activities, cultural associations, clubs, professional organizations, and charitable groups without permission or interference from government
- Individual liberty makes the individual, not the government, paramount. Socialism, on the other hand, makes the government paramount while marginalizing the individual.

To stop the rising tide of socialism and restore the America envisioned by our Founders, support only those elected officials and political candidates who affirm the importance of individual liberty tempered by personal responsibility, and who will commit to protecting it.

RESTORE ACADEMIC INTEGRITY AND TRUTH TO PUBLIC EDUCATION AT ALL LEVELS

If Americans fail to restore academic integrity and truth to public education at every level, socialist ideologues will eventually prevail and our country will follow in the sullied footsteps of Venezuela. As one of our veterans observed, we cannot win the battle with socialist ideologues as long as they control the public education system. By the time young people have been subjected to twelve years of anti-American propaganda and socialist indoctrination, winning them back to the America envisioned by the Founders is next to impossible. Then add another four or more years of college and the pro-socialism mentality becomes so deeply ingrained in young people that it cannot be dislodged by even the most obvious truths.

American students must be taught the truth about their country: the good, the bad, and the ugly. If the truth is taught in our public schools, students will realize that although America is not perfect and there have been mistakes, on balance the scales tip overwhelmingly in the direction of good and great. The owners of America's public schools and colleges—taxpaying citizens—must speak up and demand that school boards, superintendents, principals, and instructors teach the truth about our country and demand excellence from students. Don't keep your children in schools that refuse to do this.

SUPPORT A STRONG NATIONAL DEFENSE

Imagine yourself swimming in the ocean, surrounded by sharks. This is America in the twenty-first century. China, the largest shark in the water, is determined to overtake the United States militarily and economically and, having done so, dominate the world. Russia, though no longer the threat it was as the Soviet Union, is still a determined enemy, and its attitude toward America is characterized by ill will. North Korea and Iran are growing threats, and they despise America. Then there is the ongoing threat of international and home-grown terrorism.

Thinking Americans understand peace is maintained through strength, not by displaying "peace" bumper stickers on their cars. Nor does anyone with good sense depend on that most feckless of organizations, the United Nations, to maintain peace. China, Russia, North Korea, Iran, and the terrorist organizations that hate America scoff at the United Nations and view Americans with "peace" or "coexist" bumper stickers as useful fools. It is important to be willing to negotiate with our enemies, but only from a position of strength. As one veteran commented, you don't negotiate with a hungry tiger until you have subdued it and locked it in a cage.

Because socialist ideologues and their fellow Leftists support minimal national defense spending at best, thoughtful Americans must be able to convincingly state the case for military preparedness and a strong national defense. As long as hate, envy, greed, covetousness, and the lust for power reside in the human heart, there will be wars. And the more prosperous a country, the more enemies it will have; enemies covet its prosperity.

Know this: what China, Russia, North Korea, Iran, and international terrorist organizations want is not peace. The terrorists and Iran want to see America destroyed. The Chinese want world dominance. Russia wants to regain its once-powerful position in the world. North Korean officials want to be feared on the world stage. Enemy nations and terrorist organizations do not negotiate out of goodwill. They use negotiations as a stalling tactic to buy time to strengthen their positions as they plan for the demise and destruction of the United States. What these nations and terrorist organizations all have in common is this: a burning desire to bring down the United States.

America's enemies are bent on destroying our country because they do not share our values and because we stand in the way of their efforts to dominate the world. They respect and fear one thing and one thing only: strength. Consequently, any lack of strength on our part invites their aggression. In fact, just a perceived lack of will invites aggression. For example, one of the factors our enemies watch closely is the Department of Defense (DOD) budget. They perceive cuts to the DOD budget as a sign of weakness and a lack of commitment, both of which they view as opportunities.

Maintaining a well-funded DOD is going to be increasingly difficult as the extreme Left multiplies its influence on American politics. This is because socialists/liberals will want to divert military dollars into the social programs they use to attract and retain voters, programs that will make more and more Americans dependent wards of an increasingly vulnerable state. This is why it is important to support elected officials and political candidates who are committed to a strong national defense and to keeping our military properly funded, highly trained, and technologically superior.

PROMOTE THE CHRISTIAN WORK ETHIC OVER THE ENTITLEMENT MENTALITY

America is undergoing a tectonic shift in attitudes toward work. When European immigrants first came to the shores of North America seeking religious freedom, their view of work was biblical. They saw work as a gift from God that allowed them to provide for their families and improve the quality of their lives (Ecclesiastes 2:24; 5:19). Consequently, they viewed work as a good thing that should be done well and in ways that honor God. They were steeped in the Christian work ethic.

Because Americans exemplified the Christian work ethic and enjoyed unprecedented freedom, our country eventually became the most productive and prosperous nation on earth. Average Americans came to enjoy more material wealth than citizens of any other country. That's the good news. The bad news is, over time, Americans began to take for granted what previous generations had worked long and hard to attain. Many believed they were entitled to a certain level of material comfort without the inconvenience of working to earn it.

This entitlement mentality is the polar opposite of the Christian work ethic. People who feel entitled view work not as a gift from God, to be appreciated and done well, but as drudgery, a necessary evil to be avoided when possible. People with this mindset expect to enjoy the material comforts of hard work without actually having to labor. The seeds of the entitlement mentality are sown by government handouts, overindulgent helicopter parents, and school systems emphasizing inclusion instead of excellence. It results in a generation of people who:

- are overly dependent on others—including the government—in every area of their lives. They want to ride in the wagon but expect others to pull it. As the entitlement mentality grows and spreads, there will eventually be more people riding in the wagon than pulling it
- view the world as inherently unfair and themselves as victims. As a result, they often become chronically angry, then act out

their hostility in destructive ways, such as breaking and entering. Again, think of the riots, looting, arson, and anarchy that have become common in America's larger cities

- seek comfort from their self-induced failures and perceived victimhood in drugs, alcohol, and other unhealthy amusements
- believe that the government should take care of them but do not appreciate the handouts they receive because, in their minds, they deserve them.[13]

The Christian work ethic is one of the principal reasons America became the world's most productive, prosperous, and competitive country. But the entitlement mentality is steadily eroding America's work ethic. Socialist ideologues welcome this erosion.

Refuse to support politicians who try to buy your vote by offering handouts from the federal treasury. Americans are not *entitled* to them.

RESTORE CONSTITUTIONAL SOVERIGNTY AND INTEGRITY

In chapter 9, we explained how judicial usurpation, legislating from the bench, ignoring legal precedent, caring nothing for the original meaning or intent of the Founders, and applying the "living Constitution" theory are undermining the integrity of the Constitution and, in turn, its sovereignty. Judicial usurpation is turning America into a rudderless ship adrift on a sea of ever-changing cultural trends driven by a socialist agenda.

Another factor undermining the sovereignty and integrity of the Constitution is the tendency of Leftist judges to be guided by international law when making decisions. This is problematic for two reasons. First, international laws are enacted by people who typically don't share America's peerless values. Second, American citizens have no voice in the enactment of international law. To look to international law when making judicial decisions is to allow citizens from other nations to govern the lives of American citizens.

How well can you make the case for restoring the sovereignty and integrity of the Constitution? The following points underscore the importance of keeping the Constitution front and center in our judicial decision-making:

- The U.S. Constitution is the law of the land for America. No other law, treaty, or action may take precedence over the Constitution. For international laws or treaties to be valid, they *must* conform to the Constitution. The Constitution is what gives our government the right to enter treaties. This protects America's sovereignty when interacting with foreign powers. The sovereignty of the Constitution ensures the authority of the American people to govern themselves independent of foreign influence

- International law consists of laws developed and ratified by other countries and international organizations, meaning American citizens have little or no voice in their enactment. Worse yet, these other entities are often composed of individuals with values, religions, worldviews, and interests radically different from those embraced by most Americans. *Consent of the governed* is a fundamental principle of the Constitution. Therefore, laws enacted without the consent of the American people should never be applied to them

- International treaties represent a serious threat to constitutional sovereignty and integrity. Such treaties are supposed to be subservient to the Constitution, but socialist ideologues and other Leftists have no problem with treaties superseding the Constitution. Some of the international treaties proposed and supported by the extreme Left in America would deny Americans their constitutional rights in such areas as parenting, educating children, and keeping and bearing arms

- The integrity of the Constitution is a function of how it is interpreted by those empowered to do so. The battle over interpretation is a battle between advocates of originalism and proponents of the living Constitution. Unless originalists prevail in this battle, the Constitution can be made to say anything Leftist judges want it to say on any subject at any time. In other words, to those on the Left, the Constitution can say one thing one day and something different the next.

One of the principal authors of the Constitution, James Madison, had this to say about its original meaning and intent: "I entirely concur in the propriety of resorting to the sense in which the Constitution was accepted and ratified by the nation. In that sense alone it is the legitimate Constitution . . . If the meaning of the text be sought in changeable meaning of the words composing it, it is evident that the shapes and attributes of the Government must partake of the changes to which the words and phrases of all living languages are constantly subject."[14] Madison's note may be loquacious, but its meaning is clear: stick to the original meaning of the Constitution or render this hallowed document meaningless

- The value of originalism in Constitutional interpretation is it tethers the decisions of judges to the intent of the Founders and the meaning of the words as used at the time the Constitution was written. The "living Constitution," on the other hand, opens the judiciary to arbitrary, reckless, and self-interested decisions driven by ever-changing whims and potentially dangerous ideologies. Think of American society as a balloon floating in the air. As the winds change, the balloon will blow in one direction. As the winds change again, the balloon will blow in a new direction. However, if the balloon is tethered tightly to the ground, it will blow only so far before coming back to its original position. The Constitution is what tethers America to its founding principles. Originalism is what keeps the tether from being severed

- "Living Constitution" advocates like to claim the Constitution must change to match ongoing changes in American society, but they miss—or more likely, ignore—an important point. Think of America as the home you live in. Americans often make changes to their homes—color schemes, carpet, flooring, window treatments, and furniture—to accord with changes in fashion, taste, and financial status. These cosmetic changes don't undermine the integrity of the home because they don't affect its foundation. As long as the integrity of its foundation is protected, you can make all the cosmetic changes you want to your home. But undermine the foundation and the home will eventually come crashing down on you. One of the veterans surveyed for this book argues that advocates of the "living Constitution" are undermining the foundation of our country—the Constitution. We agree.

Only those elected officials and political candidates who are committed to nominating and approving originalists to the federal bench deserve your support. To support those who do not share that commitment will open the door yet wider for socialist ideologues who want to remake America into a nation the Founders would find abhorrent.

REJECT THE CANCEL CULTURE

The cancel culture, mentioned but briefly in chapter 7, is a phenomenon in which people who disagree with the views of the extreme Left are attacked, vilified, bullied, and even destroyed. These tactics are designed to suppress dissent and coerce people into either accepting Leftist orthodoxy or remaining quiet about it for fear of retribution. There has been no greater threat to freedom of speech, academic freedom, or public discourse in our lifetime. The message conveyed by the Left is, *Agree with us or shut up, or we will destroy you.* Obviously, the forty-six thousand university professors who Mao had executed didn't agree with him..

America is the most diverse nation in the world—the most pluralistic society on the globe. As a result, there will always be tension between people of different worldviews, races, genders, ages, religions, and political persuasions. This is why America's motto is "E Pluribus Unum," Latin for "out of many, one." Because we are so diverse, Americans need to look for common ground, be willing to disagree amicably, and respect the right of other Americans to hold views different from theirs. To attack and destroy people whose views are different is not just blatant tyranny; it is dangerous and will eventually backfire. Coercion never works in the long run because it inevitably leads to a backlash.

The cancel culture has rational Americans so concerned that 150 writers and philosophers signed an open letter condemning the concept. The letter was printed in *Harper's Magazine* in July, 2020. The 150 signatories represent both ends of the political spectrum and all points in between.[15] Here are a few lines from the letter: "We uphold the value of robust and even caustic counter-speech from all quarters. But it is now all too common to hear calls for swift and severe retribution in response to perceived transgressions of speech and thought. . . . Editors are fired for running controversial pieces; books are withdrawn for alleged inauthenticity; journalists are barred from writing on certain topics; professors are investigated for quoting works of literature in class . . ."[16]

Ironically, when they were vociferously attacked, becoming victims of the cancel culture they wrote about, some of those who signed the open letter recanted. This shows how powerful the cancel culture has become, as well as how weak some of its opponents are. One signatory who stood up to the attacks was author J. K. Rowling of Harry Potter fame. In the face of pressure and attacks, Rowling responded, "I was very proud to sign this letter in defence of a foundational principle of a liberal society: open debate and freedom of thought and speech."[17] Rowling makes a good point. Democrats and liberals used to be outspoken advocates of open debate, free speech, and diverse opinions.

Ironically, this cancel-culture mentality says, "If you aren't with us completely, you are the enemy" inevitably sets adherents of the same cause against one another. In August 2020, Meyers Leonard of the Miami Heat professional basketball team stood with his hand over his heart during the national anthem while other members of his team knelt. Those kneeling did so in support of the Black Lives Matter (BLM) movement. Meyers was not rejecting BLM. Rather, he was standing for the anthem of the country his brother was then serving as a United States Marine. At the time of this incident, Leonard's brother had already served two tours in Afghanistan.[18] His gesture did not mean black lives don't matter; it meant the lives of warriors such as his brother matter too, and the flag under which they serve should be respected.

Leonard was clearly troubled by the moral dilemma the situation presented. On the one hand, he understood and supported the grievances of his teammates who were kneeling in support of BLM.

On the other hand, he did not want to show disrespect for military personnel, his brother included, who put their lives on the line defending the freedoms America's national anthem symbolizes. Leonard could not understand the if-you-don't-kneel-you-are-against-us attitude he was confronted with; nor could he understand why the world had to be divided between black and white. There are a lot of Americans on the Left, in the middle, and on the right who feel the same way. Unfortunately, many of them have been intimidated into silence by the cancel culture.

Bullying, intimidation, and persecution can be effective at suppressing free speech and thought in the short run. For example, as of this writing 62 percent of Americans claim they are afraid to disclose their political views.[19] Those who are afraid to speak up are not just conservatives or Christians. The 62 percent also includes moderate Democrats who fear retribution from the extreme Left wing of their own party. But the end of this story has yet to be written. History has shown bullying, intimidation, and persecution eventually result in blowback. For example, in 2020 China's bullying of Hong Kong led to massive protests covered by the media throughout the world. This coverage embarrassed the Chinese Communist Party.

Closer to home, when the American colonists finally had their fill of being bullied by King George III of England, they decided to do something about it. Eventually, they engaged in and won the war for independence from Great Britain. King George III lost his most important colony. Almost two centuries later, in the American South, when black Americans finally tired of being browbeaten, segregated, and even lynched, a they fought back. It took the form of the civil rights movement, which resulted in legislation that changed the social, cultural, and political environment of an entire nation.

Much of the success of the civil rights movement can be attributed to the fact that it grew out of the church and was nonviolent in nature. There is a lesson in this for advocates of the cancel culture: in the long run nonviolent dissent based on universal truths will win more hearts and minds than strong-arming and harassment. Here's a second lesson: history has shown that violent sociopolitical movements inevitably turn on themselves and the members attack each other. For example, without the groundbreaking work of Leon Trotsky, there never would have been a Soviet Union. Yet Stalin turned on his fellow Bolshevik and had him killed. This kind of internecine warfare is the norm for these kinds of groups, not the exception.

REJECT MOB VIOLENCE AND SUPPORT THE POLICE

In the wake of George Floyd's tragic death in 2020 at the hands of a rogue police officer, outside agitators hijacked peaceful demonstrations in several major U.S. cities and quickly transformed them into violent riots carried out by destructive mobs. Arson, looting, and physical violence against law-abiding citizens, the police, businesses, and private property became widespread. Hundreds of businesses were either shut down or burned out by the mobs. In several cities, as incredible as this sounds, Democratic city officials actually sided with the violent rioters while condemning the police who were trying to quell the violence.

A VETERAN SPEAKS UP

The mob violence, riots, arson, looting, shootings, and criminal behavior seen in some of America's larger cities reminded one veteran of why the Founders included the Second Amendment in the Bill of Rights:

> *The Founders wrote the Second Amendment not to grant a right, but to reiterate a God-given right of all American citizens. While there is plenty to discuss on both sides of the Second Amendment debate, few of us if given the choice of being trampled, beaten, or burned out by a violent mob or having loved ones or neighbors subjected to the same fate would argue against the right to bear arms in defense of home and family.*

—Kenneth Geis, United States Army 1979–1982

Geis is a firearms and firearms safety instructor certified by the National Rifle Association.

This kind of destructive behavior soon became a common reaction to anything that riled chronically angry groups funded by outside sources bent on destroying the United States. Those who foment riots, arson, looting, and other forms of violent conduct seem determined to find new reasons for wreaking havoc on our cities. One reason agitators and their choleric minions were prepared to riot was the Donald Trump/Joe Biden presidential election in November 2020. As the results were being tallied, mobs positioned themselves and their weapons in several cities and were ready to riot should Trump be declared the winner. Their perspective on the election was, in essence: *Our candidate wins or we'll burn these cities down.*

Beginning in 2020, when mobs that demanded police departments in such cities as Seattle, Portland, Chicago, and New York be defunded, Left-wing city officials actually complied. Seeing they no longer had the support of city officials, veteran police officers in these cities resigned or retired in droves. The funding cuts to police departments—more than a billion dollars in New York City alone—coupled with the mass exodus of officers, Left citizens in these cities defenseless against violent mobs bent on looting, arson, robbery, and other thuggish deeds. Predictably, crime in these poorly led cities skyrocketed.

For example, in Chicago—a city already known for gun violence—the already high homicide numbers increased dramatically overnight, and tragically, those numbers included innocent children caught in the crossfire of hoodlums empowered by reductions in the police force. That elected officials in these major America cities would side with violent thugs, looters, and arsonists while condemning the police, many of whom were injured trying to restore order and protect citizens, is unconscionable. On the other hand, it demonstrates what can be expected when socialist ideologues are elected to political office.

Even worse than the weak local officials in these cities are national political candidates and elected officials in the Democratic Party who refused to condemn the violence and speak out in favor of law and order or even basic human decency. When asked directly if he would condemn the violence engulfing several major cities at the time—cities governed by members of his party—then presidential candidate Joe Biden not only refused to do so, but blamed the police. Only after his finger-pointing at the police caused his polling numbers to dip did he offer a half-hearted condemnation of mob violence in general while carefully avoiding specific situations and cities. For making what was at best a tepid response, Biden was condemned by far-Left radicals in the Democratic Party. His response demonstrates how far socialist ideologues have pushed the Democratic Party to the Left.

The Founders would be shocked at what is happening in some of America's larger cities, but they would be even more aghast at the inept and cowardly responses of socialist ideologues masquerading as municipal leaders in these cities. The responses of these misleaders amounted to aiding and abetting in criminal behavior. City officials who stood by and did nothing while businesses were burned, property was destroyed, and lives were lost should be held criminally liable for their lack of action. They should go to jail right beside the leaders of the mobs who committed the violent acts.

At the very least, citizens whose lives were destroyed or irreparably harmed by the actions or inaction of Leftist city officials should demand the right to sue those officials for damages. The number one duty of any elected official at any level of government is to protect the citizens he or she represents. The governors, mayors, and city councils in Portland, Seattle, Chicago, and New York failed miserably in their duty to protect the citizens of their cities. This is why we encourage you to support only those elected officials and political candidates at all levels of government who will openly and without hesitation condemn mob violence and support law enforcement professionals tasked with keeping the peace.

DEMAND TRANSPARENT ELECTIONS WHERE ONLY LEGAL VOTES ARE COUNTED

The Constitution gives state legislatures the power to determine how elections are conducted in the respective states. This being the case, a number of state legislatures have a lot of work to do. In the wake of the 2020 presidential election, numerous charges of voter fraud were alleged by the Trump campaign. A number of these cases went to court. A summary of the types of voter-fraud allegations made included false registrations, impersonation at the polls, duplicate voting, illegal assistance at the polls, ineligible voting (including votes cast by dead people), altering the vote count, and ballot-petition fraud (forging signatures).

In addition to these allegations, other irregularities were noted including supervisors of elections refusing to follow the law in allowing observers at the polls, sending out unsolicited ballots without determining if the recipients were still alive, supervisors of elections refusing to obey established procedural rules, and extending without authority the deadlines for counting ballots. As a result of these kinds of irregularities in a number of key states, many Americans lost confidence in the process.

A vote of no confidence in the election process is one of the worst things that can happen in any democratic process. Both parties are hurt when voters do not trust that elections are fair and transparent, only legal votes are counted, and ballots are counted on time. If trust in the election process breaks down, trust in our constitutional republic breaks down. What is even worse is the kind of irregularities observed and alleged are all common occurrences in socialist countries. State legislatures have the power to renew trust in the election process before the mid-term elections in 2022. We recommend all Americans in both parties as well as independents urge their state representatives and senators to begin work right now on restoring credibility to the election process and to make doing so their highest priority.

POSTSCRIPT

BIDEN PRESIDENCY: SOCIALIST AMERICA OR BACKLASH IN 2022?

Empires fall from within because of poor leadership or from the influence of outside values and influences. The United States suffers from both. Socialism focuses on the desires of the masses. But with socialism the masses seem always to suffer most. Socialists claim to divide resources equally, but the bulk of the resources always seem to go to a group of elite, powerful individuals and their close associates. Socialism takes over either by force or by voting out Democracy in the name of Democracy (Democratic Socialism). The results are always the same; power collects in the hands of a few and the masses are left out.

—Edward M. Copeland III, MD, United States Army, 1969–1971

Dr. Copeland attended Duke University and Cornell Medical College. Before entering the Army, he completed his surgical training at the Hospital of the University of Pennsylvania. During his time in the military he served at Fort Belvoir, Virginia; Saigon, South Vietnam; and the Surgeon General's Office in Washington, DC. Dr. Copeland spent most of his career as chairman of the Department of Surgery, University of Florida College of Medicine, where he was also a surgeon at the Malcolm Randall

Veterans Administration Hospital in Gainesville, Florida. He was elected by his national peers to be president of the American College of Surgeons and chairman of the American Board of Surgery. He holds the Bronze Star for his service in Vietnam and is a member of the Florida Veterans Hall of Fame (Class of 2019). Disclaimer: The thoughts expressed in Dr. Copeland's quote are his and his alone and do not originate from or reflect the views of any of the institutions or organizations in his biography.

There are several dates in history burned indelibly into the minds and hearts of most Americans. These dates include July 4, 1776, when American colonists declared their independence from Great Britain, December 7, 1941, when the Japanese launched a surprise attack on Pearl Harbor, and September 11, 2001, when terrorists attacked the World Trade Center in New York and the Pentagon in Washington, DC.

We can now add November 3, 2020, and January 5, 2021, to America's list of infamous dates. The former is the date American citizens put a political opportunist controlled by socialists in his party in the White House. That individual, of course, is Joe Biden. The latter is the date the citizens of Georgia gave Democrats control of the U.S. Senate and, in turn, control of the U.S. government. This is like giving the keys to your brand-new car to the town drunk. Socialist ideologues now have an open door for pressing their far-left agenda, a destructive agenda described in detail later in this postscript.

For decades moderates controlled the Democratic Party. The extreme Left, where socialist ideologues reside, was just a fringe element, albeit a persistent and vocal one. Over the years this has been changing. The extreme Left wing of the Democratic Party has been gradually gaining ground. Finally, in the run-up to the 2020 national elections, socialist ideologues took control of the Democratic Party.

They chose Joe Biden as their presidential candidate because he had enjoyed a forty-seven-year career in politics without adhering to any discernible principles. In fact, he had switched positions on the issues so often that his only unbendable principle was a desire to be president. Because of this the Left saw Biden, the opportunist and political chameleon, as the perfect candidate for the Democratic Party: a career politician who could be controlled and manipulated. Socialist ideologues in the Democratic Party saw him as a useful tool for advancing their far-Left agenda.

He quickly proved them right. Biden began his campaign for the Democratic nomination posturing as a moderate who could work with both parties and appeal to independents. But his stance as a moderate quickly evaporated when it became obvious he couldn't win the Democratic nomination without the support of Senator Bernie Sanders and his socialist followers. True to form, Biden quickly dropped the centrist act and adopted most of the socialist platform espoused by Sanders. He then polished his far-Left credentials by naming Kamala Harris—the most liberal politician in the Senate[1]—his vice-presidential running mate.

Taking Harris on as his running mate showed just how bad Biden wanted to be president and that he would do anything to achieve that goal. During the debates in the Democratic primary, Harris shredded him in front of a national television audience. Biden had to swallow a lot of pride to accept her on the ticket. That he did so demonstrates not just his willingness to do anything to be president, but the level of influence the Far Left has on him.

On December 14, 2020, in spite of lingering allegations of voter fraud, the electoral college made it official: Joe Biden would succeed Donald Trump as president of the United States. The Democratic Party—run by Leftist extremists—now controlled the White House and the House of Representatives. On January 5, 2021, they took control of the U.S. Senate following two run-off elections in Georgia. When Biden was sworn in as president, the Democrats needed only make good on their threat to stack the Supreme Court to control all three branches of government. The Far Left finally has what it dreamed of for decades: an open door for socialism.

As previously stated, of all the leaders of the Democratic Party, only Bernie Sanders is willing to admit he is a socialist. Biden and Harris, who ran on a platform borrowed from Sanders, steadfastly refuse to acknowledge they are socialists. This is because Biden knows more than seventy million Americans voted against him and his socialist platform. A presidential race the polls and pundits had him winning by a landslide didn't happen. Instead, Biden barely eked out a win in a closer-than-expected race clouded by the possibility of voter fraud. Instead of receiving the expected mandate from voters, Biden became known to many Americans as the "illegitimate president."

Biden knows he has a limited amount of time to move his socialist agenda forward. Come the midterm elections in 2022, he and his fellow Leftists could lose control of the government and their hold on the Democratic Party. Even without all of the clouds hovering over the presidential election, and Joe Biden personally, the party in control of the White House typically loses seats in Congress during midterm elections, and the Democrats have no seats to spare.

THE BIDEN AGENDA: VICTORY FOR SOCIALISTS — DISASTER FOR AMERICANS

Democrats—now controlled by the extreme Left—understand they may have a limited window of opportunity for nailing down their socialist agenda. Not only do they want to rush through Congress their highest-priority socialist programs; they want to alter the election process such that it will be difficult if not impossible for a Republican to ever again be elected president. To these ends, they hope to check off as many items as possible from their list of socialist programs before the 2022 midterm elections. Their high-priority list includes the following actions:

- pass "election reform" (i.e., make mailing out unsolicited ballots a permanent practice, establish automatic voter registration, and abolish the electoral college)
- end the Senate filibuster
- stack the Supreme Court
- "reform" police departments nationwide
- approve statehood for Washington, DC and Puerto Rico
- increase taxes

- open America's borders
- enact Medicare for all (i.e., socialized medicine)
- pass the Green New Deal
- restore the government regulations President Trump eliminated
- support "free" college tuition for all and student-debt forgiveness
- reduce military spending
- restrict religious liberty
- renounce President Trump's "America First" approach to international trade deals.

Pass "election reform"

By "election reform," Democrats really mean systematizing the fraudulent practices that served them so well in the 2020 presidential campaign. These corrupt practices allowed for more than 100 percent voter turnout in numerous districts; votes cast by dead people; mail-in votes counted before mail-in ballots were even sent out; counting votes that came in after the lawful deadline; the use of computer systems that erred, but always in favor of Joe Biden; and denying access to legally authorized poll watchers. In other words, the Democrats want to be able to systematically and legally manipulate vote counts as opposed to relying on the ham-fisted methods they used in the 2020 election.

End the Senate filibuster

Perhaps the biggest impediment Democrats face in trying to ram their socialist agenda through Congress is the Senate filibuster. The filibuster requires a vote of sixty senators in order to move proposed legislation forward. With a razor-thin majority in the Senate, the Democrats are not likely to get the sixty votes needed to move forward on any socialist programs they propose. This is why they desperately want to eliminate the filibuster and replace it with a simple majority vote of fifty-one. Of course, the danger here is if

Democrats lose their majority in the Senate in subsequent elections, Republicans can turn the tables on them and use the simple-majority rule to their benefit.

Stack the Supreme Court

Thanks to appointments by Donald Trump, the U.S. Supreme Court is the only branch of the federal government not controlled by the extreme Left, at least not yet. As things stand now, Republicans can count on cases coming before the Supreme Court being heard by five justices who subscribe to the "originalist philosophy" of Constitutional interpretation. This is a major stumbling block for socialist ideologues in the Democratic Party who need justices who subscribe to the "living Constitution" philosophy. Only if a majority of the court is willing to engage in judicial usurpation and legislate from the bench are socialists going to be able to completely control the government and, in turn, the people.

The Democrats' solution to this dilemma is called "court packing" or "court stacking," the process of increasing the number of justices beyond the nine that has been the norm since 1869. We use the latter term because most Americans understand what it means to "stack the deck" in one's favor, which is precisely what the Democrats intend with court stacking. Article III, Section 1 of the Constitution allows Congress to decide how many justices will compose the Supreme Court. With control of the Senate, the Democrats can arrive at any number of justices they wish and fill the new seats with anyone they wish.

The additional seats, of course, are to be filled with Leftist judges the Democrats can count on to support their socialist agenda. In other words, the new seats will be filled by judges who view the Constitution as a pliable document they can change according to the whims of the Democratic Party. A properly stacked court, from the Democrats' perspective, would give them an advantage for decades to come, if not forever.

Joe Biden and Kamala Harris have attempted to justify court stacking by claiming the Republicans are guilty of the practice. They claim that by Republicans' recommending conservative judges for Senate confirmation whenever a seat on the court is vacant, they are guilty of stacking the court. This assertion is not just lame; it's absurd. It's one more example of the kind of deception associated with the political Left in America. When in control of the Senate, both parties have long nominated individuals they believe adhere to their view of what makes a good Supreme Court justice. This is how vacancies on the court have been filled from the beginning. To do otherwise would be foolish. But this is not court stacking. Stacking the court occurs only when Congress increases the number of justices for the specific purpose of creating an unbreakable majority.

"Reform" police departments nationwide

In the aftermath of George Floyd's police-involved death in 2020, strident calls for defunding the police became the norm in big cities controlled by Democratic mayors. The most vocal proponent of defunding police departments is the Black Lives Matter organization. The extreme Left of the Democratic Party took up the banner for defunding the police, and it quickly became an issue in the national elections of 2020.

As is typical of him, Joe Biden stuck his finger in the air and went where he thought the political winds were blowing: he joined the defund-the-police crowd, at least in the beginning. Biden blamed the police for the riots, arson, and looting taking place in big cities controlled by members of his party. Then when it became obvious the defund-the-police movement was a political liability, Biden did what he has done for all of his forty-seven years in politics: he switched positions. Biden has a long history of making U-turns on issues and has no qualms about doing so. When the only principle you believe in is political expedience, taking one position today and the opposite tomorrow is not a problem.

Although Biden backed away from openly supporting the defund-the-police movement, he still refused to show strong support for police or to condemn the leaders of the big-city riots, as noted earlier. Instead, he became an overnight proponent of "police reform." Don't be misled by this political ruse. Waving the banner of "police reform" instead of chanting, "Defund the police" is the Democrats' way of pandering to the Far Left without risking pushback from the majority of Americans, who want law and order and who support the police. "Police reform" is just a euphemism Democrats use with a wink and a nod to let the extreme Left know they support efforts to handcuff police departments nationwide.

There is a civil war raging within the Democratic Party over the defund-the-police movement. The battle is between the extreme Left, led by the Black Lives Matter organization, and moderate Democrats, who attribute the Party's unexpected losses in the House of Representatives races of 2020 to the defund-the-police movement and the Democrats' socialist agenda. Under Biden and Harris, the Democrats are trying to have it both ways on this issue by quietly supporting efforts to defund the police—efforts well underway—while publicly calling for "police reform." Thirteen major Democrat-controlled cities have already made major cuts to their law enforcement budgets.

Here are a few of the police departments defunded already in Democrat-controlled cities, without a word of opposition or even a word of caution from Joe Biden:[2]

- Austin, Texas—an island of socialism in an otherwise conservative state—voted to reduce its law-enforcement budget by $150 million and use those funds for expanding access to abortion and expanding various social programs. So, if you are the victim of a home invasion in Austin, you may not be able to get any help from the police but you will be able to get an abortion
- Seattle, Washington, announced a $3.5 million cut in its law enforcement budget and the diversion of an additional $17 million into other programs. As a result, Seattle's police chief, an outstanding law enforcement professional with twenty-eight years of experience in the department, resigned
- New York City cut $1 billion from its law enforcement budget, reallocating $354 million of it to mental health, homelessness,

and education. Now New Yorkers can no longer count on police protection when confronted by criminals. However, there is one consolation for citizens of the Big Apple. New Yorkers traumatized by violent crime will now have greater access to counseling

- It should come as no surprise California leads the way in defunding its police. Los Angeles approved a $150 million reduction to its law enforcement budget, San Francisco nearly matched its neighbor to the south with a $120 million reduction, and Oakland followed suit with a cut of $14.6 million. These cities—already known for their crime rates—can now look forward to even more crime

- Washington, DC, well-known for its unenviable crime rate, cut its police budget by $15 million.

Cuts to law enforcement budgets are good news for criminals. Every dollar cut from a police budget is an open invitation for lawbreakers to murder, rob, steal, sell drugs, burn, and loot without fear of interference. Not surprisingly, wherever police budgets are cut, crime rates increase. Ironically, the higher the crime rates go in American cities, the more likely it becomes that Biden and the Democrats will face a backlash in the midterm elections of 2022.

Approve statehood for Washington, DC and Puerto Rico

When asked their rationale for wanting to grant statehood to Washington, DC, and Puerto Rico, Democrats respond that both deserve equal protection in Congress. One can only wonder how concerned Democrats would be about this issue if DC and Puerto Rico were Republican strongholds. There is just one reason Democrats want statehood for these two entities: both are reliably Democratic in their voting.

Statehood for Washington, DC, and Puerto Rico would create two new Senate seats from each, and all four would probably be controlled by Democrats. Were this not the case, Democrats would

never have raised the issue in the first place. The House of Representatives would also pick up seats from statehood. Washington,
DC, would receive one seat in the House, while Puerto Rico would
receive four. However, the total number of seats in the House of
Representatives would in all likelihood remain the same: 435. This
means several of the existing fifty states would have to give up seats
in the House.

The existing states that would lose seats in this scenario are
Florida, Texas, Montana, Illinois, and New York. The case Demo-
crats make for granting statehood to Washington, DC, and Puerto
Rico is riddled with hypocrisy. Making them states is not about
equal protection; it's about ensuring future election victories for
Democrats in the House, Senate, and White House. With this goal
in mind, Joe Biden has long been an advocate of statehood for
Washington, DC. Because Donald Trump did so well among
Latino voters in the 2020 presidential election, Biden's support of
Puerto Rican statehood can also be counted on.

Increase taxes

George H. W. Bush got himself in political hot water by stating,
"Read my lips—no new taxes," and then supporting new taxes. Joe
Biden won't have this problem. He has openly declared his intention to raise taxes. To ward off pushback from voters, Biden has
claimed his tax increases will apply only to households earning
more than $400,000 per year and to businesses. Unfortunately, as
is often the case with Biden and the Democratic Party, this claim
is just another example of Leftist deception, a ruse to make his tax
hikes seem less onerous.

The majority of Americans don't earn $400,000 per year, nor
do they own a business. Consequently, when they hear the thresh-
old for tax increases is set at $400,000 per year, they sigh in relief
and think, *No problem—that doesn't include me.* Unfortunately, many
of them are wrong. There are a lot of Americans who earn well
under the $400,000 threshold whose taxes will increase under the
Biden plan. The Democrats—aided and abetted by the mainstream
media—are so accustomed to getting away with their deceptions

they actually believe they can get away with increasing taxes on unsuspecting Americans without being caught. All it's going to take to reveal the lie in Biden's promise is one round of filings on April 15 following passage of the tax hikes.

One of the mainstays of Biden's tax-increase plan is repeal of the Tax Cuts and Jobs Act (TCJA) passed by congressional Republicans and President Donald Trump. If the TCJA is repealed, as the Democrats have promised it will be, here is what will happen:[3]

- A family of four earning $73,000 (not $400,000) will see an increase of $2,000 in taxes
- A single parent with one child, earning $41,000 (not $400,000) will see an increase of $1,300 in taxes
- Utility bills in all fifty states will go up because of the increase to corporate income taxes. This is just one of the inconvenient facts Biden and his fellow Democrats neglect to tell American voters when they claim their proposed tax increases apply mostly to "big corporations." When big corporations are forced to pay higher taxes, they pass those new expenses on to their customers in the form of higher prices and higher rates
- Small businesses, which account for 80 percent of the new jobs created in America, will see a major tax increase due to the repeal of the 20 percent deduction they now receive. Unable to simply absorb the new expense, small businesses will be forced to raise their prices or lay off employees, or both. This is another of the inconvenient facts Biden and the Democrats fail to mention when they claim most of their tax increases will affect only businesses
- The child tax credit will be cut in half for millions of American families at all income levels (not just those earning more than $400,000)
- The standard deduction that makes filing taxes easier for millions of low-and middle-income families will be cut in half, meaning an increase in taxes for everyone.

When it comes to taxes, Biden and the Democrats would do well to take a page from the playbooks of Presidents Reagan and Trump. Both of these presidents proved the government can increase its income by reducing taxes. The formula is simple: Lower taxes encourage job creation, and more jobs means more people working and paying taxes. Higher taxes lead to a higher unemployment rate with fewer people paying taxes. Further, higher taxes guarantee taxpayers will become smarter and more aggressive in finding ways to avoid taxes.

Socialists have never been able to comprehend the negative correlation between higher taxes and government income. They don't understand that actions have consequences, which is why they are never reluctant to increase tax rates. The consequences of raising taxes are almost always negative while the consequences of lowering taxes are almost always positive. When the increases they enact fail to produce enough revenue to fund their socialist programs—which is always the case—Leftist ideologues simply increase the rates again. This never-ending cycle of tax increases eventually and predictably undermines the economy, and people at all levels of income suffer. This is precisely what happened in Venezuela.

Open America's borders

Before the onset of the COVID-19 pandemic, the biggest and most controversial political issue in America was border security. President Trump and his supporters worked hard to establish control of the borders and to minimize illegal immigration. Democrats, on the other hand, fought hard and deviously to open the borders to all comers. The Democratic Party views immigrants as dependable voters for its candidates at all levels. To ensure this is the case, Democrats advocate for free health care and free college tuition for immigrants who entered the country illegally and who stay here illegally. Opening the borders is a high priority of the Democrats.

Socialize the health-care system

If Joe Biden and the Democrats have a "pet" program, it is "Medicare for All." Not surprisingly, "Medicare for All" is just a deceptive euphemism for socialized medicine, a concept tried in numerous countries with uniformly negative results. All socialized medicine has ever achieved is providing universally poor health care for all.

If Biden and his fellow travelers in Congress pass Medicare for All, physicians will be paid government rates for their services. Experience in other countries has proven over and over again that access to medical care and the quality of that care suffer when this happens. Physicians are people, and people respond to incentives. Perennially low government rates for medical services are a disincentive that will reduce access by reducing the number of people willing to enter or remain in the medical profession.

Government rates will also reduce the quality of care physicians are able to provide. Invariably, government rates result in poorer quality equipment and facilities as well as insufficient staffing. This is not mere speculation but proven fact. Ask veterans who have waited for months to be treated at a Veterans Administration clinic or hospital and then, when finally admitted, received substandard care.

Perhaps the worst aspect of Medicare for All is the rationing of health care. When there is not enough of something to go around, rationing is the typical response. This is why rationed health care is a so widely associated with socialized medicine. In addition, there are limits on what Medicare covers. For example, it does not cover long-term care, eye glasses, hearing aids, or dental care. Hence, Medicare for All amounts to less care provided and at lower quality.

Other known problems with socialized medicine include the likelihood that some hospitals will be forced to shut down, thereby reducing access to medical care. Additionally, people will be less careful with their health because they will mistakenly believe medical care is widely available and free. Finally, physicians will be forced to spend less time with each patient to keep costs within the reimbursement rates specified by the government.

Americans need to understand Medicare for All is not about improving access to health care, nor is it about improving the quality of care. Rather, it is about using the federal treasury to buy votes from Americans who naively think "free" health care is a good idea and to make those Americans dependent wards of the state. In other words, Medicare for All is not about health care; it's about politics. Every socialist ideologue's dream is to have all citizens dependent on the government for their basic needs. Because few things are more basic than health care, Medicare for All is a strategy Joe Biden and the Democrats are using to achieve their socialist goals.

Pass the Green New Deal

Looking back at the $90 billion climate package of the Obama/Biden administration, there should be no question where Joe Biden stands concerning the Green New Deal. Hold that troubling thought for a moment.

No one in Congress is more closely associated with the Green New Deal than Alexandria Ocasio-Cortez, the congresswoman who openly declared she supported Biden for president because she and her fellow extreme Left-wingers could control him. Unfortunately, it appears she was right.

Steven F. Hayward had this to day about the Green New Deal: "Alexandria Ocasio-Cortez's Green New Deal isn't even serious about environmentalism, let alone economics."[4] Like many on the Left, Ocasio-Cortez is ill-informed when it comes to the environment and economics. As a result, any environmental policy they propose is likely to be based on either scientific ignorance or political hubris. Here are just a few of the obvious problems with the Green New Deal Ocasio-Cortez, Joe Biden, and Leftist extremists either conveniently overlook or simply ignore:[5]

- To achieve its stated goal of eliminating the use of fossil fuels in a decade means all forms of power using coal, oil or natural gas will have to be eliminated and replaced with electric engines. These electric engines will have to be powered by either solar or wind. Solar and wind power have shown themselves incapable of supplying even 10 percent of the power needed to heat and cool homes and businesses. Imagine having to rely on them to power airplanes, trucks, cars, and trains. The idea of eliminating fossil fuels is not just nonsensical; it's irresponsible

- A dirty little secret ideologues hide beneath the surface in the Green New Deal debate is the issue of batteries. Forget that the best scientists have been unable to develop batteries that come even close to being able to power airplanes, trains, and cars without the boosting assistance of a hybrid engine running on fossil fuel, disposing of the millions of lithium-ion batteries that would be required by the Green New Deal would create an environmental challenge that dwarfs the issue of fossil fuels

- Advocates of the Green New Deal claim their goal is to reduce carbon emissions. Why then have they targeted nuclear power for elimination? Nuclear power is the largest source of non-carbon energy in the world. Further, if eliminating carbon emissions is really the goal of the New Green Deal, why does it contain components about socialized medicine, guaranteed employment, and ending racism? Achieving all three of these elements of the New Green Deal would have no effect on reducing carbon emissions

- Advocates of the Green New Deal demonstrate their ignorance of economics in a number of ways. Perhaps the worst is they overlook or choose to ignore the fact that eliminating the use of fossil fuels in the United States would drive down the cost of oil to unprecedented levels worldwide. With the resulting glut of cheap oil readily available, developing nations would increase their use of fossil fuels substantially in an attempt to modernize. The world's carbon footprint would increase in size almost overnight.

These are just a few of the problems Green New Dealers refuse to acknowledge, much less discuss. Nor will they discuss several realistic options for reducing carbon emissions, including nuclear power, carbon-capture technologies, or solar-radiation management. Why? Because the Green New Deal is about politics, not the environment.

Restore the government regulations President Trump eliminated

The COVID-19 pandemic changed everything, but before that crisis occurred, Donald Trump had given America the most robust economy it had enjoyed in decades. One of the tools he used for stimulating job growth, business expansion, and technological innovation was the executive order, whereby he eliminated onerous regulations that had handcuffed the private sector for decades.

On January 30, 2017, President Trump signed Executive Order 13771, titled, "Reducing Regulation and Controlling Regulatory Costs." The most significant aspect of this executive order is found in Section 1 of the document: "It is essential to manage the costs associated with the governmental imposition of private expenditures required to comply with federal regulations. Toward that end, it is important that for every one new regulation issued, at least two prior regulations be identified for elimination, and that the cost of planned regulations be prudently managed and controlled through a budgeting process."[6]

Because the cost of regulatory compliance adds twenty cents to every dollar businesses spend, reducing regulations reduced the cost of doing business for private-sector organizations. That's important because there are basically three ways to improve a business organization's bottom line: (1) increase sales volume, (2) reduce operating costs or (3) do both. Reducing regulations helped businesses achieve the second of these strategies. This, in turn, allowed businesses to invest in innovations and improvements that led to job growth, innovation, and increased sales volume.

Joe Biden's views on government regulation differ drastically from Donald Trump's. Biden is a creature of "the swamp." He has spent his entire career in Washington, DC, insulated from the everyday realities of most Americans, particularly businesses. Consequently, he views government regulations not as a hindrance to commerce and competitiveness but as good things. Hence, he can be expected to use his presidential power to give free rein to unelected bureaucrats to once again engage in their favorite pastime: the promulgation of government regulations negatively impacting the lives of all Americans.

Support "free" college tuition and student-debt forgiveness

Not surprisingly, 63 percent of American adults support "free" college tuition for all students. The idea has broad appeal, particularly among parents who have college-age children as well as among college-age students. But like so many policies proposed by the Left, "free" college tuition is a policy that comes wrapped in a soft, warm blanket of deception. "Free" college tuition is anything but free. The cost of "free" tuition in 2021 dollars amounts to more than $600 billion annually, a cost passed on to working Americans in the form of increased taxes.

Until college tuition is "free," the Democrats want to "forgive" student debt. Biden is on the record supporting student-debt forgiveness. Forgiveness is one of those concepts that appeals broadly because we have all needed it at times. Forgiving people is more than a good thing in our culture; it's a biblical admonition. But unlike biblical forgiveness, student-debt forgiveness means passing the cost of bad financial decisions along to somebody else—in this case, the American taxpayer. This is not forgiveness; it's transference. The cost of "forgiveness" that would be transferred to American taxpayers is more than $300 billion annually, and this is just the monetary cost. The cost of rewarding irresponsible behavior is even worse.

The United States is already running a $24 trillion budget deficit, a deficit that exceeds our gross national product. Our country is like a citizen whose credit-card debt exceeds his or her annual income. Joe Biden has plans for $11 trillion in new spending, and this does not include the enormous costs of the Green New Deal. Although his planned tax increases are exorbitant, they don't come close to paying for all the new spending he has planned. Adding the cost of "free" college tuition and student-debt forgiveness to the mix just ups the ante concerning how much more working Americans will be forced to pay in taxes.

There is some consolation in Biden's Leftist agenda, sad though it is. The U.S. Treasury will probably go broke before Biden and company are able to implement "free" college tuition for all and student-debt forgiveness. Biden is like the garrulous but ne'er-do-well uncle who is deep in debt and earns only minimum wage but tries to buy the affection of his nieces and nephews by promising to take them to Disney World, buy them each a new car, pay their college tuition, and give them an ample allowance for life. The losers in this situation are the nieces and nephews who believe his empty promises. The losers in Biden's America are the citizens who believe his empty promises.

Reduce military spending

To discern Joe Biden's plans for military spending, one need only look at what happened to it during the Obama/Biden administration: "National security spending includes the Pentagon's budget as well as spending by other agencies, like the Department of Energy's work on nuclear weapons. On the whole, spending increased in 2010 and 2011, but decreased [thereafter] every year for four straight years by a cumulative total of 15%. . . . In 2010, national security spending made up 21.1% of the federal budget, but in 2015 it was roughly 15.9%."[7]

In other words, soon after taking office, Obama and Biden began cutting military spending. We can expect the same thing to happen during the Biden administration as he and his fellow travelers on the Left look for ways to fund their ever-growing list of socialist programs. The socialist ideologues who control the Democratic Party like to claim the United States can afford to reduce its spending on the military because we are now in a post-9/11 and post–Soviet Union environment. The truth is, military superiority and preparedness have never been more important to the survival of the United States. We face greater threats to our national security now than ever before, threats from Iran, North Korea, China, and Russia.

China has increased its military spending more than 650 percent since the 1990s and is determined to overtake the United States economically and militarily. Joe Biden's socialist programs play right into the hands of the Chinese Communist Party. Russia remains a threat in both the Middle East and Europe. A nuclear-armed North Korea controlled by an unpredictable megalomaniac is close to developing missiles that can deliver warheads to any location on earth, including the entire United States. Finally, Iran continues to support international terrorism aimed primarily at the United States, and will eventually follow in North Korea's footsteps with nuclear weapons.[8]

The leaders in China, Russia, North Korea, and Iran know more about our military budget than do most Americans. They know when the military's budget is cut as well as how much is spent on research and development, new technologies, personnel, weapons, maintenance, repair, manufacturing, construction, deployments, and every other aspect of the defense budget. Cuts in any of these areas are viewed as a sign of weakness that just emboldens our enemies. For Biden and his fellow travelers on the Left to cut military spending is not just irresponsible, it's unconscionable.

Restrict religious liberty

Leftists in America have been waging war on Christianity for decades. The Supreme Court's decisions in 1962 and 1963 banning school-sponsored prayer and Bible reading in public schools emboldened anti-Christian ideologues, and their attacks on Christianity have been relentless ever since. In 2020 they began to opportunistically use the COVID-19 pandemic to shut down churches, claiming the closings were required in the interest of public safety. But the fact that Leftist governors and mayors allowed bars, liquor stores, strip clubs, and abortion clinics to remain open while churches were closed belied their public safety claim.

Let us be clear on this issue. Our nation was founded by Christians and built on Christian values. Half of the signers of the Declaration of Independence held seminary degrees. "The Pilgrims came for one purpose, which they spelled out in writing: 'for the glory of God and the advancement of the Christian faith.'"[9] This is why the very first amendment included in the Bill of Rights ensures religious liberty. Nevertheless, not to be dissuaded by the Constitution, Leftist extremists have done everything they can to remove Christianity from Americans' lives.

The war on Christianity continues, and Joe Biden can be counted on to side with the extreme Left of his party in carrying it out. Don't be fooled by his words about religious liberty. Rather, observe his actions. When it is politically expedient to do so, Biden claims to be a Catholic. He is adept at saying all of the right things about religion when he is backed into a corner on the issue, but his actions tell a different story. The Catholic Church—not to mention the Bible—strongly opposes abortion, and yet Joe Biden is well-known for his support of this contemptible procedure.

He attempts to have it both ways by claiming he wouldn't support an abortion personally but doesn't think his religion should stand in the way of others choosing to have one. This, of course, is a politically expedient cop-out, and a lame one at that. One could just as easily adopt the same mushy-headed stance on murder, stealing, and lying, not to mention accepting millions of dollars of unearned money from an enemy country. Under Biden, secular humanist, atheist, and agnostic ideologues will have a free hand to continue their assault on Christians and Christianity.

Renounce President Trump's "America-first" approach to international trade and diplomacy

Donald Trump made it clear during his first presidential campaign that if elected, he would ensure America came first in trade negotiations and international diplomacy. He leaned on the other NATO nations to pay their fair share of the cost of defending Europe, defunded the World Health Organization when it became obvious it was nothing but a pawn for Communist China, said no to nations hoping to use the climate debate to undermine America's economy, renounced the disastrous Iran nuclear deal put in place by Obama/Biden—a deal Iran was violating every day, and used tariffs to level the heavily skewed playing field with China on trade. Trump's America-first approach to international trade and diplomacy upset a lot of countries who were accustomed to taking money from America with one hand while slapping us in the face with the other.

Joe Biden made it clear from the outset of his presidential campaign that America won't be first under his administration. Donald Trump commanded respect from our enemies and allies, but Joe Biden appears to be more concerned with being liked by them than respected. Even before taking office, he was cozying up to countries that hate the United States as well as allies who are accustomed to exploiting us for their benefit.

Unlike Donald Trump, Joe Biden does not appear to understand his most important responsibility as president is protecting the American people. This is why the Chinese, Russian, Iranian, and North Korean governments are delighted to have Joe Biden in the White House. To the extreme Left of the Democratic Party, Biden is a useful tool. To our allies and enemies, he is a useful fool.

WHY BIDEN CANNOT UNITE AMERICA WITH HIS SOCIALIST AGENDA

Even before the electoral college made the 2020 election results official, Joe Biden was portraying himself as the president who could unite our divided nation. He even made the cover of a major magazine that claimed in bold letters Biden would unite all Americans. That Biden sees himself as a president who can unite our divided nation shows how out of touch he really is. As one of the veterans we surveyed said, it would be difficult to find a president less equipped to unite America than Biden.

We don't believe Biden eventually prevailed in the presidential election of 2020 because of his socialist agenda, but rather in spite of it. The losses suffered by Democrats in the House races support our contention. Not only did more than seventy million Americans reject Biden's agenda by voting for Donald Trump, but his own party is split over the issue of socialism. Moderates, upset at the trouncing the Democrats took in the House races in 2020, blame socialist ideologues in their party for the losses. "The setbacks prompted accusations from moderates that the party's prominent liberals, such as New York Rep. Alexandria Ocasio Cortez, had become representative of a party foreign to America's farming and small manufacturing towns."[10]

To conclude this postscript, we offer several reasons why Joe Biden cannot unite a divided America and why his socialist agenda will further divide our country. Ironically, the harder Biden pushes the socialist agenda he borrowed from Bernie Sanders, the likelier a backlash against the Democratic Party becomes in the 2022 midterm elections. This is the dilemma Biden and the Democrats now face. Democrats know they have only a brief window of opportunity before the midterm elections in 2022 to move as much of their socialist agenda through Congress as possible. Yet the harder they push their agenda, the more likely they, too, can expect a midterm backlash. In the meantime, Joe Biden's claims that he will heal our divided nation become even less credible.

To unite our divided nation, a president must be trusted. More than seventy million Americans don't trust Joe Biden. One of the reasons for this is he ran for president under a cloud of suspicion. Allegations that he used his position as vice president to feather his son's nest—as well as his own—with millions of dollars from questionable sources have yet to be answered. Adding to the cloud of suspicion is the fact that Biden went from being the self-proclaimed poorest man in the U.S. Senate to a multimillionaire as vice president and has yet to explain where the money came from. Just as Democrats demand access to Donald Trump's tax records, Republicans should demand access to Biden's financial records. Biden will never be trusted without coming clean concerning how he suddenly and inexplicably became wealthy.

To unite our divided nation, a president must be respected. Biden has demonstrated over and over he is unworthy of respect because he lacks any fixed principles or beliefs. He has no qualms about changing positions several times a day depending on what group he is speaking to. Biden's only fixed principles appear to be political expedience and personal ambition. Biden wanted to be president, and he was willing to go to any length to achieve that goal.

To unite our divided nation, a president must be viewed as a strong individual who puts the best interests of America and its citizens first. Biden is viewed by more than seventy million Americans as a weak politician who puts being liked on the international stage ahead of the interests of Americans. He is also viewed by many as a compromised president who may be beholden to China in ways that make him their puppet. As one of the veterans surveyed for this book commented, any overtures Biden makes to China and any jobs lost to that country will just increase the suspicions many Americans harbor that he is a compromised president.

To unite our divided nation, a president must put forth a platform viewed as serving the best interests of all Americans, or at the very least, most Americans. Biden is viewed by more than seventy million Americans as a politically malleable weakling, a puppet with a borrowed socialist platform who can be manipulated by the extreme Left of the Democratic Party. Many believe he was coerced by his own party into adopting a political platform that is not only bad for those who voted against him but also for those who voted for him.

More than seventy million Americans rejected the socialist agenda Biden borrowed from Bernie Sanders during the 2020 presidential election by voting for Donald Trump. The seventy million–plus who voted for Biden did so because of the COVID-19 pandemic, Trump's self-acknowledged caustic personality, the unrelenting attacks on Trump by the mainstream media, purposely biased political polls, and ignorance born out of years of indoctrination, not because they buy into socialism. Many who voted for Biden know little to nothing about socialism; they don't know what it is, what it isn't, and what it will do to them and our country. Unfortunately, with Leftist ideologues now in control of the government, they are about to find out. What will be interesting is to see how fast Biden's supporters turn on him and the Democratic Party once they begin to feel the negative effects of socialism.

NOTES

INTRODUCTION

1. Winston Churchill, speech in the House of Commons, October 22, 1945, WinstonChurchill.org, accessed April 8, 2021, https://winstonchurchill. org/resources/quotes/vice-of-capitalism/.
2. Lydia Saad, "Socialism as Popular as Capitalism among Young Adults in U.S.," Gallup, November 25, 2019, https://news.gallup.com/poll/268766/ socialism-popular-capitalism-among-young-adults.aspx.
3. Hannah Hartig, "Stark Partisan Divisions in Americans' Views of 'Socialism', 'Capitalism,'" *Fact Tank* (Pew Research Center blog), June 25, 2019, https:// www.pewresearch.org/fact-tank/2019/06/25/stark-partisan-divisions-in-americans-views-of-socialism-capitalism/.
4. Megan Brenan, "American Pride Hits New Low; Few Proud of Political System," Gallup, July 2, 2019, https://news.gallup.com/poll/259841/ american-pride-hits-new-low-few-proud-political-system.aspx.
5. Brenan.
6. Transcript of Ronald Reagan's Farewell Address to the American People, January 12, 1989, New York Times Archives, https://www.nytimes. com/1989/01/12/news/transcript-of-reagan-s-farewell-address-to-american-people.html.

CHAPTER 1

1. Gerald R. Ford, in an address to a Joint Session of Congress, August 12, 1974, Gerald R. Ford Presidential Library and Museum website, accessed April 9, 2021, https://www.fordlibrarymuseum.gov/grf/quotes.asp.

2. William Howard Taft, quoted in Marlene Rimler, *Great Words from Our Presidents* (Woodbridge, IL: Great Quotations, 2005), 13.

3. William Bradford, *Bradford's History of Plymouth Plantation: 1606–1646*, ed. William T. Davis (New York: Charles Scribner's Sons, 1920), 146.

4. David Barton, *Exceptional: America's Keys to Greatness* (Aledo, TX: Wallbuilders, 2004).

5. See Wikipedia, s.v. "Constitution of France," https://en.wikipedia.org/wiki/Constitution_of_France; and "Constitutional History of Germany," Constitution.net, https://constitutionnet.org/country/constitutional-history-germany, both accessed accessed April 9, 2021.

6. Albert P. Blaustein, "Influence of the American Constitution Abroad," Encyclopedia.com, 1986, https://www.encyclopedia.com/politics/encyclopedias-almanacs-transcripts-and-maps/influence-american-constitution-abroad.

7. David C. Gibbs, III and Barbara J. Weller. UNDERSTANDING THE CONSTITUTION, (National Center for Life and Liberty: Flower Mound, Texas), 2014, pp. 25-29.

CHAPTER 2

1. Arifa Akbar, "Great Leap Forward 'Killed 45 Million in Four Years,'" *Independent* (UK), October 23, 2011, https://independent.co.uk/arts-entertainment/books/news/maos-great-leap-forward-killed-45-million-in-four-years-2081630.html.

2. Andrew Henderson, "Pol Pot's Killing Fields and the Progression of Overnment Tyranny," Nomad Capitalist, last updated December 30, 2019, https://nomadcapitalist.com/2013/09/11/pol-pot-killing-fields-and-the-progression-of-government-tyranny/.

3. Bret Stephens, "Yes, Venezuela Is a Socialist Catastrophe," *New York Times*, January 25, 2019, https://www.nytimes.com/2019/01/25/opinion/venezuela-maduro-socialism-government.html.

4. Roberto González and Liza Gellerman, "Venezuela: Economic Collapse and Tyranny Were Predictable," *National Review*, April 30, 2019, https://nationalreview.com/2019/04/venezuela-tyranny-economic-collapse-predictable/.

CHAPTER 3

1. Paul, Rand. THE CASE AGAINST SOCIALISM, BROADSIDE BOOKS, an imprint of Harper Collins Publishers, 2019, 190–193.
2. Rose Fitzgerald Kennedy, *Times to Remember* (New York: Doubleday, 1974), 29.
3. Kennedy, 30.
4. Kennedy, 30.

CHAPTER 4

1. This veteran was referring to the "tithe," a mandatory contribution of one-tenth of their wealth that God required from the ancient Israelites. (See Leviticus 27:28–33.) Many churches teach that the tithe is still required of Christians today.

CHAPTER 5

1. Bao Ruo-wang (Jean Pasqualini) and Rudolph Chelminski, *Prisoner of Mao* (New York: Coward, McCann & Geoghegan, 1975).
2. Ruo-wang and Chelminski, 27–35.
3. Ruo-wang and Chelminski, 58–63.
4. Newt Gingrich, *Rediscovering God in America: Reflections on the Role of Faith in our Nation's History and Future* (Nashville: Integrity House, 2006).
5. Gingrich, 81.
6. Gingrich, 2.
7. Gingrich, 39.
8. Gingrich, 54.
9. Gingrich, 44.
10. Gingrich, 45.
11. David Barton, America's Godly Heritage, 3rd ed. (Aledo, TX: Wallbuilder Press, 2017), 4–9.

12. Barton, 4–5.

13. Barton, 17.

14. Barton, 21.

15. Barton, 21.

16. Richard Dawkins, *The God Delusion* (Boston: Houghton-Mifflin, 2006), 27.

17. Christopher Hitchens, *God Is Not Great: How Religion Poisons Everything* (New York: Twelve, 2007), 36.

18. Sam Harris, *The End of Faith: Religion, Terror, and the Future of Reason* (New York: W. W. Norton, 2005), 72.

CHAPTER 6

1. Alexis de Tocqueville, *Democracy in America* (New York: Bantam Books, 2000), 9–15.

2. Ford, address to joint session of Congress (see chap. 1, n. 1).

3. M. R. R. Ossewaarde, *Tocqueville's Moral and Political Thought: New Liberalism* (London: Routledge, 2004), 156.

4. Tocqueville, *Democracy in America*, 14.

5. Winston Churchill, quoted in "'Socialism is the philosophy of failure . . .' —Winston Churchill," The Churchill Project, July 30, 2015, https://winstonchurchill.hillsdale.edu/socialism-is-the-philosophy-of-failure-winston-churchill/.

6. The Economist Intelligence Unit, *Democracy Index 2019: A Year of Democratic Setbacks and Popular*

7. *Protest*, 2020, https://www.in.gr/wp-content/uploads/2020/01/Democracy-Index-2019.pdf, 13, 35.

8. Kira Goldring, "Social Welfare: Do Its Advantages Outweigh Its Disadvantages?," The Perspective, updated 2020, https://www.theperspective.com/debates/living/is-social-welfare-necessary-or-does-it-discourage-productivity/.

9. Goldring.

10. Goldring.

11. Goldring.

12. Goldring.

13. Benjamin Franklin, quoted in art. 8 (October 1844), *North American Review* 59 (Boston: Otis, Broaders, 1844), 475.

14. David W. Kreutzer, "Taxes, Regulations Hurt Economy," Heritage Foundation, August 18, 2017, https://www.heritage.org/taxes/commentary/taxes-regulations-hurt-economy.
15. Kreutzer.
16. Kreutzer.

CHAPTER 7

1. Peter Benesh, "Horace Mann Lifted America through Education," *Investor's Business Daily*, May 21, 2012, https://www.investors.com/news/management/leaders-and-success/horace-mann-boosted-education-democracy-citizenship-public-schools/.
2. Willona M. Sloan, "What Is the Purpose of Education?," *ASCD Education Update* 54, no. 7 (July 2012), http://www.ascd.org/publications/newsletters/education-update/jul12/vol54/num07/What-is-the-purpose-of-education%C2%A2.aspx.
3. David Horowitz, "Academic Bill of Rights," accessed April 13, 2021, http://la.utexas.edu/users/hcleaver/330T/350kPEEHorowitzAcadBillTable.pdf.
4. David Barton, *4 Centuries of American Education*, 3rd printing (Aledo, TX: Wallbuilder Press, 2018), 6.
5. Abraham Lincoln, "Gettysburg Address," November 19, 1863, https://voicesofdemocracy.umd.edu/lincoln-gettysburg-address-speech-text/.
6. Bret Stephens. "Diversity, Inclusion and Anti-Excellence," *New York Times*, August 2, 2019, https://www.nytimes.com/2019/08/02/opinion/university-campus-diveristy-inclusion-free-speech.html.
7. Nicolas Kristof, "A Confession of Liberal Intolerance," *New York Times*, May 7, 2016, https://www.nytimes.com/2016/05/08/opinion/sunday/a-confession-of-liberal-intolerance.html.
8. See Tom Stafford, "How Liars Create the 'Illusion of Truth,' BBC Future, October 26, 2016, https://www.bbc.com/future/article/20161026-how-liars-create-the-illusion-of-truth.
9. David Barton, *The American Heritage Series*, 10 DVD set (Aledo, TX: Wallbuilders, 2007), disc 5.
10. Barton, disc 5.
11. John Marshall, *The Papers of John Marshall*, ed. Charles Hobson (Chapel Hill: University of North Carolina Press, 2006), 12:278, quoted in David Barton,

Separation of Church & State: What the Founders Meant (Aledo, TX: Wallbuilders, 2007), 4.

12. Harry S. Truman, "Address at the Lighting of the National Community Christmas Tree on the White House Grounds," December 24, 1946, National Archives, Harry S. Truman Library & Museum, https://www.trumanlibrary. gov/library/public-papers/271/address-lighting-national-community-christmas-tree-white-house-grounds.

13. Alexis de Tocqueville, *Democracy in America* (London: Saunders and Otley, 1838), 2:144.

14. Thomas Jefferson, letter to the Danbury Baptist Association, January 1, 1802, in Steve Mount, "Jefferson's Wall of Separation Letter," USConstitution.net, https://usconstitution.net/jeffwall.html.

15. David Barton, *Separation of Church & State: What the Founders Meant* (Aledo, TX: Wallbuilders, 2007), 13.

16. Barton, 15.

17. Drew Desilver, "U.S. Students' Academic Achievement Still Lags That of Their Peers in Many Countries," *Fact Tank* (Pew Research Center blog), February 15, 2017, https://www.pewresearch.org/fact-tank/2017/02/15/u-s-students-internationally-math-science/.

18. Barton, *4 Centuries of American Education*, 6.

19. Matthew Lynch. "How Dumbed Down Education Is Creating a National Security Crisis, the Edvocate, August 20, 2019, https://www.theedadvocate. org/how-dumbed-down-education-is-creating-a-national-security-crisis/.

20. Valerie Strauss, "Here's the Famous 1895 Eighth-Grade Test from Kansas. See How You Would Do," *Washington Post*, October 15, 2015, https://www. washingtonpost.com/news/answer-sheet/wp/2015/10/16/heres-the-famous-1895-eighth-grade-test-from-kansas-see-how-you-would-do/.

21. Charlotte Thomson Iserbyt, *The Deliberate Dumbing Down of America* (Ravenna, OH: Conscience Press, 1999), xiv.

22. Iserbyt, xv.

23. Iserbyt, xv.

24. Iserbyt, xv.

25. Iserbyt, Ibid, page xvi.

26. Iserbyt, xvi.

27. Aleksandr Solzhenitzen, quoted in Iserbyt, xiii.

28. Solzhenitzen, in Iserbyt, xiii.

CHAPTER 8

1. Paul Kengor, "Liberal Reverance for Tolerance Is Selective to Exclude Faith," *Garner News*, October 6, 2014, https://gardnernews.com/liberal-reverance-for-tolerance-is-selective-to-exclude-christian-faith/.

2. Kengor.

3. Kengor.

4. Kengor.

5. Jeffrey J. Selingo, "College Students Support Free Speech—Unless It Offends Them," *Washington Post*, March 9, 2018, https://www.washingtonpost.com/local/college-students-support-free-speech--unless-it-offends-them/2018/03/09/79f21c9e-23e4-11e8-94da-ebf9d112159c_story.html.

6. Selingo.

7. Selingo.

8. Selingo.

9. Foundation for Individual Rights in Education, *Spotlight on Speech Codes 2007: The State of Free Speech on Our Nation's Campuses* (Philadelphia: Fire, 2007), https://www.thefire.org/presentation/wp-contentuploads/2016/05/17121611/Spotlight-on-Speech-Codes-2007.pdf, 3.

10. Emerson Sykes and Vera Eidelman. "When Colleges Confine Free Speech to a 'Zone,' It Isn't Free," *Speak Freely* (ACLU blog), February 7, 2019, https://www.aclu.org/blog/free-speech/student-speech-and-privacy/when-colleges-confine-free-speech-zone-it-isnt-free.

11. Sykes and Eidelman.

18. Sykes and Eidelman.

12. Voltaire, in S. G. Tallentyre, *Voltaire in His Letters: Being a Selection of His Correspondence* (New York: G. P. Putnam's Sons, 1919), 65.

CHAPTER 9

1. At least, that's the story. The metaphor itself has been proven untrue, but according to J. Whitfield "Whit" Gibbons, professor emeritus of ecology at the University of Georgia, "that does not diminish the truth of the message that the accumulation of imperceptible changes can have a significant effect on the . . . environment." Gibbons, "The Legend of the Boiling Frog Is Just a Legend," Savannah River Ecology Laboratory, University of Georgia,

December 3, 2007, https://archive-srel.uga.edu/outreach/ecoviews/ecoview071223.htm. In our illustration, the "environment" that is significantly changing is America and its politics and culture.

2. Don Frost, "Socialism Will Creep Up on Us," *Daily Herald (Chicago)*, November 12, 2011, http://www.dailyherald.com/article/20111112/discuss/711129957/.

3. Rod Dreher, "Jumping through the Overton Window," *American Conservative*, February 19, 2014, https://www.theamericanconservative.com/dreher/jumping-through-the-overton-window/.

4. See "Official US Executive Branch Web Sites," Library of Congress Newspaper & Current Periodical Reading Room, accessed April 14, 2021, https://www.loc.gov/rr/news/fedgov.html.

5. A-Z Index of U.S. Government Departments and Agencies. Retrieved from usa.gov/federal-agencies on April 18, 2021.

6. Clyde Wayne Crews Jr. "How Many Rules and Regulations Do Federal Agencies Issue?," *Forbes*, August 15, 2017, https://www.forbes.com/sites/waynecrews/2017/08/15/how-many-rules-and-regulations-do-federal-agencies-issue/#74e122f11e64.

7. Crews.

8. Crews.

9. Michael Snyder, "12 Ridiculous Government Regulations That Are Almost Too Bizarre to Believe," *Business Insider*, November 12, 2010, https://www.businessinsider.com/ridiculous-regulations-big-government-2010-11.

10. Snyder.

11. George Bernard Shaw, *Everybody's Political What's What* (London: Constable, 1944), 261.

12. Jim DeMint, "The Coming Crisis: How Government Dependency Threatens America's Freedom," Heritage Foundation, May 8, 2001, https://www.heritage.org/political-process/report/the-coming-crisis-how-government-dependency-threatens-americas-freedom.

13. Gene Falk, Karen E. Lynch, and Jessica Tollestrup, *Federal Spending on Benefits and Services for People with Low Income* (Congressional Research Service, February 6, 2018), https://fas.org/sgp/crs/misc/R45097.pdf.

14. Falk, Lynch, and Tollestrup, 1.

15. Falk, Lynch, and Tollestrup.

16. Falk, Lynch, and Tollestrup..

17. HealthSherpa, "Top 10 Government Programs for Low-Income Families," *HealthSherpa* blog, accessed April 14. 2021, https://www.healthsherpa.com/blog/top-10-government-programs-for-low-income-families/.

18. Ronald Reagan, quoted in DeMint. "The Coming Crisis."

19. DeMint.

20. Dinesh D'Souza, *United States of Socialism* (New York: All Points Books, 2020).

21. Mark Pullum, "The Quandary of Judicial Review," *National Review*, April 8, 2015, https://www.nationalreview.com/2015/04/quandary-judicial-review/.

CHAPTER 10

1. From the home page of Black Powder Holdings, accessed April 14, 2021, https://www.blackpowderholdings.com/.

2. George Washington, *Quotations of George Washington* (Bedford, MA: Applewood Books, 2003), 26.

3. Matthew Spalding, "A New American Fusionism: Recovering Principles in Our Politics," Heritage Foundation, March 17, 2009, https://www.heritage.org/political-process/report/new-american-fusionism-recovering-principles-our-politics.

4. Matthew Spalding, "Reclaiming America: Why We Honor the Tea Party Movement," Heritage Foundation, July 15, 2010, https://www.heritage.org/political-process/report/reclaiming-america-why-we-honor-the-tea-party-movement.

5. Washington, *Quotations of George Washington*, 26.

6. This quotation has been variously attributed to Winston Churchill and to British prime minister Margaret Thatcher. According to Snopes.com, Thatcher's actual words were "Socialist governments traditionally do make a financial mess. They always run out of other people's money." Jim Fulkrod, *Economics and Gods Truth Are Not Rocket Science* (n.p.: Xlibris, 2016); Dave Mikkelson, "Margaret Thatcher on Socialism," Snopes, July 7, 2009, https://www.snopes.com/fact-check/other-peoples-money/.

7. John F. Kennedy, "Address and Question and Answer Period at the Economic Club of New York," American Presidency Project, December 14, 1962, https://www.presidency.ucsb.edu/documents/address-and-question-and-answer-period-the-economic-club-new-york.

8. Diane Katz, "Here's How Much Red Tape Trump Has Cut," Heritage Foundation, October 17, 2018, https://www.heritage.org/government-regulation/commentary/heres-how-much-red-tape-trump-has-cut.

9.   See also Jeffrey Dorfman, "Ten Free Market Economic Reasons to Be Thankful," *Forbes*, November 23, 2016, https://www.forbes.com/sites/jeffreydorfman/2016/11/23/ten-free-market-economic-reasons-to-be-thankful/?sh=5186fe456db7.

10. You can read the text of James Madison's *Federalist* Number 10, dated November 22, 1787, at Founders Online, https://founders.archives.gov/documents/Madison/01-10-02-0178.

11. Benjamin Constant, The Liberty of Ancients Compared with That of Moderns (1819), ebook (Good Press, 2020), https://www.google.com/books/edition/The_Liberty_of_Ancients_Compared_with_th/XF4OEAAAQBAJ?hl=en&gbpv=1&kptab=overview.

12. U.S. Constitution, Tenth Amendment.

13. Jake Lawson. "Accepting Personal Responsibility," Retrieved from www.livestrong.com on July 23, 2020.

14. "From James Madison to Henry Lee, 25 June 1824," Founders Online, National Archives, https://founders.archives.gov/documents/Madison/04-03-02-0333. (Original source: *The Papers of James Madison*, Retirement Series, vol. 3, *1 March 1823–24 February 1826*, ed. David B. Mattern et al. [Charlottesville: University of Virginia Press, 2016], 338–39.)

15. "A Letter on Justice and Open Debate," *Harper's Magazine*, July 7, 2020, https://harpers.org/a-letter-on-justice-and-open-debate/.

16. "A Letter on Justice and Open Debate."

17. Nicole Russell, "Harper's Open Letter Critical of 'Cancel Culture' Should Be Applauded, Not Canceled," *Daily Signal*, July 10, 2020, https://www.dailysignal.com/2020/07/10/harpers-open-letter-critical-of-cancel-culture-should-be-applauded-not-canceled/.

18. Tim Reynolds, The "Heat's Leonard Stands for Anthem, Explains Why," Associated Press, August 1, 2020, https://apnews.com/article/ap-top-news-race-and-ethnicity-san-antonio-spurs-denver-nuggets-racial-injustice-47bae68b6ea8ff83ce86ad7c3a026591.

19. Emily Ekins, "Poll: 62% of Americans Say They Have Political Views They're Afraid to Share," Cato.org, July 24, 2020, https://poseidon01.ssrn.com/delivery.php?ID=29606400308602302303011906400700302305108405104406802200910007802711903006511710702506100111110550100011211250310310180160961181260460360510780200651220650700071203209000707907011410309111507906709211402802708511901908712507002512208109500112&EXT=pdf&INDEX=TRUE.

POSTSCRIPT

1. Karen Townsend, "GovTrack.US: Kamala Harris is the most liberal politician in the U.S. Senate," Townhall Media, August 13, 2020, https://hotair.com/karen-townsend/2020/08/13/govtrack-us-kamala-harris-liberal-politician-u-s-senate-n347161.

2. Jemima McEvoy, "At Least 13 Cities Are Defunding Their Police Departments," *Forbes*, Autust 13,2020, https://www.forbes.com/sites/jemimamcevoy/2020/08/13/at-least-13-cities-are-defunding-their-police-departments/.

3. John Kartch, "Biden: 'If You Elect Me, Your Taxes Are Going to Be Raised," Americans for Tax Reform, February 29, 2020, https://www.atr.org/biden-if-you-elect-me-your-taxes-are-going-be-raised.

4. Steven F. Hayward, "Five Reasons the Green New Deal Is Worse Than You Thought," *Bulwark*, February 12, 2019, https://thebulwark.com/five-reasons-the-green-new-deal-is-worse-than-you-thought/.

5. Hayward.

6. Executive Order 13771, "Presidential Executive Order on Reducing Regulation and Controlling Regulatory Costs," January 30, 2017, https://trumpwhitehouse.archives.gov/presidential-actions/presidential-executive-order-reducing-regulation-controlling-regulatory-costs/.

7. James Clark, "A Look at Military Spending Under the Obama Administration," Task & Purpose, December 15, 2015, https://taskandpurpose.com/news/a-look-at-military-spending-under-the-obama-administration/.

8. Brian Thomas. "U.S. Military Struggles with Obama Administration Funding Cuts," Federalist Papers website, October 11, 2017, https://thefederalistpapers.org/us/u-s-military-struggles-obama-administration-funding-cuts.

9. Jerry Newcombe, "Religious Freedom at Risk," American Vision, November 19, 2020, https://americanvision.org/25095/religious-freedom-at-risk/.

10. Thomas Beaumont, "Biden's Win Hides a Dire Warning for Democrats in Rural U.S.," Associated Press, November 27, 2020, https://apnews.com/article/election-2020-donald-trump-tom-bakk-iowa-minnesota-01881b095d7a8b0d7b61923c4a93627d.